Lipstick and Autism

Not All Days Are Rosy And Pink

Lauren Ratcliff

Library of Congress Control Number:		2023917122
ISBN:	Hardcover	979-8-3694-0698-4
	Softcover	979-8-3694-0697-7
	eBook	979-8-3694-0696-0

New Revised Standard Version (NRSV)
New Revised Standard Version Bible, copyright © 1989 the Division of Christian Education of the National Council of the Churches of Christ in the United States of America. Used by permission. All rights reserved.

Print information available on the last page.

Rev. date: 09/06/2023

To order additional copies of this book, contact:
Xlibris
844-714-8691
www.Xlibris.com
Orders@Xlibris.com
855738

Contents

CHAPTER ONE..1

CHAPTER TWO..8

CHAPTER THREE..18

CHAPTER FOUR..27

CHAPTER FIVE...40

CHAPTER SIX...46

CHAPTER SEVEN..52

CHAPTER EIGHT...59

CHAPTER NINE...69

CHAPTER TEN...80

CHAPTER ELEVEN..90

CHAPTER TWELVE..101

CHAPTER THIRTEEN..115

CHAPTER FOURTEEN...127

CHAPTER FIFTEEN..134

CHAPTER SIXTEEN...143

CHAPTER SEVENTEEN...151

CHAPTER EIGHTEEN..158

CHAPTER NINETEEN..172

CHAPTER TWENTY..191

CHAPTER TWENTY-ONE...207

CHAPTER TWENTY-TWO...219

CHAPTER TWENTY-THREE..233

SYMPTOMS OF (HFA/AS) PLUS BENEFITS AND TIPS......245

GLOSSARY..255

This book is dedicated to Autistic people and their loved ones.

CHAPTER ONE

*The time is coming when I will gather those who are disabled, announces the Lord. I will bring together those who were taken away as prisoners. I will gather those I have allowed to suffer. I will make the disabled people my faithful people. I will make into a strong nation those driven away from their home. I will rule over them on Mount Zion. I will be their King from that time on and forever. (*Micah 4:6-7 NirV)

My birthday party of 2021 was an epic birthday party. On July 23rd of that year my family had a surprise birthday party for me at the campground where they park their camper every summer. I never expected to have such a huge turnout for my birthday party. It was a day I will never forget.

"Sis" said my younger sister, Lacey, the day before the party, "I would like you to come and eat dinner with us at the campground tomorrow night and I have a shirt for you to wear."

"Ok, but I'm going to work out first if you don't mind," I said not knowing that my whole family had a surprise birthday party planned for me for my 40th birthday that would take place later that day and exactly a week and a half before my real birthday.

The next day everyone was rushing to get stuff done. I felt grumpy and tired due to getting home late from a concert the night before and begged to take a nap first, then go to the gym and workout before heading to what I thought was just a dinner with my family. My Dad wanted me to ride with him to our campsite instead of us driving separate cars so I packed my iPad, phone, and stuff to charge them with because I knew I would be using them a lot, so I thought.

When Dad and I got to the campground he parked the car near their camper while I walked up near the picnic center and laid down my phone and my iPad before heading to the bathroom to wash my hands. It was at that moment that I heard Lacey and one of my cousins yelling for me to come back to the picnic area first.

"Surprise! Happy Birthday Lauren," everyone yelled loudly as I entered the picnic grove.

"Oh My Gosh," I said out of sheer shock with intense happiness and excitement.

"Did you know what we were doing? Did we fool you good enough," asked Lacey, with excitement.

"Yes," I said. I never expected this. Thanks so much," I yelled out of excitement.

Mom and Lacey invited all of our close relatives locally and those out of state to my special birthday party. Forty years is a blessing. After greeting everyone, eating, and thanking everyone for coming to the party I opened my gifts. I felt more blessed than I had ever felt in my life. I got lots of gifts that I loved but the best part was a surprise birthday with the people that I knew and loved so much.

The number 40 has an important biblical meaning. The Old Testament mentions that the Israelites were in captivity for 40 years and they celebrated when they were released from captivity. Three of the gospels mention that Jesus spent 40 days in the desert where he fasted and was tempted by Satan. While I was at that particular birthday party, I was able to reflect on many miracles and blessings both large and small that have I experienced in my personal life.

My parents and Lacey have always been so amazing in their support of me. I, like many other people, have made my fair share of mistakes in my youth and young adult years, but I live a good life and my family is the reason that has been possible. It was not always easy for me or my family. I feel as though my life has been a turbulent and bumpy roller coaster ride of high hills and low valleys that were difficult to ride through at times.

I was diagnosed with High Functioning Autism. My diagnosis of High Functioning Autism has been very challenging for me, and this party felt like a celebration of accomplishments for me. Reflecting on this birthday party, I realized that I had overcome so much more than what my parents ever thought I would achieve! I was able to earn my driver's license when I was a teenager, graduated high school, cosmetology school, and college, speaking about my experience with Autism at our local county autism awareness walk, and being able to mentally survive the challenging impact of the COVID 19 pandemic. Getting a driver's license and graduating with any form of a college degree is something that many families take for granted but these are major accomplishments for people with special needs including Autism. A wise doctor that I saw as a patient at Cleveland Clinic told my mother that she would learn to appreciate things that other parents took for granted. Although I have accomplished a lot, I have often been misunderstood which has resulted in social misconceptions, and difficulties obtaining education and employment.

My family has helped me achieve many of my accomplishments even though they have felt like throwing in the towel and giving up at times, but we managed to pull through. My Dad worked with me all through high school on learning how to drive so I could get my license when I got old enough and I feel very thankful for that. Mom always helped me with school and tried to manage my High Functioning Autism in the way physicians advised. My grandmothers were very influential in my childhood. Lacey and I spent a lot of time with both of my grandmothers as children. Our grandmothers were always there for us through thick and thin. My maternal grandmother (Nan) was like another mother figure for Lacey and myself because we spent so much time with her. She babysat us when Mom and Dad worked, and I loved staying with her on the weekends. Whenever Mom and Dad came to get Lacey and I at my maternal grandmother's house after work she always made a delicious meal for all of us. She was always able to help me calm down from meltdowns and was my rock on on my worst days. My paternal grandmother (Mamaw) always told me not to cry whenever she caught me in the midst of a meltdown. If they were still alive for this special birthday and my other special moments both of my grandmothers would have been celebrating with joy along with me and everyone else. My paternal grandmother passed away in 2006 and my maternal grandmother passed away in 2014.

Celebrating holidays and birthdays were always important to my family. My maternal grandmother (Nan) always made popcorn balls and lots of goodie bags for trick or treaters on halloween. Everyone in the neighborhood flocked to her house to get popcorn balls and goodie bags. Birthdays for Lacey and me were always celebrated at our house with cake and ice cream and our favorite food with all of our local friends and family. Christmas was equally fun but sometimes emotionally stressful for me. Mom and Dad always got Lacey and I nice gifts for Christmas but the excitement of everything would just send me into meltdown mode by the end of the day. Poor sleep from too much excitement because I could not wait to wake up early on Christmas and open my new gifts to having a meltdown over having to pitch in and help clean the house or wondering whether anyone liked their gifts if I purchased any. My Mom's brother from out of state, my uncle always came home at Easter to celebrate with us. Whenever Easter came Mom and Dad always got me and Lacey Easter baskets filled with goodies and whenever possible we always went to church on Easter Sunday. Easter weekend was always spent at my maternal grandmother's house, and this always included an Easter meal and for the kids an Easter egg hunt. My parents were not rich, but they always did their best to make holidays special for Lacey and me. Mom was a bargain shopper, hitting the sales and stashing our treats until the respective holidays.

I am an Amusement Park and roller coaster fanatic. Since I was old enough, I have asked my parents to take me to different amusement parks every chance that we could go to one and if I had the time and money, I would travel to all of the different amusement parks in the United States and Canada. I am thankful that Lacey has volunteered to be my side kick at amusement parks. Over the years I have learned to be meticulous about saving money for stuff like this, including saving change and one-dollar bills, and using credit card points.

I was diagnosed with Asperger Syndrome, which used to be lumped under a category of disorders called Pervasive Developmental Disorders (PDDs) in 1994. Asperger Syndrome was introduced into the Diagnostic and Statistical Manual IV (DSM-IV) for Psychiatric Disorders in 1994. Prior to that I was given a diagnosis of Pervasive Developmental Disorder Not Otherwise Specified (PDD-NOS) by a team of doctors at Cleveland Clinic in Ohio in 1987. The DSM periodically gets updated and as of the current DSM Autism Spectrum Disorders are grouped into a category now called autism spectrum disorder classified with levels one through three based on the severity of the symptoms. Now Asperger Syndrome is called Level One Autism, meaning that it is a high functioning form of Autism.

I grew up in an area and time period where little was known about classic Autism, let alone High Functioning Autism. Because of this my parents used parenting techniques that they were raised on, which often work well for other children. This includes teaching techniques as well as discipline and reward techniques and most of these techniques did not work well for me. For example, removing a privilege for having a meltdown or appearing as if I was not listening did not work for me.

As of this publishing the Center for Disease Control (CDC), (www.cdc.gov) and Autism Speaks, have confirmed that as many as 1 in 36 children in the United States and 1 in 100 children globally has some form of Autism and the numbers continue to rise.[1] In 1981 when I was born 1 in 10,000 kids had Autism. In the 1990s numbers rose to 1 in 1000 kids. In the early 2000s numbers rose to 1 in 250 kids.

High Functioning Autism (HFA) is referred to as a hidden disability because the symptoms of it are less noticeable than the more severe types of Autism. A person with High Functioning Autism can easily pass off as Normal until they have a meltdown because they tend to have Normal intelligence and normal appearance and some of them can function independently for the most part. Many of them have communication and mild speech issues. This type of Autism is less common than the more severe forms of the disorder.

1

Although there are classic criteria that qualify an individual for a diagnosis of Autism the disorder affects each person differently. Some children will struggle with one symptom while others may struggle with another symptom. The disorder is more common in boys than in girls.

Having a child or a spouse with Autism increases the risk for marital problems that often result in divorce. My parents have been able to work through any issues and have maintained an amazing relationship. I have come into contact with other families of special needs children/spouses where the relationship has resulted in divorce.

Hans Asperger was an Austrian pediatrician who identified a group of young male patients in 1944 who exhibited intense special interests, lack of empathy, poor coordination, and poor social skills. These children that were patients of Hans Asperger would have been diagnosed with what is known as level one Autism today. The condition Asperger Syndrome was named after Hans Asperger. Asperger believed that the behavior patterns he observed in his patients were genetic even though to this day no single genes have been identified as a cause of Autism. He believed that the condition is polygenic, meaning that his syndrome is caused by several different genes.

Child Psychiatrist Leo Kanner first identified Autism in 1945 and since then ongoing research from different sources have suspected that the biggest risk factors for autism spectrum disorders are genetics and advanced parental age. There is no known cause or cure for autism spectrum disorders. When started early enough treatment can be effective. Autism Spectrum Conditions are NOT mental illnesses even though they are classified as Psychiatric Disorders. The DSM 5 lists Autism under a category of conditions referred to as Neurodevelopmental Disorders. They are neurological based disorders that look like mental illnesses on the surface. These disorders do not show up on imaging tests such as CT, MRI and blood testing. Autism of any type is a congenital and lifelong disorder but with effective treatment techniques and family support a person with the disorder can function independently and live a somewhat normal life. According to Autism Speaks the majority of Autistic adults still remain unemployed yet many companies are now hiring Autistic employees.

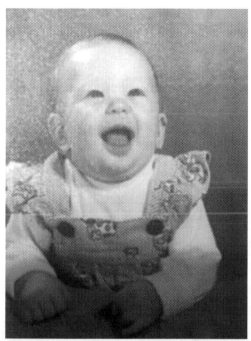

I was about eight months old here and it was in the spring of 1982

CHAPTER TWO

Before I formed you in your mother's body, I chose you. Before you were born, I set you apart to serve me. I appointed you to be a prophet to the nations. (Jeremiah 1:5 NIrV)

My roots begin in a small rural eastern Kentucky farming area where everyone knew each other. This area is considered to be part of the Bible Belt area where religion always has and continues to be important. Families often attended church services on Sunday. Poverty was and still is a social issue in this area due to limited employment opportunities, drug use as of the more recent years, and lack of resources outside of a school setting. Traditional homes, getting married young, and having large families was the norm. Farming was a way of life for a lot of families. More specifically that was how my parents, were raised. Mom was the youngest of four kids, two boys and two girls. Dad was next to the youngest of five children, one girl and four boys. Mom was a nurse at a local hospital and Dad was a coal strip mine inspector, even though he earned a teaching degree. Despite being raised in poor and hardworking families my parents both earned college degrees, unlike so many other people of our area and time period. For a side hustle Dad farmed in the evenings and weekends, and still does to this day. He and his brother Milt Ratcliff, who is my uncle and lives across the road from us, own a family farm together.

What was the world like in 1981? There was little to no research known on classical autism, let alone the high functioning type. Psychiatric illness of any type was considered to be a taboo topic, especially in our area in my opinion. It was the dawning of a new decade. There was no internet, smartphones, tablets, and few home computers. The nearest public libraries were in nearby counties. Prince Charles and Princess Diana got married. My mother became pregnant with me and halfway through the pregnancy my maternal grandfather passed away with Leukemia. Then, here I come making my way into the world in August of that year.

It all began one summer night August 1, 1981. My mom went into labor with me and felt as if it were the worst pain of her life, yet she felt extremely excited that her new baby would be here soon. Her original due date to deliver me was four days prior but she did not go into labor until the night of August 1st, 1981. She was 27 years old, and Dad was 31 years old. Mom and dad had been married for two years. Ultrasounds were new in 1981 and used for diagnostic purposes only, Mom allowed the technicians to practice their ultrasound skills on her. She was excited to see the baby, but wanted the gender to be a surprise, she said she felt that was just one of life's surprises and mysteries that she wanted to experience. Dad drove Mom to the hospital to have me and Nan rode with them. After the nurses assessed my mother, they felt like her labor would be rapid because she had such intense contractions. Fifteen hours later, to the nurse's surprise, along with a Pitocin infusion and forceps delivery, I arrived. Wide shoulders and my position were attributed to why Mom experienced some difficulties in delivery. Besides that, she had no delivery or pregnancy complications with me. I was born late in the afternoon on Sunday August 2nd. It was a long and arduous night and day for my mom. There were no cell phones or iPads in the labor rooms for distraction from the discomforts of an ineffective epidural long and exhausting. When she held me in her arms for the first time, she said it was one of the two happiest days of her life (The other being when Lacey was born.) She wanted to name me Lauren Rae. My first name "Lauren" is a derivative of Larry, my middle name was after my maternal grandfather. My mother said that she grieved that her father, who became sick and passed away during her pregnancy, was not here to see me.

Six weeks later Mom went back to work at her nursing job. My Nan Nan babysat me every day while Mom and Dad worked. Since she did not drive, mom and dad brought me to her house every day on their way to work and for Nan it was a treat for her to babysit me. Babysitting me helped her to deal with the loneliness brought on by losing my grandfather just a few months earlier. If Nan Nan did not babysit me, which was a rare occasion, I stayed with my Uncle Milt and his wife, my aunt Joyce and their two children who were our closest neighbors.

My parents said I was a good baby except for having colic for the first two weeks of my life. My mom didn't notice anything abnormal about me other than the fact that I was a bit more socially reserved than other babies were. I appeared to be a healthy and happy baby or so my family thought, achieving all of my milestones. All of the information I know about myself from when I was an infant was based on what my parents and my grandmothers can remember about me. My Mom and my Nan later told me that I got Chicken Pox when we went on our first family vacation to Florida when I was 8 months old. Most kids do not get Chickenpox until they are school aged, but unbeknownst to my mom, the spot of poison ivy rash she had was actually an outbreak of Shingles and she gave me Chickenpox before she realized she had anything wrong with her.

During my first ever family vacation I was in the midst of a Chickenpox outbreak and Mom and Dad had to take me to a local emergency room because Mom felt like I needed something more than just Tylenol for my fever. That was where they confirmed that it was Chickenpox. I had a severe case of Chicken Pox. The ER doctor gave me a prescription for Benadryl. Many medications that are now considered to be common, household medications for children such as Benadryl and Dimetapp were only available by prescription.

My first vacation consisted of Tylenol every few hours for my fever, Benadryl for my itching, baking soda baths, avoiding the sun, staying hydrated, and a lot of worry for a new mother. Both of my grandmothers were with us on that vacation and that allowed Mom and Dad to go to the beach and get some sun. We came back home after a week in Florida and life went back to normal. Mom and Dad went back to work and

Nan continued to babysit me. Four months later in August of that year I turned one year old.

Around that time my Nan Nan remembered me being afraid of a ceramic nativity shepherd boy, a figurine that my (Mamaw) painted for her. I was for sure too young to remember this. She said that I would duck or crawl around the figurine to avoid one of her favorite Christmas decorations. She told me this when I got older.

For the first two years of my life mom and dad rented the house next door to the one that we currently live in. I was too young to remember anything that happened when we lived in the smaller house. My first and second birthday parties were held at that house and mom has pictures of those events.

My mom told me she noticed that as I grew into my toddler years, I was slightly different from other children but at the time she did not feel as though it were anything to be concerned about. She attributed this to me being a little socially isolated from other children because I stayed with Nan Nan everyday while She and Dad worked.

I developed a series of ear, throat, and bladder infections (not together) and I was frequently on antibiotics for those (Amoxicilin and Septra). I was about two years old whenever I developed these infections. This was late 1983 and the Spring/Summer of 1984. It was at that time that I developed my uncontrollable emotional responses. My symptoms were strange and the fears irrational. I also developed an intense interest in anything with a fan blade in it such as hairdryers and ceiling fans. I also had very good memory for details. My speech and vocabulary development were very good according to my parents, but rarely talked.

My mom remembers taking me to my pediatrician one day whenever I had an ear infection and a cold. Dad had to work that day. Since it was snowing that day and because Mom did not want to drive in the snow, we rode with My Uncle Milt and his wife because their son had an appointment at the same doctor's office that day. The doctor prescribed me an antibiotic for my ear infection and advised Sudafed for my cold symptoms. When we got back from the doctor appointment Mom gave me the first dose of both my Antibiotic and

Sudafed. As she was trying to rock me and get me down for a nap, she said that I looked around the room and looked as if I had seen something that was not there. She said that I screamed and clung to her hiding my face and peeking back again at nothing that she could see, she wondered if I was having visual hallucinations. She thought that maybe I could have had a reaction to the Sudafed because that was the first time that she gave me Sudafed. Episodes like this continued, but my mom never gave me Sudafed again.

Around late 1983 we moved into the house that we currently live in today which is beside the one that we lived in during the first two years of my life. In the spring of 1984, my paternal grandfather (I called him Papaw) died in May of that year from complications of a heart condition. I was two years old, and mom was pregnant with Lacey. I barely remember my papaw but from what I can remember and what my mom and dad remember was that my papaw dearly loved me. Even though they never babysat me as much as my (Nan Nan) did, my paternal grandparents lived very close to us, within walking distance and I got to see them on a regular basis. One day in the summer of 1984 Mom was off from work because Dad was in the hospital due to a kidney stone, and she was trying to get some housework done before heading to the hospital to be with Dad, she was eight months pregnant with Lacey. She said that while she was washing dishes, I started looking at something (unseen to her) in the kitchen, with a look of pure panic, as if I saw something horrible, grabbed onto her legs burying my face in her legs, screaming and crying in sheer terror. I could not tell her what was bothering me. She once again could not figure out what was wrong with me, but I hadn't had Sudafed, and thought maybe there could have been a fly in the house.

My Nan Nan remembered a similar incident to those above. My mom's brother, (my uncle Jack) and his family came to visit my Nan Nan later that summer around the first week of July just like they always did, back then. Myself, my mom and dad were there visiting with them and my Nan Nan one day while they were there. I always loved spending time with them. When we left to go home on that particular night after visiting with them everything was fine until we got inside the car to leave. I screamed in sheer panic when we got inside the car to leave. A moth got inside the car as Mom was buckling me in my seatbelt and it scared me.

During the same summer and around the same time I had another incident like the ones described above and yes, I remember it. I went to Mamaw's house with Mom and Dad while they picked beans from the garden one afternoon. We were sitting outside on Mamaw's back porch and Mom was stringing beans that Dad picked. At one point she took me inside the house. As we walked inside the house, I noticed the wall mount heater and inside the heater it looked as if it had something with eyes in it.

I screamed as I saw what looked like eyes inside the wall mount heater. I knew logically that it was not a set of eyes that was going to jump out and get me, but I just happened to notice it and it scared me. "You must have gotten spooked at something inside that heater," said Mom, not expecting this to happen. I could never tell my parents what scared me, they only guessed. I just acknowledged what she said but did not respond to her. There were so many incidents like this one and the three previous ones I mentioned that I cannot remember all of them. My Mom said the problem with having these reactions were not the reactions themselves so much but for hours, and sometimes days later I was very unsettled, timid, excitable, fearful or nervous.

Little things that most people would forget about would just spook me out to the point of startling me to death even though I knew that they were not dangerous. I suffered from hypersensitivity to stuff that I saw and heard such as something in the corner of the room or some odd noise whether anyone else noticed it or not. I was scared of noises such as hair dryers, sweepers, and the loud sound of public toilets flushing but at the same time I was fascinated with the hum of a fan and loved having it blow against my face. As much as I loved relaxing and playing in the pool whenever I had the chance to go to a pool at the same time, I was terrified at the thought of ducking my head under the water. Seeing something like a moth gave me an eerie feeling and to describe that type of feeling would be like watching something horrific to a normal person. Those eerie feelings caused me to get weird sensations all over my body such as chills, shock sensations, and weird feelings in my stomach whenever I would see something like this or hear a weird noise.

Mom also told me that I had poor eye contact when I was very young, but I was unaware of it. I was also afraid to touch a plant leaf and certain types of ribbon. I was a finicky eater and would only eat certain foods. I used to have phobias of black toilet seats and could not stand dirty public bathrooms when we traveled, which often led to me withholding urine and feces until I had an accident. Feelings of guilt and frustration ran through my mom's mind, trying to understand why I reacted this way, and wanting to do the right thing but not knowing what to do. There are other symptoms, but these were the main ones that I could think of.

My fear of touching a plant leaf, fear of ducking my head underwater while swimming, perceiving things that I see or hear as spooky, finicky eating habits, and feeling uneasy using black toilets and or dirty public bathrooms are caused by poor sensory processing. Poor sensory processing is a symptom of Autism even though some individuals with Sensory processing disorders are not Autistic. Whenever I would react fearfully for unknown reasons Mom and Dad just thought that I had panic attacks and other people could not understand me. Whenever I experienced this, I would get so overwhelmed with emotion that I would scream as I did in all of these incidents that I described. My screams were as loud as Macauley Culkin's screams in the movie, home alone but I was never home alone of course. Whenever I had these attacks of sensory fears as I call them, I would scream and cry uncontrollably and it was for sure hard to explain what was bothering me even though I did not have any speech issues and was completely verbal. Mom and Dad tried calming techniques that would work for other children, but they were unsuccessful for me because I could never explain to them what I was terrified of. Mom and Dad tried to figure out what was bothering me whenever this would happen and because I was not able to explain my fears, they felt frustrated because they knew I was terrified of something, and they wanted to help me. In the case of being fearful of a moth butterfly the shape of the butterfly and the way it moved spooked me even though I knew logically that it was harmless.

I can vaguely remember my third birthday, but it was at that point that I knew for sure that I loved birthday cake! It continues to be one of my favorite foods to eat. I didn't show it, but I liked having people sing Happy Birthday and it was exciting to open gifts. I can remember details of so many events that happened in my life and when I had a conversation with anyone, I was able to remember details like days of the week, dates, times, and the particular outfit I wore to a specific event. This used to surprise my family and everyone else that I knew when I cited specifics. Whenever I stayed with my Nan Nan she liked to teach me the Alphabet, Numbers, Colors, and shapes, while I played with building blocks. It was at that time that I learned all of that and I used to just repeat it back to myself. One day my dad came after work to get me from Nan's house and was so surprised to find me naming the multiple colors of a plastic toy keychain when I was two. (More information told to me by my Nan).

dad, mom, and me
I was about two years old in the pic and Lacey was not yet born

CHAPTER THREE

Train your children, because then there is hope. Do not do anything to bring their deaths. (Proverbs 19:18 NIrV)

For the remainder of the summer of 1984, I continued to have those strange fears and the other symptoms that I described in the previous chapter. My lack of social development became more noticeable to my family when Lacey was born. Nan felt like this was all related to jealousy of Lacey; I have always been jealous of her, but Mom felt like that was not the case. When I would have a reaction to something that would make me feel fearful it took me several days to recover from it. It seemed like the dark intensified my sensory fears especially during the times when they were acting up on me. I still have to have a night light when I sleep.

I would be up prowling the house at night and when lying in bed I would constantly be tossing and turning and hiding under the covers because I thought I saw something spooky in the corner of the room. I always slept with mom and Dad because I felt less afraid but even then, I always felt terribly spooked by the dark without a light of sorts. Tired from a long day at work and wanting to do what was best for me and wondering why I was reacting the way I did Mom was very stressed out.

As the summer of 1984 progressed it was time for my mom to give birth to Lacey. August 19th, 1984, mom went into labor with Lacey. Uncle Milt's wife, my aunt Joyce babysat me and later took me to Nan's house for me to spend the night while Dad went with Mom to the hospital to have Lacey. While Mom was in the hospital after delivering

Lacey, my mom's brother, My Uncle Melvin brought me and Nan Nan to see Lacey before Mom and Dad brought her home. Mom and Nan remembered me calling my new sister Baby Aunt Sylvia (because my mom was trying to find a name that went with Sylvia), and that I wanted to go see her. Two days later Mom and Dad came home from the hospital with my new sister, Lacey Richelle, not a baby Aunt Sylvia after all.

While Mom was recovering from having Lacey, Nan-Nan stayed in the guest room of our house to help Mom take care of both me and Lacey while Dad worked. Six weeks later after recovering from delivering Lacey Mom went back to work at her nursing job. Nan Nan continued to babysit Me and Lacey. Since she still did not drive, Dad would go get Nan before work and took her home after work, because Mom had to go to work earlier than Dad.

I liked giving Lacey a bottle and changing her diaper. When she got old enough to discover my stuff I did not like when she would get into it. I was very particular about anyone else handling my stuff and I still feel that way today.

I have severe jealousy toward Lacey, but Mom and Dad could always determine if I was having weird fears or feeling jealous toward Lacey. I was always jealous for attention whenever I got the impression that Lacey got more attention than me even when she got sick. Whenever this would happen, I would cry and complain about wanting Mom and Dad's attention. Jealousy towards Lacey is an issue that is overpowered with love for her. I love her so much and enjoy spending time with her.

I started looking at the Sears and JCPenney catalogs every season and fantasizing about all the things I wanted, especially the section where the fans were located in the spring/summer catalogs and the toy section of the holiday catalogs. I continued to be fascinated with the hum of a fan and the way it felt against me. I called fan blades a Lalada. I became very fascinated with red lipstick and nail polish. Whenever my Mamaw's sister from California would come for a visit, she always had the prettiest looking bright red toenails and fingernails with matching red lipstick. I always asked her to pull her shoes off so I could look at her toenails.

I liked a lot of the things that were popular during that time period but not quite as much as other people did. I really liked Punky Brewster and watched her show. TV programs that required an outside satellite source were emerging and people that were fortunate enough to have this type of TV system enjoyed TV stations like Disney channel, music channels like CMT, MTV, and VH1, Cartoon Network, and more as well as the basic channels. In the country we had to have a satellite system in order to access more TV channels. My parents had a satellite system installed on our TV.

I loved books and I still read a lot today. The Smurf's and the Muppet Babies were my favorite characters of that time period. I didn't watch them much on TV, but I listened to their theme songs constantly and would sing it quite a bit. I played with my Smurf collection of toys a lot. Like many kids in that era, I owned my fair share of Care Bears, Cabbage Patch Kids, my little ponies, Smurf's, Sesame Street characters, muppet babies, and so on. I got a Smurf every year for Christmas from my aunts and uncles on my mother's side of the family until I was almost five years old. I can remember the Christmas I got my most prized stuffed animal present from my Nan Nan. It was Christmas 1984. It was a fairly small sized plush Papa Smurf. Lacey was an infant at the time. One day before Christmas of that year my Nan Nan told me she was getting me a big Papa Smurf in a box. Little did I know that she wrapped him up inside a Nike shoe box waiting for me to open on Christmas Day. "I got you a big Papa Smurf put up in a box," said Nan Nan one evening close to Christmas of 1984 when I was at her house. I didn't tell anyone that Nan even mentioned that she bought me a Papa Smurf for Christmas.

After celebrating Christmas as a family of four and opening gifts Dad drove us to my Nan Nans house and the air was filled with Christmas excitement. Nan as usual cooked a big Christmas meal and made gift filled stockings for all of the kids that were there. My Mom's sister Sylvia along with her husband and daughter and My uncle Melvin and his wife and two children were there to celebrate. I played with my cousin Aaron and his older sister Amber (my uncle Melvin's children) and Tara (Aunt Sylvia's daughter). Aaron was exactly one year younger than me and Amber was four years older than me, and we were very close because we spent a lot of time together. Growing up Aaron stayed with us so much that he was like another sibling to Lacey and I. Aaron and I played with Nan's ceramic nativity set for hours.

Then it was my favorite time, to open the presents. Everyone gathered in Nan's living room. When it was time to open gifts, Amber handed out the gifts. When I got mine, I ripped it open in sheer excitement.

"Woo Woo Woo, I said as I opened my Papa Smurf from the Nike Shoe box and held him up against my face." From that day on that Papa Smurf became my favorite stuffed animal. That particular Christmas I got other presents from my aunts and uncles including some Smurf stuff, but I was in love with my Papa Smurf. I made my Papa Smurf howl like a wolf and meow like a cat. I just loved his soft plush body against my skin. I don't know if this is part of the autism spectrum or not. He slept with me at night and if I were to stay with Nan Nan he would go with me and if I were at home, he was also right there with me. Whenever we would travel anywhere, he would always go with me as one of my number one toys to take with me. If I were to have any emotional meltdowns or feel any of the weird sensory fears Papa Smurf was a comfort to me as well as my other stuffed Smurf's.

Shortly after that I developed a strange type of inflammation in my left hip joint that I can remember, and it was pure agony. It hurt so bad that I could not walk. Nan Nan remembered me waking up on the first morning that I had pain and how I was trying to walk from my bedroom to the living room and had to get on my knees and crawl because it hurt to walk. Mom took me to my pediatrician, as well as her doctor friend at the hospital that she worked at. I had to get an X-ray of my hips to see what was going on.

The X-ray of my hips didn't show any abnormalities according to my mom. I was referred to a local orthopedic specialist and he told my mom that I had Synovitis that usually follows an upper respiratory infection in kids. It went away shortly after, and this case was fairly mild.

My weird fears continued and, they came intense one night during a family vacation to Florida during the spring of 1985. I was having trouble sleeping as usual and Mom and Dad got up with me while Nan, Mamaw, and Lacey were sleeping. It felt like I was seeing at least two different items that were spooking me out of my mind in the living room of our condominium that we stayed in. On one side of the room there was a closet with the door open and inside that closet was a crumpled up black garbage bag that if I looked at it it reminded me of a scary creature. On the other side of the room there was the window, and it was slightly cracked to allow cooler air in. The knob that opens the window also looked like a scary looking creature.

I wailed in sheer terror as I walked into the living room of our condominium holding my beloved Papa Smurf and noticed the crumpled-up garbage bag in the closet of the living room.

I wailed again in sheer terror as I sat on the living room couch in our condominium and looked in the opposite direction of the closet toward the window.

"Lauren, what are you so afraid honey," said my dad as he held me trying to comfort me while Mom wiped the tears from my eyes and tried to figure out what was bothering me. I continued to scream looking at both directions of the objects that spooked me out not knowing how to tell Mom and Dad about the objects that I perceived as eerie looking but clutching both Mom and Dad and my Papa Smurf. I knew logically that none of those items were harmful but that didn't take away my spooky feelings to look at them.

Our sleepless night passed, and we continued to enjoy the rest of the vacation. I of course enjoyed the beach and playing in the ocean. Nan Nan liked to hunt for shells while Mom and Dad looked after Lacey and Me, and Mamaw just enjoyed being at the beach.

I started to develop another special interest that became an intense interest. Every year for as long as I could remember we would take regular family trips to our local amusement park where I rode my first roller coaster. Sometimes my parents would take us there several times in one season in addition to the annual trip we always made with my mom's siblings and their families. That's where I developed my obsession with amusement park rides, mainly roller coasters. My mom always took Lacey, myself, and my two closest cousins, Amber and

Aaron to the local amusement park several times in one season. Going to amusement parks to enjoy my special interest with my family was one of my favorite pastimes when I was a kid. I rarely had a meltdown of any type at an amusement park because I was too busy riding the best thrill rides available.

Lacey and I continued to stay with my Nan Nan while Mom and Dad worked full time. Preschool/Head Start was not required for kids back in the 1980s in our area. My mom recognized my need to be away from my Nan and with other children, so she tried to enroll me in our local head start program because she felt like I needed to be around other children. I couldn't go because my parents worked. There were no other preschools then.

Whenever I turned four years old in August of 1985, I continued to have my strange and out of sync symptoms. Lacey was developing normally, and she was always happy and a very social baby. As a toddler she was turning into a tomboy and liked to hang out with my dad on the farm whenever he was off from work on the weekends. I liked to go shopping with Mom and Nan Nan at the local Kmart store and the grocery store on the weekends. Nan always bought me a new book because she knew I liked to read. Mom didn't like for us to get toys unless it was a special occasion. It was common for us to spend the weekends at our house or Nan's house with my cousin, Aaron and his older sister Amber. I began to recognize that I was different, and afraid of unusual things from spending time with my cousins. Although when we were together, we always had fun. Aaron took it upon himself to protect me because of all my fears and Lacey because she was the baby.

As fall turned into winter my sore throats and earaches got worse too. I was never tested for the Strep bacteria that causes sore throats. I was always suspected of having it and just got prescribed antibiotics every time I got a sore throat and Lacey started getting ear issues too. In January of 1986 the space shuttle launched and exploded killing the astronauts and teacher on board. According to my mom that was the day that Lacey and I had surgical procedures done. She had tubes in her ears, and I had a tonsillectomy and adenoidectomy plus ear tubes. Speech disorders are common among people with Autism and hearing disorders. I feel so blessed that I never experienced any speech issues. No more strep throat for me after that but the worst of my issues was still there.

Lacey and I both healed from our procedures and the winter passed. Nan continued to babysit in the daytime as needed because Lacey was still an infant and I was only four years old. Mom and Dad as well as Nan Nan started talking to me about what it would be like to start school in the fall of that year. We watched my cousins across the road get on and off of the school bus on a regular basis.

My unusual interest in fans continued as well as my strange fears. One night in the early/mid spring of 1986 Uncle Milt and Aunt Joyce invited invited my family to a basketball game at the Elementary School where both of their children went to school. I knew that I would be going to school there shortly because my family had talked with me about it. My parents, myself, and Lacey, went to that particular basketball game. I never dreamed that I would see a picture in the gymnasium that would incite such fear in me that I would never get over it. There was a picture of a wildcat hanging on the wall of the school gymnasium that terrified me to look at. Wildcats were the school mascot. From that night until the last time, I saw it, I was terrified to look at that particular picture of the wildcat. I never told anyone that I was mortified to look at it.

Just a few minutes after the ballgame was over, we left and shortly after we got in the car, I screamed in horror like I have done plenty of other times whenever something spooked me, and the picture of the Wildcat was no different. I screamed out of sheer terror even as we drove away from the ballgame and the wildcat. I was sitting in the backseat of the car while Mom and Dad were in the front seat of the car with Dad driving. It was dark by the time we got done and of course when we got home, it took quite a while to recover from the fearful incident.

As subscribers of the Sears and JC Penney catalogs, we got the Spring catalogs from both companies. I peeked through both catalogs when we got them. It was the Sears 1986 spring and summer catalog that I peeked through frequently that had different types of fans in it. There were desktop fans, box fans, stand up fans, window fans, ceiling fans, etc. I still never asked for any of these particular fans that I saw in that particular Sears catalog, but I would just find the pages that they were located on and just look at them and talk obsessively about them with whoever was with me. I kept that particular Sears Catalog for about another five years or so because I still liked looking at that one particular page that had the fans. Within just a year or so that catalog started to look shabby. After about five years of me being fascinated with it mom eventually tossed it. Yes, we got other Sears and JC Penney catalogs on a regular basis, and you bet I spent hours looking at their fan selection. By that point everyone knew that I was the girl with the weird interest in fans. Every time we would go shopping, I always wanted to look at the fan section because I still craved the sensation of a fan blowing against my face and listening to the hum of a fan. Since I was a girly girl, I wanted small, cute fans in bright pastel colors and mom got me one for every occasion, when she could find one. I think that was the year I got one in every color.

Sometime near the end of that spring Mom got me a cutoff sweatshirt with a cute picture of a Smurf on the front of it at our local dollar store. I was obsessed with that shirt. I would sneak and wear it every chance that I could even if it didn't match what I was wearing. I kept it for about two years or so and I believe it aged faster than normal because I wore it so much. Mom would have to sneak it away from me to launder the shirt.

Summer 1986 came, and I did the same things I did every other summer. Mom, Dad, Lacey and I went on a beach trip with my mamaw and my dad's older sister and her family. I loved playing in the ocean despite my weird fears acting up one night. Of course, I brought my beloved Papa Smurf, but my Nan Nan did not go. I do remember that Lacey somehow got a nasty ear infection while we were there, and she had to be on antibiotics and ear drops for it when we got back from vacation. When we got back, summer went on as usual, and we went to the local amusement park as much as possible in addition to the annual trip to the local amusement park with my mom's siblings and their families.

I got a medium sized brown desktop fan for my 5th birthday as one of my gifts. I liked it a lot and whenever I would have it on, I liked the feel of it against my face. This particular fan did not come from the Sears Catalog that I constantly peeked through. My mom got it from our local Kmart store.

A couple of days after my birthday party I had my fan turned on. It was a hot summer evening the first week of August 1986 and I was sitting on our kitchen island with the attached bar stools adjacent to my fan. Mom was carrying in groceries and Lacey, and I were in the kitchen. I tried to stick my tongue near the fan. Mom panicked when she saw me sticking my tongue against the fan and scolded me about how dangerous that is.

Shortly after that it was almost time for me to start Kindergarten and for Lacey to celebrate her second birthday.

My nan nan and me

CHAPTER FOUR

There is a time for everything. There is a time for everything that is done on Earth. (Ecclesiastes 3:1 NIrV)

I started Kindergarten in August of 1986. One of my major problems that I experienced was severe separation anxiety starting the day of my kindergarten evaluation. Mom and Dad talked with me about school for several months, I thought I was ready. I woke up that morning feeling very nervous about leaving my family, my home and being in the school situation.

Mom took off from work to go with me to my Kindergarten evaluation. It was a hot summer day in the middle of August 1986 and anxiety swept over me as we drove the five-minute drive to School for my appointment for a Kindergarten evaluation. I was greeted by my teacher, Mrs. Lycans and the Kindergarten aide, Mrs. Smith. After a few minutes of testing tears welled up in my eyes and Mrs. Lycans and Mrs. Smith tried their best to calm me down.

"I want to leave," I said, with anxious tears in my eyes.

"Honey, it's ok. You are almost finished for the day," said Mrs. Lycans as she tried to calm me down while we finished the assessment.

After my kindergarten evaluation my mom, myself, Lacey, Nan Nan, and my cousins, Amber and Aaron, that stayed with us frequently on weekends went out for ice cream later that day. When we got back home, we ate our ice cream and that's when I noticed that I lost my first tooth. That scared me quite a bit and of course my Nan Nan comforted me. No one warned me about losing teeth, but I had my first dental visit over the summer. Most kids are at least six years old when they lose their first tooth but not me. That night I got a dollar under my pillow because I lost a tooth, and I cherished that dollar.

A week after kindergarten evaluations it was time for me to start kindergarten. Mrs. Lycans and Mrs. Smith happily greeted all of the incoming Kindergarten students, including me and the day happened to be a great first day. I met all of my classmates/friends the day I first started Kindergarten. I was fine my first two days of school and I think that I just happened to have a bad day on that day that I started crying all day. When I experienced a bad day for any reason it often led to a bad week and multiplied.

"I miss my mom and Dad and my Nan Nan," I said, sobbing in panic mode for two hours of being at school one day.

"Kids come and gather around me please," said Mrs. Lycans as she motioned the class in a circle for story time and discussion. Here I was crying and sobbing uncontrollably while the other kids felt excited to listen to the story, lesson and discussion.

While the other children in my class gathered around Mrs. Lycans for story time, Mrs. Lycans excused herself from the other children and led me to the other side of the room to sit where it was quieter in hopes of trying to calm me down and to be less of a distraction for the other kids in the class.

"You have cried uncontrollably all morning and I want you to sit here so you can hopefully calm down and rejoin the class, said Mrs. Lycans. You cannot cry like this honey. You have to go to school. I am very sorry you feel this way."

"Why is Lauren crying," asked one of the other kids.

"She is just very nervous about coming to school. She will be fine," said Mrs. Lycans.

Days like this continued and as much as I disliked it the constant crying only worsened. My separation anxiety was so severe that it caused me to cry uncontrollably about stuff that I feared but would most likely never happen. I knew what I felt but describing my worries felt very difficult for me because I did not know how to explain them to anyone in a way that I felt like others could understand. I wanted to play with the other kids in my class during recess, but it was difficult due to my severe emotional distress caused by severe separation anxiety. This caused many people that knew me to think that I did not want to socialize with other kids, which was not true.

Mrs. Lycans told my mom that during school one day another little girl in my class tried to console me and I pushed her away from me and I did not realize that I pushed her away from me. If I realized at the time that I was pushing this other little girl away from me, I would have stopped and apologized.

Whenever I was in kindergarten in the fall of 1986 parents had the option of sending Kindergarten students to school five days a week while some kids went to school three days per week. I was one of the students that went to school 3 days per week. When I was in early elementary school the kindergarten through fourth grade classrooms were placed in double wide trailers outside the main building of the school. The trailers surrounded the main building of the school, which housed the gymnasium and cafeteria in the same room, the principal's office, and the fifth through eighth grade classrooms. There was one small bathroom for the girls and one small bathroom for the boys in the trailer classrooms and we shared them with the class on the other side of the trailer. This along with my weird sensory issues caused me to be very uncomfortable to use the school bathroom that was in our classroom. I always felt that the school bathrooms in the trailer classrooms were dirty, too small, and there was not enough privacy. I would hold it back if I needed to use the restroom while at school. Sometimes I ended up having accidents and that frustrated my parents. I later learned that other children with autism spectrum conditions and comorbid disorders have bowel and bladder control issues due to sensory processing issues.

It became clear to my mom when I entered kindergarten that I had some sort of issue that was causing me to have daily emotional outbursts as well as unusual fears. Mom told me that one day whenever I was in Kindergarten that she drove to my pediatrician's office after work one day without me and had a consultation with him about me having all of these issues in school. Mom had great faith in our pediatrician and prayed as she drove to the consultation without me. It made sense to my mom that Dr. Robinson would have answers for her about my problems. Dr. Robinson had been mine and Lacey's Pediatrician and we always went there for regular checkups and sick visits.

Mom tearfully explained all of my symptoms in detail to Dr. Robinson and expressed how she felt concerned that I was different from other children. She even handed Dr. Robinson a note written by Mrs. Lycans that expressed her concerns that I was having trouble in class.

"Lauren is just a bit nervous about being in school. It just takes some children longer than others to get used to being in school and Lauren is one of those children. Dr. Robinson had strong feelings about five-year-old children being in class all day. He recommended half days. She just turned five years old and that is a bit young for kids to be in school all day. She will eventually catch up to her peers."

Leaving the office that day, Mom thought he didn't understand. She was so frustrated as she left Dr. Robinson's office that fall afternoon. Because he was such a good doctor, kind and compassionate, Mom wanted him to be right but, in her heart, she felt that he just did not understand how bad the situation was. There is something not right about Lauren, I know it, I am her mother, Mom thought.

It was obvious to Dr. Robinson that I had no signs of any major medical problems. Upon all of my exams by Dr. Robinson I appeared to be ok and met all of my physiological milestones besides having sore throats that required a tonsil and adenoidectomy with tubes placed in my ears. I did not have any speech delays. That says how much doctors knew about the different types of Autism when I was a child back in the 1980s. My parents didn't even have the type of video cameras that were popular in 1986. For those that had video cameras back in the day no one videoed their child acting up. As embarrassing as it is, being able to document behaviors on video as well as keeping a diary, is one of the best ways to provide important clues about your child to a doctor.

Over the next few days my mom talked to Dr. Singh that worked with her at the hospital where she was employed at. Pediatrics was not his speciality but he has seen my problems and has gotten to know my family over the years. He agreed with her that I had something going on and that I needed to be checked out. During his free time Dr. Singh worked on composing letters detailing my symptoms and Mom gathered up more information from Mrs. Lycans. Dr. Singh sent a long-detailed letter composed of several pages of notes to a team of pediatric specialists at Cleveland Clinic in Ohio to evaluate my case and to get me an appointment there. They got me in for a two-day evaluation there with a team of doctors for January 1987. Until it was time for my appointments at Cleveland Clinic, Mom and Dad focused on the upcoming Christmas season and school Christmas program.

I remember our school Christmas program of that year. My class sang the Christmas song "When Santa Claus Gets Your Letter" and each of us had to dress up as a Christmas character. I was dressed up as Rainbow Bright, while the other kids in my class were dressed up as reindeers, Santa Claus, elves, one student was dressed as a Christmas tree, and another one was dressed as a present.

Lacey and I went shopping with my mom and my Nan Nan at our local mall for Christmas gifts. Like most kids of that time period, I loved going to the toy store and getting a new toy. That particular day I saw Nan purchase her Christmas gifts for Lacey and Me at the Toy Store. It was Oopsy baby dolls. I mentioned to Mom that I saw Nan purchasing us some new Oopsy baby dolls and Mom told me that she was just getting boxes as a way of trying to playfully trick me.

Christmas of 1986 came, and Lacey and I got our fair share of other Christmas presents. Later that day we went to celebrate Christmas at my Nan Nan's house and with my usual extended family. When it came time to open presents, I found that my gift as well as Lacey's gift was that Oopsy Baby doll that I saw Nan Nan purchase at the mall earlier in the month. People always say that Autistic People are not aware of what is going on around them. In that moment I was highly aware that Nan purchased those Oopsy baby dolls, but I just did not tell anyone that I saw her buy them earlier in the month when I opened the gift.

I learned sometime over the Christmas Holiday season of that year that I had a new baby cousin. She was born five days before Christmas. Nan Nan told me about her and of course I heard everyone else talking about her too. Nan did her best to get me excited about going to visit family and about visiting my new baby cousin. I had no clue that my trip to see my cousins would also coincide with a trip to Cleveland Clinic for me.

The first week of January 1987 I went back to school, and I displayed my usual behavior patterns. As the month wore on, I got more excited about meeting my new baby cousin, Amanda. Finally, it was the day to leave to go visit our family or so I thought. It was a cold wintry day in late January of 1987, and we were packing up to leave. I did not understand that we were first going to be spending two full days at Cleveland Clinic to find a diagnosis for me. As they were packing for everyone to leave for the trip to Cleveland Clinic and to visit family, anxiety and and anticipation filled my parents, especially Mom. After days of little sleep, packing and confirming hotel accommodations, weeks of getting all of my health history put together and working through health insurance woes it was time for that trip to Cleveland Clinic that would change my parents lives forever.

Snow flurries floated around outside in the late January air as Mom and Dad loaded up the car with our luggage. We picked up Nan and her stuff from her house and we were on our way to Cleveland Clinic. Dad and Mom sat up front while Nan Nan, Lacey and I sat in the backseat trying to keep ourselves somewhat entertained with books, coloring books, paper and our favorite small toys.

Mom prayed as we traveled to Cleveland for doctors that could find out what was wrong with me and be able to help me. She prayed that there would not be anything seriously wrong, and that it would be something treatable. She wanted to find treatment that I would have happiness and be able to go to school like other children, and that it would be something that i could overcome.

After making a couple of stops for gas and snacks it was getting dark. I noticed that when we stopped it didn't look like a house. It was a hotel. I thought we were lost. Mom reassured me and although she had told me about the doctors, I thought we would be staying at my Uncle Jack's house. She reassured me that after we stayed in the hotel for a couple of days, we would be going on to see our family for a few days. I was a little frustrated, waiting for Dad to check us in. Mom explained again that we needed to see doctors there to see if there was anything we could do to help with the crying and sadness.

We were all crammed into one hotel room together. Lacey and I argued over who got to sleep with Nan Nan, Lacey won. Mom was trying to comfort and get me to sleep. Sleeping was always a problem for both mom and Me. Mom was way too worried about all of my doctor appointments to sleep, and Dad seemed to sleep well.

The streets were snow covered on the morning of my first appointment at Cleveland Clinic. We got up and ate breakfast from a local McDonalds and as it was time to leave for my first appointment Dad drove Mom and Me the few blocks from the hotel to Cleveland Clinic Children's Hospital section in the snow. Nan Nan and Lacey stayed behind at the hotel to watch cartoons and play with the toys we brought along.

I listened as Mom and Dad discussed the sequence of my appointments that day. I was to see Dr. Erinberg, the director of Pediatric Neurology first. Mom read directions to Dad as he navigated the Cleveland address and street names, there was no Google Maps or GPS then.

My Mom said she was so nervous as we walked in the building and headed to the department of pediatric neurology for my first appointment. She checked me in at the registration desk and proceeded to fill out a ton of papers while Dad sat down in the waiting room with me, and I played in a two-story playhouse with a slide. After riding down the small slide in the playhouse several times it was time for me to go back into the exam room.

Mom accompanied me in the exam room while Dad sat outside in the waiting room. The nurse took my vitals and took more information to be given to the doctor and left the room. I was fascinated with a fan I heard humming somewhere in the building and I started a conversation with Mom about it while we waited on the doctor. A few minutes later Dr. Erinberg entered the room.

After greeting us warmly and making introductions, he began to clarify the information that he already had. Mom said it was obvious that he had reviewed all the material that had been sent ahead of our visit thoroughly. He did a detailed history in his interview with Mom. She discussed her concerns about my strange phobias, trouble socializing and the inability to control my emotions. They discussed my intense interest in fans and hair dryers. She also verbalized her concern regarding my lack of awareness of other people to the point of rudeness, despite teaching me manners. Dr. Erinberg questioned extensively about speech development, but that had all been good. He took extensive notes (no computers then).

Dr. Erinberg then performed a thorough neurological examination on me. He noted a few small things about me such as my left pupil being larger than my right pupil and clyndactily, meaning that my little fingers were significantly shorter than my ring fingers. Mom was most impressed with his thoroughness and skills with a 5-year-old. At the conclusion of his history and exam he advised that he also would like to get a head CT to make sure there was nothing going on there.

Dr. Erinberg explained that he had read the letters sent from our family doctor and the notes from my teacher. He said that he was aware of the distress that occurred with parents when a child does not conform to the normal classroom environment. He told my parents that based on the letters he read from Dr. Singh, the notes from my teacher and his findings that he felt like I had a condition called Pervasive Developmental Disorder. He was aware that I also had further appointments with the Psychiatrist and Urologist and told us that he would compare his findings with that of the Child Psychiatrist at the completion of the other appointments. Dr. Erinberg was very kind and informative with my parents.

We went back to the hotel to check on Nan and Lacey and then we all went out to get some dinner at a nearby restaurant. Night two at the hotel was cramped again with poor sleep for Mom from going back and forth between beds with Lacey and me. Disappointment about my diagnosis and anxiety over the next round of appointments and testing ran through Mom's mind all night long.

The next morning, we got up early and had breakfast, preparing for a big day ahead of us. A big snow blanketed the ground that morning in Cleveland and it was a very cold and a typical January day. Lacey and Nan once again stayed at the hotel while Dad drove Mom and me back to Cleveland Clinic for day two of appointments and testing after breakfast.

We walked outside in the bitter cold weather to the car and drove back to the Cleveland Clinic. Mom explained to me that I would be seeing Dr. Rue for my first appointment. Mom assured me that all he would be doing was to talk to me, and also probably Dad and her. She explained that after that we would have that "fancy x-ray" done of my head. After that we would be having an appointment with another doctor. I could not wait for these appointments to end so we could go visit my new baby cousin as we had planned.

We checked in at Cleveland Clinic Department of Child and Adolescent Psychiatry for my appointment with Dr. Rue, the chairman of Child and Adolescent Psychiatry. Cleveland Clinic was a big place that was easy to navigate because we were assigned to follow a line based on colors of where we were supposed to go to. Mom filled out more paperwork while Dad and I sat in the waiting room. Anxiety over seeing another doctor ran through my body and tears were gradually filling waiting to spill out my eyes, and I now know that my mother was probably just as anxious as me.

Dr. Rue proved to be another kind person as he escorted me and my parents back to his office. He was very welcoming, inviting me to play with the toys in his office as he and my parents were seated comfortably. After introductions he went over the information he had received from my doctor, the teacher, and Dr. Erinberg. He inquired of my parents what their concerns were, and what behaviors I displayed that concerned them. He proceeded with a long line of questioning of his own.

While Mom and Dad were still talking with Dr. Rue I climbed up into Mom's lap and started sobbing and crying uncontrollably and told Mom that I wanted to go back to the hotel and see Nan Nan. Mom was trying to calm me down while talking to Dr. Rue at the same time. She could barely hear what Dr. Rue said because I was crying so loud. So, Dr. Rue ended up mostly talking to Dad while Mom was trying to console me.

"This is what I recommend for Lauren if you are willing to try it," said Dr. Rue to Mom and Dad. A low dose mood stabilizer medication or antipsychotic and I would also recommend play therapy services that involve trying to gradually get her to engage with others around her while she is playing."

After a consultation with Dr. Rue, it was time for my appointment to have a CT scan of my head. Again, we followed the assigned color of lines to the designated area in Cleveland Clinic. Mom checked me in at the Radiology department while Dad and I waited on her.

A few minutes later I was called into the CT room. Mom went inside with me while Dad stayed outside in the waiting room of the Radiology Department at Cleveland Clinic Children's Hospital. Mom had to wear a lead apron to protect her from potential radiation while I was getting my CT scan. Terrified about having a medical test done and seeing a huge machine in that room I had no idea what that thing would do with me inside it. After several minutes of trying to get me calmed down the technicians handed me a flashlight to hold while the table slid me into the CT scanner machine.

After the CT scan of my head, we went to lunch at the cafeteria while we waited on my appointment with the urologist, Dr. Kay. It was then time to head to the urology department for my appointment with Dr. Kay. A third round of paperwork about my medical history for Mom to fill out while Dad and I sat and waited in the waiting room.

Dr. Kay recommended an ultrasound of my urinary tract because he felt that although my exam was normal that there could be something causing my chronic urinary tract infections. I had the ultrasound done and that test as well as the CT scan of my head was normal even though Dr. Kay later wrote in a note back to Dr. Singh that I needed further testing and more antibiotics for my chronic Urinary Tract Infections.

Later that day we went back to Dr. Erinberg's office to discuss the results of the CT scan of my head. Dr. Erinberg confirmed the diagnosis of Pervasive Developmental Disorder to Mom and Dad. He assured my parents that they did nothing wrong, it just happens, that it is not life threatening, but there is not a cure. He assured my parents that with having a child like me, they would celebrate milestones and skills that other parents take for granted.

"Pervasive Developmental Disorder" refers to a group of disorders that are neurological in nature but can affect the development of a child. These disorders usually cause mental health symptoms despite being neurological in nature.

At the end of the trip to Cleveland Clinic I had a confirmed diagnosis of Pervasive Developmental Disorder by both Dr. Erinberg and Dr. Rue. Dr. Rue also felt like I may have Schizoid Disorder of Childhood and Dr. Kay felt like I had chronic urinary tract infections without any known cause.

Relief, but frustration at the same time swept through my parents as we headed to visit with family two hours away in Pennsylvania. We stayed there for the weekend, and I was so glad to see my long-awaited baby cousin Amanda and hold her and visit with family. I have always loved my Uncle, Aunt and cousins so much. After a nice visit, we headed home.

I continued Kindergarten and I still had my issues of autism spectrum disorder/PDD. Mom and Dad did their best to help me to succeed and to follow the recommendations from the doctors at Cleveland Clinic. It was difficult because both of them worked full time. Dr. Rue and Dr. Kay wanted me to come back for follow up appointments, but it was hard due to distance, time constraints and of the fact that our health insurance only covered so much out of network expenses.

I followed up with a local urologist as advised and took a low dose antibiotic long term for my Urinary Tract infections. Atarax was prescribed for premedication for dental appointments, or procedures. The atarax was too sedating to use while attending school.

Our school Kindergarten Easter egg hunt was held on the week of Easter. I was always good at finding eggs when we would have our family Easter egg hunts at my Nan's house, but the school Easter Egg Hunt was totally different. I was nervous and frustrated about not being able to find a lot of eggs. It was the school environment, I was not used to being in competition for the eggs, and there probably were not as many eggs.

One month later, in May of 1987 we had Kindergarten graduation. It was common in the 1980s to have Kindergarten graduation ceremonies. I was nervous about my Kindergarten graduation ceremony, and I was the only girl seated amongst all of the boys in my class on one side of the stage while most of the girls were seated on the other side of the stage and whenever we had to sing our songs I didn't participate. I just stood there. As a way of celebration our class took a field trip to our local amusement park, the day after our graduation; I had looked forward to that day forever. A few days after kindergarten graduation and the class trip to the amusement Park it was time to end school for the 1986-1987 year and begin summer vacation.

My aunt Sylvia, my mom's sister, came to visit us. She knew that I had a weird fascination with fans of any type. She said that she would pinch my nose off every time that she heard me say the word fan. From that point onward she would do this to me if I mentioned fans anytime I was around her. I knew that she was teasing me in a fun way, and I loved hearing her say that. "Fan," I would say whenever I would approach Aunt Sylvia just to hear her say that she would pinch my nose off and tickle me.

My family went on a beach vacation just like we did every year since I was born but this time we went sometime near the middle of July. I was beyond thrilled to be at the beach and loved being around my cousins and Aunts and Uncles. It was fun and this time we had my mom's entire family except for my Aunt Sylvia and her family with us. We did all of the other summer stuff that summer that I liked including going to our local amusement park whenever we could.

Family picture of the four of us in spring 1986
Dad is holding Lacey and I'm standing against mom

CHAPTER FIVE

A cheerful heart makes you healthy. But a broken spirit dries you up.
(Proverbs 17:22 NIrV)

Six and three years are good numbers. Mom decided to celebrate our birthdays together that year. Sometime around the second week of August between mine and Laceys birthday of 1987 Mom decided to have Lacey and me a birthday party together instead of two separate parties, nine candles total to blow out, six for me and three for Lacey. My family from out of state as well as all of our local friends and relatives were invited as usual to our birthday party. Before the birthday party I went with Mom to shop at our local Kmart store. I picked out a puzzle map of the United States and asked Mom if she would get it.

The day of the birthday party arrived. Mom came home after work that day with a huge cake that said Happy Birthday Lauren on one corner and Happy Birthday Lacey on another corner. When it came time to blow out the candles Mom wanted everyone at the party to wear a party hat. I had worn party hats before, and I did not like the way they felt against my face. It was a sensory thing related to Asperger's, but I refused to wear a party hat. Each of us had our own stack of gifts to open and the puzzle map was one of the gifts in my stack. I loved that puzzle and played with it constantly and ended up learning all of the different states and Canada with that map.

I started first grade in August of 1987. It was a hot sunny day in mid-August of 1987 and Mom took the day off of work to drive me to school and get me used to the idea of a new classroom. I didn't know that I would progress to first grade. I thought I would be back in kindergarten. Mom started explaining to me a bit about transitioning to first grade the day before school started and continued as we drove to school the next day. If Mom had a day off from work, she always drove me to school and came back to get me. On days that she had to work I always rode the school bus and it felt like a treat for me whenever Mom drove me to school and came to get me at the end of the day.

I didn't know what to expect with school and being in first grade. I asked my mom where my friends from kindergarten would be. Mom explained that they would be in first grade too, and that I would have a new teacher and she would be very nice. Mom was very encouraging to me on our five- or ten-minute drive to school. She walked me to my trailer classroom, wished me a great day and assured me she would be waiting for me that evening.

As I walked inside the first-grade classroom, I saw Mrs. Burton at her desk and all of the kids from my Kindergarten class eager to get started back to school. If Mom had not explained to me about the transition to first grade, I would not have known what to do. I would have just gone to school feeling very confused and late for class and learned the hard way about promotion to the next grade. I was glad that Mom primed me ahead of time about what to expect because navigating changes like this is harder for kids with any form of Autism as compared to normal kids.

I still suffered from severe separation anxiety and felt embarrassed when I had to use the bathroom at school. Despite the fact that I was severely emotionally disturbed by Separation Anxiety I always completed my assignments at school and usually got fairly good grades. Mrs. Burton was a great teacher and I really liked her as a person. I still had my crazy interest in fans and tried to break Nan's portable electric heater just to see the fan blade yet at the same time my interest with fans gradually started to decrease at that point.

During first grade I developed a fear of the weather at school. I didn't like bad weather anyway and I have always felt insecure about it. Bad weather at school always made me feel more anxious about changes in routine. If the weather was nice my emotional issues and worrying about change in routine still affected me but it was less severe. The two boys in the class ahead of me that were the school bullies would tease me and call me a cry baby during lunch and recess because they still had the same recess and lunch as my class.

It was at that time that I also discovered that I suffered a math learning disorder but excelled in other areas like Spelling and Reading. I would get frustrated easily and that usually ended up in some kind of meltdown. Mom bought me math workbooks and to help me improve in Math she would work with me for long periods of time on learning math.

Try as I might I could never rationalize with the thoughts that caused my separation anxiety. I never saw myself as a mentally challenged kid even though I knew that I was different from other kids. I just thought I was timid. Mrs. Burton would allow me to go to the school office and talk to some of the people in that part of the school whenever I felt like I needed a break from the classroom, and it worked for the most part. I would stay in the office or wherever talking with whoever was willing to talk with me and calm me down. It usually lasted for anywhere from a few minutes to a full hour. Even if I was crying out of control, going to the school office helped me to calm down and the school principal that we had during my kindergarten and first grade years was awesome when it came to helping me calm down on my worst days.

Mrs. Burton and the reading teacher felt like I should visit the reading classroom once a day to try to help me refocus and calm down because I really liked to read. It worked. There was a particular series of books that the reading teacher had that I really liked, and I found myself reading that particular series of books quite a bit when I visited her classroom.

In the Spring of 1988 Mom signed Lacey and me up for gymnastics class. We took it for about two months. She thought that we would like gymnastics because we always liked to watch our cousin Amber practice her flips. I was terrified of the idea of flipping over and I wanted so badly to not have that fear, so I could learn the flips. To make matters even more nerve wracking there were a large number of other children in the class. I believe I would not have been quite as afraid if I had taken a private class. The instructor and my mom thought that I just didn't like it but that was not the case. I was scared to have my body in space not knowing where I was going, and I knew that if I were to do it once that I would overcome that fear. I now believe that I would have performed much better if Mom signed me up for a private class to start, but I did not know how to express my feelings.

Right around the end of February and the first week of March 1988 I had another episode of the transient synovitis infection in my left hip joint that I had three years earlier. It struck me one night and like before it really hurt to move, it was horribly painful. The pain continued to worsen for the next few days and one night it took a turn for the worse. Dr. Singh was gone the following day and Mom felt like I needed to be seen so she called our pediatrician, Dr. Robinson and we got in later that day. Dr. Robinson immediately referred me to an orthopedic surgeon and he admitted me to the local hospital for X-rays, more bloodwork and a biopsy of my hip synovial fluid to check for a bacterial infection. I had my leg in traction in a hospital bed for the next three days, took antibiotics and aspirin every four hours. I was miserable. Children on the Autism spectrum do not tolerate changes in routine, and hospitalizations are scary for everyone. Mom stayed with me the entire time and Dad came in every day after work to visit. It was confirmed that I had a severe case of recurrent transient synovitis. When I got home, I had to use crutches and continue the aspirin until I went back for a followup with my orthopedic surgeon that saw me in the hospital.

Later that spring I learned that my mom and my dad both earned college degrees prior to getting married and having me and Lacey. I started asking people where they went to college, including some of the teachers at my school during recess and lunch. It turns out everyone that I interviewed went to school at Morehead State University. Asking people about their educational background became kind of an obsession for me. I also developed a fascination with geography thanks to the puzzle map I got for my birthday several months earlier and figuring out how to get to different places.

When I healed up from my hip problem, I wanted a hula hoop. Hula hoops were a popular toy back in the 1980s and one other student in two grades ahead of me brought her hula hoop to school for her friends to use at recess as well as herself. One day shortly after school let out for the year Mom and Dad took Lacey and I on a small overnight trip to a local hotel with a pool for one night. The next day we went to the local Walmart, and I found a hula hoop that I wanted, and Mom got it for me. I wanted to learn how to hula hoop and for several days after that I practiced and got good at it within a week or so.

We took our annual beach vacation that year just like we always did. That year Uncle Milt, Aunt Joyce and their two children, Mamaw and Nan Nan also went. I loved playing in the ocean. Playing in the ocean helped me to deal with the weird sensory fears. One night while we were on that particular beach vacation, I thought I saw what looked to be a wolf looking inside from the front door of our beach house. I thought a wolf ran up the stairs of our beach house and decided to look inside. It turns out it was just the way that the light was reflecting from the kitchen of the beach house to the screen door of the entrance.

At our annual family reunion of Nan Nan's family that July I asked everyone that I encountered about their education experience. (Back then it was a two-day event. The first day we had an auction and a soup bean dinner and the following day it was a food and fellowship only event and there were a lot of people). I became obsessed with earning a college degree like my parents did and that dream continued for the next twenty plus years of my life. I was still somewhat interested in fans too but not quite as much because by that time it started to fade even faster than what it would if I would have tried to control it.

"Where did you go to college? Did you go to kindergarten when you were a kid," I asked about everyone that I got a chance to visit and chat with while we were at the reunion on both days. I knew the answer to most of everyone's questions. The majority of those that I asked said they did not earn a college degree, and some did not even finish High School. Most of them just got married young and had large families instead. I loved hearing the sounds of how people's voices sounded when I heard them talk. I told everyone that I was going to go to Morehead State University because Mom and Dad went there, and I was going to drive a green California Raisins car.

Me and Lacey around December of 1986

CHAPTER SIX

In this world you will have trouble but be encouraged. I have won the battle over the world. (John 16:33 NIrV)

Second grade begun like any other school year for me. I continued to cry every day at school. School started around the middle of August. I continued to visit the reading teacher's classroom as recommended once a day as a way of helping me to redirect my feelings because reading always seemed to help me. Since I was very good at reading the reading teacher one day wanted to see if I could recognize and pronounce words that were harder than second grade level. I did. The professional term for this is called Hyperlexia. Hyperlexia is a term that refers to a child being able to recognize and pronounce words that are beyond his or her age level and at the same time having difficulty understanding the meaning of what they read. Hyperlexia is common among people with autism spectrum disorders.

As recommended by Mrs. Sparks the second-grade teacher, the special education teacher and the math teacher also allowed me to come to their classrooms at certain times of the day as a way to get my assignments done and it worked. My anxiety continued and I started biting on pencils whenever I got frustrated doing homework and whenever I felt like I could not master it, especially math homework and I still gnaw on pencils today. I was able to function well with our math teacher that year and she was able to help me improve my math skills. Mrs. Bond was our math teacher, and she was not only good at helping her students succeed, but she was also patient with me and that helped me to keep my emotions stabilized.

I still did not understand how to tie my shoes at that point and was behind in that area. My Mom came up with a different idea to help me to learn how to tie my shoes and it worked. Shortly after school started that year my mom fixed up a shoe box lid with shoestring size holes in it to help me learn how to tie my shoes the correct way. My dad was the one that taught me how to tie my shoes. One evening when Dad got home from work, he told me "Lauren," we are going to learn how to tie shoes." I practiced it every day and it worked. I learned how to tie my shoes without any help in a about a week.

The previous principal took a new job, and a new principal had taken over. During the fall of 1988 my second-grade teacher was pregnant with her son, and she took maternity leave during late September through mid-November of that year. We had a substitute teacher for that period. Our substitute teacher was the primary substitute teacher for the entire school and by that point she had gotten to know me well enough to know my needs. There was a particular day I was crying uncontrollably, and she sent me to the principal's office in hopes of trying to calm me down because it normally helped me.

I spent the entire day in the principal's office. While in the principal's office, I received a paddling for crying so much, which only made my reaction worse. Punishment for my meltdowns has always been counterproductive. I was given a lecture by the principal explaining how she felt like my behavior was wrong. I never told my parents about the paddling, but I never told them anything specific, just answered yes or no when they asked if I had cried that day. That night, getting in the bathtub, Mom saw the bruises on my bottom.

"Honey said Mom in a calm but well-meaning voice. You have to find a way to control your crying. Daddy and I love you very much and want you to be happy. It makes us feel sad when you are upset. Lacey also loves you very much too. You make other people worry about you. When you cry like that you disturb the other kids in your class."

While I went back to school the following day and repeated another day in the principal's office at school Mom went to work feeling tired from lack of sleep caused by feeling frustrated and worried about me. Struggling to contain her composure and focus on taking care of her patients, Mom confided in Dr. Singh whenever possible on that day about what happened to me.

During the next several days mom tried to remain calm about my punishment despite feeling very upset about it. The rest of the family was very upset about it too. Lacey was too young at the time to understand all of this, I never told anything to anyone about school.

A week later I had a doctor appointment with another specialist for an unrelated problem at the time. Mom took the day off from work just like she always did whenever I had one of my many appointments.

We drove to Dr. Singh's office that morning before heading to my appointment. Dr. Singh always went to the hospital to see patients during the morning hours or did work in his office and saw patients in the office in the afternoon hours. When we got to Dr. Singh's office I stayed with his secretary and she gave me lots of stuff to draw pictures on while Mom talked with Dr. Singh privately about my punishment by the school principal while gathering my medical records for my afternoon appointment, and to discuss options for local mental health referrals. While waiting on Mom I was content to color and draw pictures because I liked art anyway and was good at art. About a month or so earlier I drew an entire map of the United States.

I developed an intense fear of dogs, especially large dogs like German shepherds. Nan Nan always warned Lacey and me about her neighbor's dog being mean and about diseases spread by animal attacks. She always worried about us. We were with Nan at her house one Saturday while Mom was working, and Dad was doing work on the farm when the neighbor's dog happened to come up to Nans' house. It was at that point that I started feeling the sensory issues around dogs and inability to control my intense feelings of fear without screaming and crying.

Mrs. Sparks came back to school shortly before Thanksgiving break and soon after the Thanksgiving break it was time for our annual school Christmas program and our two-week Christmas break.

The two-week holiday break from school was a relief and I enjoyed getting new stuff for Christmas and spending time with my family.

After the two-week Christmas break, we went back to school on the first week of January of 1989. My sensory fears that I mentioned in previous chapters came back and they were debilitating as usual but as I got older, I was able to control them better sometimes.

One weekend near the end of January in 1989 my weird fears were acting up. I started on a Friday evening with uncontrollable screaming the whole weekend because I felt as if everything I saw or heard in the corner of a room would be some weird animal just like I had before during these episodes.

"Please Lauren, calm down and tell me what you are so terrified of," Mom asked.

It really was hard to explain, and I was not able to explain these feelings to Mom and Dad They were frustrated because they wanted to help me but didn't know how. If I didn't have those sensory fears, I had the other emotional control symptoms. I mostly experienced the sensory disorder fears at home, and it was really frustrating to try to control them without screaming and crying.

School provoked anxiety and stress related to completing my assignments, and fear of not being able to master the work, especially Math assignments. Separation anxiety continued. It was during the second semester of second grade that I started to experience low self-esteem and social isolation. I was unaware of it, but I was later told that I even made the honor roll once or twice that year. Students that earned honor roll status for their grades and/or perfect attendance for a certain grading period got an ice cream bar for their treat at lunch time at the end of a particular grading period every six weeks but, I must have been absent from school on the days that Ice Cream was given to students who earned honor roll/perfect attendance status.

Mom and Dad tried Counseling with me in the Spring of second grade with a recommended private PhD counselor. He was actually a child psychologist. His office was located in the same building that housed the Autism Society of America at the time and more than likely he had some affiliation with the organization. The psychologist was an elderly man, and I am sure a nice person, but I just did not feel comfortable talking to him. He tried to engage me in play therapy during his counseling sessions, but I was distracted. I felt fearful of the sound from a fan in another room that felt loud against my ears. If that fan was on, I ran past the room where it was located into the psychologist's office.

Toward the end of the therapy session Dr. Mock would usually bring Mom and Dad back inside the room for a family counseling session. After one session he told them that he was concerned about some irrational fears that I expressed toward the fan in another room of the department. My parents were surprised about this because I liked fans. Mom asked me about it one day on the way to one of my appointments with Dr. Mock. I couldn't explain it. That particular sound was scary to hear.

One day Mom and Dad went to an appointment with Dr. Mock without me. They explained all of my symptoms and he told them that some of my behaviors were learned behaviors. He recommended some books for Mom and Dad about parenting, they felt frustrated but were willing to try to help me.

Despite me developing new symptoms such as poor self-esteem and old symptoms such as my fascination with fans fading away, I was able to end my second-grade year without any academic issues. The second-grade class went on two school trips that year. The first-class trip we went to a small zoo about an hour away and during the first week of June that year we went to our local theme park. I enjoyed that and my mom always made sure that she was able to go on all of mine and Lacey's school trips.

Summer of 1989 was an interesting summer as always. My family took our annual beach trip and stayed in a beach house. This year we went with my Aunt Sylvia and her daughter Tara, my dad's niece and her family and both of my grandmothers, Nan Nan and Mammaw. It was during that trip that I went to my second amusement park, and I loved it. The beach and amusement parks always made me happy. The night we went to the amusement park I felt like I was on cloud nine riding lots of rides including a small roller coaster that I rode twice. The summer continued to be great, my parents continued to take us to the local amusement park periodically. Aunt Sylvia and Tara spent a few weeks of the summer with my Nan Nan after we got back from the beach that year, and my Uncle Jack and family visited that summer too.

As the summer continued, Mom spent time preparing Lacey for Kindergarten since she would turn five years old in August of that year. About two weeks before school started Mom took me and Lacey to get our annual checkups for school at Dr. Robinson's office and also shots because Lacey had to have her immunizations for kindergarten, and I needed a shot too. Later we did the annual back to school shopping trips for our new clothes at our local Sears store.

Summer 1988
I was almost seven years old and Lacey was almost four years old

CHAPTER SEVEN

Love your enemies. Pray for those who hurt you. (Matthew 5:44 NIrV)
Be fair when you judge other people. Then you yourself will not be judged.
You will be judged in the same way you judge others. You will be measured
in the same way you measure others. (Matthew 7:1-3 NIrV)

What happened in the world in 1989 and 1990? The ending of a decade and the beginning of another one is one way to put it. After three years of completion two new shopping malls in our area opened up. New Kids on The Block were all the rage and I fell in love with them the minute I had seen pictures of the guys and seen a video of them. Lacey started Kindergarten that year and loved school. TV shows such as Saved by the Bell, 90210, and Melrose Place became popular among teens and preteens. I watched some of the episodes of Saved by the Bell. Nintendo's became a household game and my closest cousin, Aaron owned one, but I was not yet interested in a Nintendo.

Third grade started off like any other school year. I went to school dressed in my new school clothes that Mom bought me. The school bullies continued to harass me at recess and lunch since our classes shared the same recess and lunch periods.

Lacey was excited to start Kindergarten and had no trouble adjusting to school. Whenever Mom was off from work, she would drive Lacey and I to and from school just like she had always done with me the previous three years. One day whenever Mom was off from work Lacey asked her to let us ride the school bus home and I was not happy about it, yet I agreed to ride the school bus with her. It was different because it was a change in routine. Mom believed in playing fair and I grew up believing that it's important to give equal attention to kids. It is important to figure out ways to be fair to other children that will not cause anxiety in your child that is on the spectrum.

My meltdowns continued and I still suffered from Separation Anxiety. The sensory fears were still there but not as bad and I tried to hide them as best I could. There were other symptoms that increased. This included pressure to succeed, fear of failure, unrealistic expectations, and low self-esteem. This caught up with me and not only was I crying all the time; I went through a phase where I was not sleeping or eating enough. This caused me to get Shingles. Shingles normally does not affect young people, but it got me because I was so stressed out about school and could not control my emotions. Once you have chicken pox, the virus never leaves your body, and stress can cause it to flare, but instead of chicken pox, you get shingles. It was three painful patches of blisters on my side that my mom discovered getting me out of the bathtub.

Mom knew that Lacey contracted chicken pox from my outbreak of shingles. She had to stay with Nan Nan. The first day she stayed home from school she took a hot bath because she felt bad. When she got out of the tub the chicken pox had popped out all over her face. Nan Nan got tickled at what she had told her when she looked in the mirror, "Oh no, my life is over!" She was sick with the chicken pox for a week and had to be out of school. She loved school and didn't like missing.

One day I went to the school office because I could not control my crying. I spent the majority of the morning in the principal's office. She sat me down and had a chat with me this time and I was allowed to go to the cafeteria for lunch but at a time before my class went to lunch. I was told to come back after lunch and when I got back to her office, I noticed that she had someone in the room with her. I can remember this particular September day back in 1989. I was not told ahead of time that I was getting a teacher's aide. She introduced me to Miss Bernice and told me what would happen the rest of the week. Miss Bernice told me that there wouldn't be much she would do today, but that she would meet me in the classroom when I got to school tomorrow.

I really liked Mrs. Bernice. She was a very nice person and she spent most of the school day in the classroom beside me and was there when I needed her. There were some benefits of having Bernice with me. She helped me whenever there would be unpredictable situations that would arise at school that would worsen any meltdowns. That was a blessing to me. She helped me to be able to complete homework assignments and to prepare for other school stuff. I am not saying that Mrs. Bernice was a crutch to me. What she did was to help redirect me whenever I would have a meltdown or needed a break from something, and it really worked. My anxiety and social issues were still there and as long as she was there to redirect me, they were not as bad. My grades significantly improved and for two grading periods I was able to earn honor roll status.

My mom signed me and Lacey up for piano lessons in November of 1989 and I really liked piano lessons even though I did not practice as often as I should have. Lacey did not like piano lessons as much as I did and after a month of sessions, she wanted to quit but I wanted to continue. It was stressful to complete a piece of music for every piano lesson session but practicing my piano lessons also proved to be therapeutic for me. Mom and Dad got a first ever camcorder video camera that year shortly before Christmas and they used that on a regular basis.

Its difficult for kids on the spectrum to learn lessons but I learned a lesson that Christmas about asking Santa Claus for a doll that I wanted. I learned that some toys did not always work in the way they were advertised. I asked for a Betsy Wetsy doll that I saw in the toy section of the Sears holiday catalog and received it as a gift. Betsy Wetsy was a doll that was supposed to pee in its pants after feeding it if you squeezed its hand. Mom followed the directions that came with the doll but she could not figure out how to make it work in the way that the directions said, and she even enlisted help from my Uncle Melvin later that day at our Christmas dinner. He could not figure it out either. Mom was disappointed for me about what happened with my Betsy Wetsy doll and pondered on taking it back to the store to exchange it. Kids with any form of Autism usually believe anything they read about or hear about, and I was fooled into believing that a Betsy Wetsy doll that pees its pants when you squeezed its hand would be the coolest thing ever. I did not play with Betsy Wetsy as much as I did my Barbie Dolls and my Kitchen, and it was at that point that I felt like I should have just asked for Barbie stuff and New Kids on The Block tapes since they were extremely popular, and I loved them a lot.

After being out of school for two weeks it was time to go back to school. Our first day back at school we had a math test and I got frustrated about it and cried because I felt like I could not master it. My teacher aide had to be gone that day for some reason and I did okay for the most part without her except for getting frustrated when I blanked out during the Math test. Yes, this did result in a meltdown.

During March of that year, it was determined that Ms. Bernice could not be my aide anymore and the school had to get a different aide. There were certain requirements for education that changed at the time, and she did not meet those new qualifications and the board of education could not afford to pay her. Ms. Bernice was a wonderful person and I wanted her to continue being an aide for me and she did not want to quit. The other students in my class liked her too. My class had Mrs Bernice a going away party with gifts, as well as pizza and cupcakes. My Mom brought cupcakes for the party and had them to school at the time for the party. The party happened around 2pm in the afternoon and students handed Mrs Bernice gifts and artwork that they created. She thanked us all and told us she enjoyed her time with us.

The other Aide at the school already employed became a fill-in for me throughout the remainder of the school year. I still continued to do good with the presence of the aide. She was very nice and great with kids too. I was still not where I needed to be developmentally and emotionally but having an Aide in my classroom in third grade was the best thing that ever happened to me in elementary school.

At the end of the school year in third grade I earned a science fair award. I tied with another girl two grades ahead of me as the overall winners of the School Science fair. My science fair project was based on a plant turning color when you mixed food coloring in the water.

Skip It toys were popular that year and I played with the one I got when it was nice outside.

Lacey's class had their Kindergarten graduation in May of that year, and I was able to leave class long enough to attend her graduation. Nan Nan, Mamaw, Mom, Dad and I went to her graduation. Mom videoed the ceremony with the video camera that she got in December.

During the summer between third and fourth grade I finally got up the courage to learn how to ride a bicycle and that helped me to feel more confident in myself. Thanks to my Nan Nan I was able to learn how to ride a bicycle. Mom was so surprised to find me riding a bike when she stopped by Nan's house after work to take Lacey and me home. She told me how proud she was of me. When my cousins would come for a visit Lacey and I would always have fun riding bikes with them at my Nan Nans house, she had the perfect place to ride bikes.

This was the first summer that my family did not take our annual beach vacation. Instead of going on vacation Mom and Dad used their vacation money to upgrade our basement and add an extra living room and another bathroom.

I continued taking piano lessons for the summer while Lacey had long since quit. I made progress on that front too. One day that summer Mom, Lacey and I were sitting in church during the Sunday School preliminaries listening to the piano for the singing portion of the service, "Do you think you can play the piano that well someday," Mom whispered in my ear while trying to participate in the singing portion of the service."I hope so," I said.

My extended family came that summer for our annual family reunion with Nan's brothers and sisters. One of my cousins had a new baby that summer and she brought the baby for us to see. My weird interest with fans and with people's educational backgrounds was still there but it decreased significantly without any effort. Over the years I noticed that my older cousins wore makeup whenever they would visit us. That, coupled with me admiring the red lipstick and nail polish that my great aunt Gladys from California wore made me want to wear makeup. One day while my Aunt Sylvia was home, she wanted to take Lacey and I shopping at our local Kmart store to buy us something. I wanted makeup but she did not want to get me any makeup without consulting Mom about it first but since Lacey just wanted a Barbie doll, she got one for her.

About a week later we had another family reunion, different relatives (my grandfather's family). Aaron, Lacey, and I along with bunch of other extended cousins were playing. It was almost time to leave, and I took my shoes off because it was really hot in the building. Aaron was trying to be funny by trying to hide my shoes and I was crawling across the slick floor trying to get one of my shoes before Aaron found it and I ended up falling and breaking my front tooth. Aaron was freaking out and I was beyond terrified. Aaron ran screaming to Mom. I was wailing of course. "Put it in milk, " said one of the women at the reunion as she got Mom a glass of milk for the remainder of my tooth. Mom called the dentist as soon as we got home, they instructed her to put it in milk, and they got me in on the next business day and repaired my tooth.

Mom told me that she wanted to try to get me and Lacey tickets to go and see New Kids on The Block in concert for our birthday because I loved them so much, but they were already sold out. I came near having a total meltdown, but I just went ahead and asked for the rest of my birthday gifts anyway.

I had my first piano recital, and I was mildly nervous but at the same time very excited. I was not as nervous as most people about stuff like this. The recital came and went, and I remember telling Nan Nan and Mamaw about it and they always loved listening to me practice piano. "Oh Lauren, if you stumble just keep going," Nan said when I told her that I felt nervous about messing up while playing my recital songs. The day of the recital came, and I did well. I enjoyed playing my songs for an audience and had no anxiety.

I wanted a camera for my birthday and Mom got me one. It was a yellow 110 film camera, and I liked it even though it didn't take the best pictures. I really enjoyed that camera and took pictures of everything. I would even pose my dolls or my stuffed animals and take their pictures.

The weekend before school started, I got a perm in my hair at the beauty salon at our local mall. Permed hair was in style during the late

80s and early 90's and my mom thought I would look cute with a perm in my hair. My shoulder length hair was perfect for a perm.

About a day or so before school started, I felt back to school anxiety with concerns about what would happen to me since I didn't have an aide to redirect me yet. I had lots of concerns, and Mom told me to just to do my best and try not to cry. I wanted to wear makeup to school that year, but Mom wouldn't let me.

CHAPTER EIGHT

If you judge someone else, you have no excuse for it. When you judge another person, you are judging yourself. You do the same things you blame others for doing. (Romans 2:1 and Matthew 7:1 NIrV)

The fall of 1990 and a new school year arrived. What happened in 1990-1991? Some girls from my school moved in the house next door to my family and I liked that because it was nice to have friends to hang out with after school and on the weekends whenever we did not have anything to do. The school had a cheerleading squad in addition to their boys' and girls' basketball teams for the first time since I was a student there. They had cheerleading there on and off in the past. Academic and Spelling Teams, 4H, and Girl Scouts were some of the clubs that were offered for certain grade levels and age groups. My Mom enrolled myself and Lacey in Girl Scouts. I was the only student from my class in Girl Scouts and I didn't like that part of it. I still continued with my weekly piano lessons.

I started fourth grade and Lacey started first grade and she was beyond excited to start back to school. I wore my new backpack that I got for school. It was a New Kids on the Block backpack and in my backpack, I had several other New Kids on The Block themed school supplies, including a trapper keeper, pencil bag, and folder. New Kids on The Block were still the hot band of 1990, and I was obsessed with them like a lot of other girls were. I went to school that morning trying to hold my emotions together and doing everything to keep from crying. I asked my friends in my class about their summer and their family every time I had a chance in order to keep myself from crying.

"I like your perm in your hair," said Teccoa, one of the other girls in my class.

"Thanks," I said.

"How was your summer," I asked Teccoa.

"Great, said Teccoa. How was your summer?"

"Good," I said.

Lunch came and then after lunch I crumbled, I had held it together as long as I could.

"Alright class, '' said Mrs. Miller, as everyone settled into their seats after lunch. "Please get out your social studies book and turn to the first page of Chapter One." Mrs. Miller was the fourth-grade teacher.

As I got out my Social Studies book, I could feel my heart beating out of my chest, knots in my stomach, and started breathing harder trying not to show that I was ready to cry. It was at that moment that I bowed my head and tried to hide that I was crying, and it didn't go well because Teccoa sat in front of me, and she noticed that I was upset and asked me what was wrong. Everyone in the classroom knew that I was crying again, and Mrs. Miller also asked what was wrong.

I didn't say anything because at that moment I was trying to stop the tears. It didn't work.

About an hour or so later we went to our science class in a different classroom, with the fifth-grade teacher, Mrs. Bentley while the fifth-grade class came to Mrs. Miller's classroom for Social Studies. I felt a little bit better at that point knowing that in about an hour or so it would be time for the school buses to arrive to take the students home for the evening. We had Science from around 1:30 to 2:30 and on Wednesday from 2pm to 2:30 because the the fifth-grade class went to the library during that time period. That bothered my anxiety because I thought that we would have to stay at school longer for the day. I would try to rationalize with myself on this issue, but it was extremely difficult like many of the other issues I faced. If we had science tests on Wednesdays that always made a bad situation worse for me.

Well Lauren how was school today, asked Mom as she walked in the door. She noticed that I cried today because my eyes were swollen, and I had dark circles under them. Please tell me that you didn't already start crying again."

"Sorry Mom, I cried today," I said.

"I wish you would not cry so much at school, said Mom. You will always get to come home at the end of the day. It hurts me when you cry, and others worry about you too. We love you and want you to be happy. You need to try to figure out ways to deal with your anxiety."

My weird interest in fans from when I was a toddler was already on a tremendous decline naturally and without any assistance, but it was still there to an extent. I still needed Ms. Bernice as my classroom aide, but no one was able to find an aide in time for school of that year. Things started to get harder for me in fourth grade as far as my grades go. I had always struggled to keep my grades up any way and really had to work hard. I still went to the special education room daily and usually worked on my assignments there. Because I was not able to have Ms. Bernice as my aide again in fourth grade things took a turn for the worse. I slipped back in the cracks and cried every day again just like I did before I had a teacher's aide.

One day when I was crying really hard in school, I admitted that I wanted Ms. Bernice to be my aide again. I cried so hard that I urinated in my pants. I was crying uncontrollably while heading off to the main building of the school from our classroom. One of the other Aides that occasionally visited my classroom to check on me walked me to the main school building that day. She told me that Ms. Bernice was not able to be there and that I needed to find ways to deal with things.

Changes in routine at school always worsened my Separation Anxiety. In fourth grade Physical Education was combined with our Health class. Health and PE classes were alternated on certain days of the week. We would have health class twice a week and PE three times a week for one week and vice versa. This happened through the remainder of our fourth-grade year. I had a difficult time participating in Physical Education (PE) class because I was still terrified of the picture of the wildcat that hung on the wall inside the school gymnasium. I was still not able to admit that I was terrified of that picture of the wildcat. I always did my best to participate in PE, but it was a relief if I had to sit down on the bench and wait my turn for something. I would try to redirect my fear of the wildcat picture by either drawing in my notebook or reading my weekly library book. We always had our PE classes after our afternoon recess and since it was the last class of the day on days that we had PE instead of Health class everyone in my class brought their stuff to the gym with them in order to walk straight to the rooms where students stayed while waiting on the busses. It was a relief on days that we had Health class instead of PE because I would not have to see the picture of the mascot in the gym that bothered me so bad.

"What's up Lauren, " said Chandra, one of the other girls in my class one day during PE class as I had my notebook out drawing in it and waiting for my team to be in the lead again in dodgeball.

"Oh nothing. Just drawing a picture in my notebook," I said, trying not to let Chandra know that I was terrified to look at the picture of the mascot hanging on the wall.

"Come on, it's your turn. Our team is up to play," said Chandra.

"Ok," I said, joining the part of my class on my dodgeball team while watching the clock to see how long it would be before we left for the day and hoping to not notice the picture of the wildcat.

When my first report card of the year came in Mom was glancing at it.

"Lauren, you need to start participating more in PE class honey. PE is part of your grade." I knew she was right, but I did not want to tell her the truth.

By the time I entered fourth grade everyone knew that I was the girl that cried every day at school. Other kids started asking me frequently why I cried all the time, and I knew that those kids were just curious. I did my best to be kind to those kids and explain things that would make it simple for them to understand.

One day on the bus ride to school another girl sat down beside me because that was the first seat that was available for her.

"Lauren, may I ask why you cry all of the time at school," said the other girl out of curiosity and by no means bullying me in any way.

"I just stay stressed out," I said, trying to keep things simple because it was too complicated to explain everything in detail on a noisy school bus.

"If you feel too stressed out just take a break and lay your head down," said the girl.

I developed tics around October of 1990. It was annoying and frustrating to deal with. My tics symptoms include strange grunting noises, feeling the urge to constantly take a deep breath, talking out loud to myself when I didn't realize that I was and that makes people think that I am talking behind another person's back.

"Why are you grunting," said Dad one night as he and Mom were helping me study for some tests. I don't know, but I don't know I am doing it, I can't help it" I said. Mom and Dad, I know felt frustrated and wanted to help me with the tic sensations that I had at the time. Try as I might to control them, they are just as hard to control as the intense emotional outbursts. I was never medically diagnosed with Tourette Syndrome or any other form of tic disorder. I still have tics to this day, and I am most often unaware that I am having them until someone else mentions them to me. The next day at school the tics continued, and it was a disturbance to everyone in my class as well as my constant crying.

As fourth grade progressed Mom and Dad decided to try some alternative approaches with me. In November of 1990 I was homeschooled for almost a month, and I had a very hard time staying motivated to do my schoolwork. Resources for homeschooled students were very limited during that time period. Both of my parents still worked full time and the homeschooling teacher for our area at the time only came to a student's home once a week for about an hour to show what kind of assignments needed to be done. It was hard for my mom and Dad to work full time and work with me at the same time. My Nan Nan helped me with my schoolwork as needed. I completed the same criteria as the other students in my class even though I was homeschooled. I just did my assignments at home and at a different pace. Lacey on the other hand still went to school every day and continued to perform well in school.

I went back to regular school around the week before Thanksgiving and my anxiety set back in. I believe it was better for me than being homeschooled. We got ready for the annual Christmas program at school and our class sang the Christmas song "Deck the Halls." The first-grade class (Lacey's class) sang "Rudolph the Red Nosed Reindeer" and wore reindeer masks made from construction paper. Mom took off from work early that day to come straight to our Christmas program. She videoed the whole thing with the video camera that Dad got her the previous Christmas. Our main gift that year was a Barbie doll house for both of us. I played with it constantly for the next several years. After our two-week Christmas break it was time to head back to school for the Spring semester.

Mom had even considered switching me to a private Christian School near the hospital where she worked as a nurse. She had found out about that particular school from one of her nurse friends at the hospital whose son went to school there. The rules of that particular school were much stricter than the rules at my current Elementary School. Mom had done some research from her friends on this particular school for me and the research was startling. Crying caused by severe separation anxiety would never have been tolerated there, and my dad would not permit my mom to have me on the road that much, and he thought it was too unsafe.

One day that spring while I was in class one of the school aides came to get me in class.

"Excuse me, Mrs. Miller Mrs. Smith wants to talk to Lauren for a few minutes."

"Ok. That's fine. Lauren go on down to the gym please," said Mrs. Miller.

"Lauren, I was wondering if you would want to talk to me for a few minutes," said Mrs. Smith.

"Yes," I said.

"Would you be willing to talk to me about why you cry while you are here at school and what we can do to help you not to cry so much," said Mrs. Smith.

It was at that moment that I opened up so much of my feelings and why I cried so much while I was at school. It was such a relief to be able to have someone at the school sit and listen to me without having to send me to a mental health professional. Yet I still refused to mention that I was terrified to look at the picture of the wildcat mascot on the wall in the gymnasium because that was still way too difficult for me to talk about. Within a few minutes I started feeling better and even asked Mrs. Smith about her family and her children.

Mom went shopping at a local store that spring and while shopping she happened to run into a lady who knew about me from school. "There is nothing wrong with Lauren. You have spoiled her to death," said the lady. Mom felt very hurt and embarrassed and left the store, but she did not say anything.

Times for me and my family were tough, but my parents truly cared about me and wanted me to get the best education possible. Hardships are part of having any chronic problem and there are times when it will flare. When coming into contact with someone on the autism spectrum or their loved ones its okay to ask whats wrong, but do your best to show kindness.

Mom and Dad enrolled me in therapy services. Part of my treatment plan involved working with a case worker who would visit my home about once a month and regular counseling services once a week either at my school or at the clinic with my counselors. My caseworkers held monthly meetings at school with my teachers, the school administrators, and my parents. The treatment plan also consisted of me participating in a summer program for emotionally disturbed children.

One psychologist consulted by the same agency recommended that I be homeschooled for the remainder of the school year. He felt that I was traumatized by school. For the last nine weeks or so of my fourth-grade year I was placed in a nontraditional homeschool environment with a different aide, Mrs. Pack who was an amazing person. She was a retired teacher who loved working with children. My Nan Nan always stayed with me on days when Mrs. Pack would come to the house, while my parents worked, and Lacey went to school. Mom had made a classroom in the basement, with a school desk, chalk board, and things she thought we would need in the family room. Mrs. Pack came to my house, and we had school there in the basement of our house in the mornings on certain days of the week. I still had to follow the school criteria such as end of the year school assessment testing, which I disliked because it never affected your grade, and it was always incredibly boring. Mrs. Pack drove me to go to school twice a week and we would have class in a different room in the school and I would have PE and lunch with the kids in my class.

I had a good summer and spent a lot of time hanging out with the girls next door, Rachel and Donna. Rachel was a year older than me, and Donna was a year younger than me. They would come over in the day and oftentimes they would spend the night with Lacey and I on a regular basis. I continued with Piano lessons and at that point had no intention of stopping.

Twice a week I attended the program for emotionally disturbed children. The morning of the first day of my group outing with the local group of emotionally challenged kids came.

"Are you ready to go have some fun," said Kim, the director of the program when Mom opened the front door.

"Yep, I said ready to leave. Bye Mom. I love you; I said as I left in the van with the other kids.

For the outings in the group for the emotionally disturbed children we always went to the main building for about two hours until around 12 noon. We would usually do artwork and talk about how to deal with our feelings, McDonalds for lunch around noon and then to the local YMCA for about an hour of exercise and an hour of swimming in the pool at the YMCA before returning home for the day. Mom couldn't wait to hear about my day. I told her it was a good day, and I made some friends.

We did not take a beach vacation because Mom started classes working on her master's degree. I was okay with that because Lacey and I had Rachel and Donna to hang out with almost every day when we were home. That very same year we also had Mamaw a surprise birthday party in our newly remodeled basement with all of my dad's brothers and one sister and all of their families, Mom's side of the family that was already in for the Fourth of July holiday, and a couple of Mamaw's siblings. I played "Happy Birthday" on my piano as Mamaw entered the room to blow out candles on her cake.

Near the end of the summer program for emotionally disturbed kids I happened to have a bad day and ended up quitting after that. It had absolutely nothing to do with anyone else in the program or any of the employees. It was almost over for the year anyway and it ended during the last week of July.

I still loved New Kids on the Block and by that point one of my new kids on the block VHS tapes was nearly torn up because I watched it so much. Toward the end of July, I had my second Piano recital, and I did well. I began focusing on my upcoming 10th birthday and making a list of all of the new toys I wanted. One item that I wanted was a Magic Nursery Newborn doll. Magic Nursery dolls were a popular toy item in the early 1990's. Lacey started collecting the collector's edition Barbie Dolls and one doll in particular that she asked for as a birthday gift was a Happy Birthday Barbie doll. Because I was interested in doing hair and makeup Aunt Yvette who is Uncle Melvin's wife gave me some beauty supplies from her beauty salon.

Lacey's birthday fell the day before school started and Mom and I went to our local Kmart store to do some last-minute shopping for school and Lacey's birthday party about a day or so before. We happened to run into Charlie, a boy in my class who was also school shopping. He and I talked about going back to school and what fifth grade would be like.

"Are you ready for school to start back," said Charlie.

"No," I said. What about you?

"Fifth grade is going to be hard," said Charlie.

"I agree," I said.

The day of her birthday Lacey had an amazing birthday party and she got nice gifts and had a Little Mermaid themed cake. She loved all of the Walt Disney classic movies, and The Little Mermaid is still one of her favorites.

The very next morning school was starting for the 1991-92 school year and the stress and worry of starting back to school had already set in for me. I started crying and told Mom how I dreaded how hard fifth grade would be.

"It's going to be ok, said Mom. Calm down. If you want me to, I will try to come home earlier."

"Ok," I said, continuing to cry.

That night as Mom and Dad helped me, and Lacey get ready for bed and get our school stuff ready to start back to school in the morning Mom decided to have a chat with me.

"Lauren are you aware of the fact that there are parents that do not want to send their kids to school because of your behavior," said Mom.

"No, I said. I don't mean to be mean, and I would never hurt anyone."

"I know honey, but you need to do your best to stop crying so you won't scare anyone else and make them think that you're mean when you're not."

CHAPTER NINE

Lord, who can live in your sacred tent? Who can stay on your holy mountain? Anyone who lives without blame and does what is right. They speak the truth from their heart. (Psalm 15:1-2 NIrV)

I had never dreaded the first day of school as much as what I did for fifth grade. By the time that the school year started that year I had already learned to dread going back to school and my separation anxiety that came with it. As I entered the classroom on the first day of fifth grade with all of the other kids that I had gone to school with for the past five years, my anxiety was at an all-time high and I just felt like there was no way that I could control it.

"Welcome back students, " said Mrs. Bentley as she explained to us what would happen for the school year. She explained that we would have different teachers for Math and Social Studies and that we would take typing class whenever the school computer lab opened up. We then began our first-class session of the day. I immediately started crying because the anxiety, and frustration about not being able to complete assignments kicked in at full force.

For the first week of fifth grade, I was placed in the regular education setting with my teacher and the rest of my classmates from the past five years. It was then determined that Mrs. Pack should be with me again from around 11am until the end of the day every day. Mrs Bentley had different ideas than the other teachers did about dealing with me. My anxiety and the pressure to succeed was so intense that I screamed and cried even on the school bus in the mornings, and I was normally well behaved on the school bus. Because of this the bus driver wanted me to ride the handicap bus in the mornings.

Until that point, I was never intentionally disrespectful to teachers, and I was very disrespectful (unintentionally) to Mrs. Bentley one day out of frustration while we were working on a science assignment in class.

"Alright class, " said Mrs. Bentley. Please get out your science books and turn to chapter 2 and begin reading. Then I have some questions for you to answer."

"Oh no, I said, crying hard again. I don't think I can do this. Can someone please help me? I just want to leave. I don't like this!"

Mrs Bentley explained her concerns about my behavior to me. My heart was pounding out of my chest from both frustration and anxiety. I stood up wringing and grinding my hands and reacted disrespectfully to Mrs. Bentley. She and most other teachers did not know how to deal with kids like me. No one knew how to deal with kids like me back in those days.

About an hour later it was time for Mrs. Pack to come and work with me for the day. The day went on and Mrs. Pack and I did ok. I continued to wring my hands and gnaw on pencils every time I felt frustrated about not being able to master an assignment as well as any other time, I felt frustrated or anxious. I still have the stemming behaviors today. Suppressing the urge to stem when upset in any way has never helped me. Besides biting on pencils if I were working on Math, I never had stemming behaviors until that point. When I got home from school that afternoon Mom noticed that I was grinding my hands up. My mom was very concerned and like many Autism moms she worried over me doing that and felt worried that I would damage my fingers.

"Lauren please stop doing that with your hands, " said Mom.

"What will happen if I don't stop," I asked, still feeling frustrated over the homework assignment that I was working on earlier.

"You will injure your fingers, " said Mom trying to reason with me. Now get upstairs and finish your homework so we can go eat supper with Nan Nan.

What happened that school year? Kindergarten and Preschool classes were added and held for half a day. We had a cheerleading team at my school in addition to basketball for the second year in a row since I was a student at there as well as 4H, academic teams, and Girl Scouts. Lacey and I were still members of Girl Scouts, and I was still the only student from my class in girl scouts. I was never a cheerleader or a basketball player, I just couldn't with my weird sensory issues. Seventh and eighth grade classes were moved to our new junior high school, which housed grades seven through ninth grade at that time.

Mrs. Pack felt that it would be good for me to read to the preschool class in the afternoon on certain days of the week and I started that shortly after school started for the year. A few minutes later I went to the school library and picked out a kids book to take to read to the preschool class.

As I walked inside the preschool and Kindergarten classroom Mrs. Lycans introduced the class to me.

"Class this is Lauren, and she is going to read us a story," said Mrs. Lycans.

I started reading the story and all of the kids had their eyes on me as an audience. Whenever I finished the story, I asked the kids what they thought.

"Did you like it," I asked, smiling at the kids.

"Yeah," said one little girl and the other kids nodded their heads yes.

"Thanks for coming to read to them, " said Mrs. Lycans. You are welcome to come back every week."

It was at that point that I discovered that I really liked children. From that point on despite me having issues it was a relief to spend a few minutes reading to the preschool class on a weekly basis.

A few weeks later we got our first report card of the school year. I looked at it and noticed that Mrs. Bentley wrote in one section where I was being very disruptive in class. I knew what it meant without asking. As I got home that evening, I handed my report card to Mom, and she glanced through it before putting it back inside my backpack.

"Lauren, do you know what this means? Mom said as she showed me the notes written in the conduct section of my report card. I knew that it was because of the incident that day in science class.

My doctor and my mom decided to try me on the Haloperidol twice a day in the form of drops, that had been suggested previously by the psychiatrist. The goal was to keep me on it during the school season and wean me off of it during the summer sessions. I learned that medication can be used to treat psychiatric disorders that week. It gave me unpleasant side effects at first.

My Mom gave me the medication with Dad close by. A few minutes later I went to the garbage can and vomited. Mom told me I had probably picked up a virus at school. The vomiting episodes did not prevent me from having dinner.

I continued to vomit on a daily basis for the first two months of taking haloperidol and my mom thought it was sinus drainage. I would usually vomit once or twice in the mornings before school and keep the remainder of my food down for the rest of the day. On a bad day I would vomit at school or on the bus usually in the mornings in addition to crying. I really believe it was the medicine that upset my stomach somehow.

One day I vomited after lunch break while Mrs. Pack was working with me on a math assignment. I began to believe that it was sinus drainage that was causing me to vomit because that is what Mom thought it was. Mrs. Pack asked me if I needed to take a break, wondering if I was tired or getting stuck on the assignment and trying to redirect me from having a meltdown. I grabbed the nearest garbage pail and vomited in the midst of doing a math assignment.

A psychologist came to school in September and performed a psychological evaluation on me. I had been riding the handicap bus to school in the mornings for a few weeks and not long after that my caseworkers felt like it would be best if Mrs. Pack would teach me full time, drive me to school an hour later and leave an hour earlier than the other kids at my school. I later had to go to the main office of the local mental health clinic for some more psychological testing. Those test results helped to further confirm my diagnosis of Pervasive

Developmental Disorder and where I stood developmentally compared to other kids my age.

During the mornings I stayed with Mamaw until Mrs. Pack got there and during the afternoon, she would drop me off at Nan Nan's house. I still did the same lesson curriculum and assignments as the other students but with modifications. I was still able to participate in PE, lunch, and recess with the rest of the kids in my class as well as read to the preschool class once a week. Traditional homeschooling did not work well for me, and it was at that point that mom and Dad, and Mrs. Bentley decided that working with Mrs. Pack, in a different room of the school, was the best option for me.

One evening during the fall in late October I overheard Mom and Dad discuss taking me back to Cleveland Clinic. I asked if that was what they were discussing. Mom explained to me it was to follow up with the same doctor to see how they thought I was doing.

In November I went back to Dr. Rue, the Child Psychiatrist that I saw five years earlier at Cleveland Clinic in Ohio for a follow up visit that needed to be done more regularly but could not be done due to time constraints and distance. That visit went well, Dr. Rue was pleasantly surprised at my progress, according to Mom and Dad. My parents continued to take me to therapists and doctors in our area and they would communicate with Dr. Rue.

During that appointment at Cleveland Clinic, Nan and Lacey stayed behind so Lacey could go to school. Lacey was not happy that we had to leave for a trip to Cleveland Clinic. I was not happy about it either, but I knew that if I wanted to live a somewhat normal life, I had to do it. Mom explained to Lacey that it was to help me, and assured her Nan would be with her.

Then Mom, Dad and I left for the five-hour drive to to be with family before heading to my appointment at Cleveland Clinic on Monday reluctantly leaving Nan and Lacey behind. When we got there everyone was glad to see us and I hung out with my cousins Amanda and Richelle, who were five and six years younger than me. My aunt took Mom, her granddaughter, Amanda and myself shopping at a local Walmart for fun.

"Ring around the roses, pocket full of posies," Amanda and Richelle sang as I danced with them and held hands in circles while outside playing the night before my appointment.

"Ashes, Ashes I have to go to Cleveland Clinic tomorrow," I thought to myself as we continued playing.

The next morning Dad wanted us to leave early so that we would have enough time to check in at the hotel and grab some lunch if needed. My aunt and her family owned a restaurant at that time, and she was scheduled to work that day. On our way to Cleveland that morning we stopped at her restaurant for breakfast. I had gravy and biscuits with orange juice, and she showed me around her restaurant. Then it was time to take the hour and a half drive to the appointment.

"Dear Lord, Mom prayed. *Thank you for safe travels and a good visit with family. I pray that you will bless this appointment and that Dr. Rue will do what is best for Lauren. Please get us back home safely and watch over our family back home until we get back, in Jesus's name, Amen."*

We got to our hotel and checked in. This time our hotel was connected to Cleveland Clinic. A few minutes after we got settled into our hotel room it was time to go to my appointment with Dr. Rue. Luckily, we were able to walk to my appointment. When we got to my appointment Mom checked me in, paid the bill, and filled out paperwork to update my chart since it had been five years since I had been there. Then it was time to go back to be seen with Dr. Rue in his office.

"Lauren," said Dr. Rue as he came out to get us.

"Come on back, " said Dr. Rue as he motioned us back to his office. How have you been doing? It has been a while since I saw you?"

"Good I guess," I said with tears in my eyes complaining to Mom and Dad as Dr. Rue welcomed us into his office.

"Lauren I would like for you to come over in this corner and play with this dollhouse, said Dr. Rue. I want to see if you can rearrange the furniture in this dollhouse. While you rearrange the furniture in this dollhouse I am going to talk to your parents." I began to think how to rearrange furniture in the little tikes dollhouse while trying not to listen to the conversation between Mom and Dad and Dr. Rue.

"So, what has been going on with Lauren. How has she been doing since I last saw her five years earlier," Dr. Rue asked Mom and Dad.

"She seems to be stable for right now. She is taking Haloperidol twice daily and I have not noticed any major side effects other than some nausea with it. It does seem to help her sleep better. She still has the emotional outbursts, but they seem to be less severe now that she has private schooling," said Mom.

"I have read the notes from Dr. Singh and Lauren's teachers, and I would like for you to continue giving her Haloperidol and consider adjusting the dosage as needed. Based on her symptoms that you have described and from the notes from Dr. Singh and the school board she does have Pervasive Developmental Disorder. I am happy with Lauren's ability to communicate and how much she has improved. I arranged for her to be evaluated by one of our speech pathologists, but I have now decided that she does not need it. I will make some recommendations for the counselors at your local mental health clinic and the school board for Lauren and I would like to continue follow ups with her as needed.

We then headed back to the hotel and ate dinner at the restaurant downstairs before going to the hotel room for the night in preparation for a six-hour drive back home the next day. We got up bright and early the next morning, had breakfast and left around 8am and got home around 3pm. Nan and Lacey were happy to see us, and my mom was really happy to see Lacey.

When we got back home from Cleveland Clinic the counselors came to my school once a week to talk to me. Mom and Dad continued with the services that we used in fourth grade, including monthly meetings, and having caseworkers come to our house.

Even though I found myself liking makeup and noticed that other girls my age had already outgrown playing with Barbie dolls I still continued to play with Barbie dolls.

One night before December Mom drew an outline of mine and Lacey's feet. I wondered why she was doing this and asked why. "I just wanted to see what size shoe you wear just in case I decide to ask Santa to bring you some shoes this year," said Mom.

Turns out we got Roller skates for Christmas and that's what Mom was measuring us for. Roller skating was lots of fun once I got good at it. I was constantly roller skating in our downstairs hallway in our basement listening to music. Now that we had our own roller skates, we didn't need to worry about renting a pair of skates whenever Dad would take us to our local roller-skating rink. Rachel and Donna still hung out with Lacey and I on Saturdays if we were free.

I developed what I thought was a crush later on in the year on one of the boys in the class ahead of me, but it turned out that it was not a real crush. I was open and honest about my crush, but I never obsessed about him. It was more of a status symbol crush instead of a real crush.

That Spring some girls in the class ahead of me started bullying me at lunch and they thought it was funny to tell me to do stuff just to see if I would respond or not. The boy that was the biggest bully in school continued to bully me and one of the other girls in my class too sometimes. I got up the nerve to tell Mrs. Pack that we needed to talk to the principal about the bullying. Our school principal took a leave of absence for the remainder of the spring year, and we had a fill in principal, whom I really liked. The boy that bullied me got into trouble for it and the principal talked to the teacher of the other class about the issue of me getting bullied. This worked, and these kids did not bully me anymore.

The room that Mrs. Pack and I used was split into halves by a divider and the other side of the room was used occasionally for the school speech pathologist and her students. One day a boy with nonverbal Autism about five years younger than me and his therapist used the other side of the room. That was the first time that I had ever heard of Autism as a disorder and for the next few years I always thought of Autism as a disorder that affected speech and communication even though I knew that I was developmentally delayed. My mom bought Child craft books, encyclopedias, dictionaries, and medical yearbooks that year and I really enjoyed reading them. It was nice having encyclopedias and child craft books to use when me or Lacey needed to do research projects for school because we did not have a local public library other than the school library. I was a research minded person who liked to read about how stuff worked. None of these books contained any valid information about about my type of Autism/PDD. One book had an article about the various types of mental disorders and in that article, there was about two paragraphs on classic Autism. That was all of the information available about the Autism Spectrum. She also got us our first personal computer that she used quite a bit because she went back to school to earn her master's degree in nursing.

All of my mom's siblings came to visit for Easter, both the local ones and those from out of town. I wanted a new Easter dress to wear to Church on Easter. About a week or so before Easter of that year Mom took Me and Lacey shopping for a new Easter dress at our local Sears store. On Easter Sunday of that year, we all went to Church as a family, and I was excited to show off my cute new Easter dress at Church to everyone in the congregation. After church we went back home to get ready for our family Easter dinner later that afternoon. I enjoyed spending time with my cousins and finding easter eggs when Mom hid them.

Rachel and Donna's family had to find a new house to rent. Lacey and I were both very disappointed because it was so convenient to have friends so nearby. We still remained friends, but it just wasn't as convenient.

I still continued my weekly visits with Julia, my counselor who came once a week to my school. I developed low self-worth at the end of the school year. I began blaming myself for everything and continued to feel insecure about myself compared to others. These kinds of thoughts are very draining to experience and worsen anxiety and depression. My problem with self-worth felt magnified by previous experiences that would seem insignificant to other people because I have a detailed memory as part of having Asperger Syndrome/High Functioning Autism.

The school year ended, and summer began. The doctors and counselors felt that I did not need to take my Haloperidol in the summer and advised Mom and Dad to taper me off of it if they wanted to. I tapered off my Haloperidol for the summer and did fine for the most part. Toward the middle of June my family went on a beach vacation for the first time in three years. We drove to Florida and Nan and Mamaw went with us. We stayed for a week and Lacey mostly liked to play in the pool at our condominium. I loved the pool but at the same time felt terrified of the idea of sticking my head underneath the water to swim like Lacey did. Every chance that we got I went over to the beach to play in the ocean and build sandcastles in the sand. One day we went to an amusement park about 30 minutes away from where we stayed, and they did not have much back then. I was thrilled to death to be going there but I did not know that they had a roller coaster at the time, nor did I even notice it when we were there. Otherwise, I would have been asking Mom and Dad to let me ride it.

Lacey and I went to Girl Scout camp that summer and I was not impressed with Girl Scout camp. Unlike the previous summer I did not participate in the program for emotionally disturbed kids, but I went to counseling on a regular basis with the same counselor that I had seen in my school once a week.

Me and my aunt on Easter Sunday 1992

Easter Sunday 1992

CHAPTER TEN

Blessed is the person whose lawless acts are forgiven. Their sins have been taken away. (Psalm 32:1 NIrV)

What was going on in my 6th grade school year. It was my last year in elementary school. First, second, and third grade students at our Elementary School were grouped together in mixed age groups for different teachers called the primary block. Preschool, Kindergarten, and fourth through sixth grades were not included in any type of category. I still continued to have the same school services as what I did in fifth grade, and I did alright for the most part. I continued to have PE, break time and lunch with the rest of my class and read to the Preschool class in the afternoons on Mondays. I took Karate for a month in October 1992, a therapist had recommended it to my mom. Although I was not that crazy about Karate, I regretted it when I quit it even though I did not tell anyone. The main reason I dropped out of Karate was because I was the only female in my class and everyone else was younger than me. When I dropped Karate, I started back in Piano lessons after a six-month break.

I developed an interest in the Sweet Valley Twins and Babysitters Club book series. I was always a reader anyway and reading those books helped me to redirect my anxiety at school if something were to pop up. I still cried out of anxiety when I was in sixth grade, but it seemed to have calmed down thanks to interventions that were taken.

Another therapeutic treatment suggestion was the Big Buddy program. Melanie, a student from Kentucky Christian University was assigned to be a Big Buddy for me. I liked that a lot. We would meet once a week based on her school schedule, and we would go out to dinner and do some fun stuff. She always had crafts or different activities planned for me.

One day in September 1992 Mrs. Pack dropped me off at Nan Nan's house an hour early just like she always did. Nan told me that Mom was picking me up early to go meet someone coming to the house to meet me. Nan made supper for me, but it was earlier.

A few minutes before 4pm Mom came and got me to bring me home for my meeting with the case worker and Melanie. I went up to my room and a few minutes later I noticed Melanie and my caseworker come to the door from my window. I went downstairs to meet them.

"Welcome," said Mom as she answered the door. Come on in and have a seat."

"This is Melanie, " said Katrina the caseworker. She is Lauren's big buddy from our big buddy program.

"Nice to meet you," said Mom as she shook Melanie's hand.

"Nice to meet you too," said Melanie.

"Lauren, " said Mom, as I stood beside her feeling a bit shy because it was the first time, I met Melanie. This is Melanie. She is assigned to be your big buddy through the big buddy program.

Then as we settled into the meeting Katrina discussed my goals and updates to my treatment plan while I was eager to get to know Melanie better. I thought it was cool getting to know Melanie. That evening Melanie spent some time with us. She talked to us and got to know me, and Lacey too. Melanie was in college to become an elementary school teacher. Kentucky Christian University partnered with local mental health clinics to employ college students to participate in big buddy programs for special needs children.

A week later after school Melanie came to the house to get me for her first weekly outing with me. I was excited to go out with her and meet her friends. I had fun hanging out with Melanie and her friends. Melanie started to reinforce the idea of learning manners with me and how to act socially appropriate yet in a way that was easy for me to understand.

Halloween came and I wanted to dress as a pumpkin while Lacey dressed up as a fairy. Our costumes actually matched due to the fact that Cinderella went to the ball in a coach shaped pumpkin by her fairy godmother. We had no intentions of matching in any way, I now see that.

There were still times that I would cry and would nearly refuse to tell anyone why I was upset and because I either didn't want to be judged and I was taught that you have to always use kind words when you say something. I still do this today and when it happens it shocks those around me. One day this happened while I was in class with Mrs. Pack. She was shocked at why I was crying and feeling agitated and asked me questions about what was bothering me. When I finally told her what was bothering me, she talked with me and listened to my worries, and we were able to get the problem solved. The day later tuned out to be a good day.

During the early part of November of that year Mrs. Pack felt like I needed to visit the Junior High School on a regular basis. She talked to my caseworkers and the school officials, and they agreed to let me visit the junior high school on Fridays. The case manager, teachers, and Mrs. Pack felt like it was a good idea to wean me back into riding the school bus to and from school on Fridays and made plans to do that.

The first morning that I rode the school bus back to school Dad walked Lacey and me out to the school bus stop at the end of our driveway like he always did. Lacey was very nervous about me crying on the school bus and she kept looking back at me wondering if I was going to start crying as we got on the school bus. She didn't say anything. No tears from me on this bus ride to school. That afternoon after visiting the Junior High School Mrs. Pack brought me back to School and I rode the bus home from there.

Our school always had good Christmas programs anyway and this year was our best Christmas program so far in all of my seven years in Elementary School. Lacey's class put on a performance of dancing and singing to the tune of "Rocking around the Christmas Tree." The fourth, fifth, and sixth grade classes did a Christmas play together about Santa Claus with the Elves working at the North Pole to create toys. I had the role of one of the many elves. The school academic team put on an amazing Christmas play too, and the younger grades also did amazing during their program performances. The program ended with everyone in the whole school singing a Christmas song.

I wanted a new camera for Christmas and a Geo Safari because we had one in our classroom in fourth grade, and I really liked playing with it. My other camera that I got two years earlier was not good and I didn't like the pictures. When we opened our gifts that morning, I discovered that I got the new camera like I wanted and some accessories for it along with other gifts. The GeoSafari was the main gift for Lacey and Me.

My mom's local family came for Christmas and after our afternoon Christmas dinner everyone gathered in the living room to open gifts. When I opened my gift from my Aunt Sylvia, I found that it was a photo album and some film. Mom told her secretly that she was getting me a camera for Christmas. I got holiday gifts with my extra allowance money for everyone that came to our house on Christmas as well as Mom, Dad, and Lacey. Toward the end of the evening all of the holiday action wore me down and I started feeling worried that I made a huge mistake by buying everyone Christmas presents. About an hour or so after everyone opened their gifts I went into the TV room, laid down on the couch and cried.

"Lauren said Aunt Sylvia as she walked in behind me. Why are you so upset?" I didn't answer for the longest time. I just ignored her because I did not feel like explaining why I was upset. My Mom asked her sister what was wrong.

"I don't know. She won't answer me," said Aunt Sylvia in concern. Post-Christmas letdown was an issue I always dealt with and still is.

In January 1993 I developed sensory related fears and intolerances that I never had before. I developed a strange fear of a picture of some owls in our living room that I never had before. It was a mother owl and a baby owl. The baby owl had eerie looking eyes. I developed an inability to tolerate the ticking of our pendulum clock and was afraid to look at clocks that ticked for some reason instead of a digital clock. So, because of that mom had to remove our pendulum clock and the owl picture from our living room to the garage. Mom had told me not to look at the owl picture and to not focus on listening the clock, the attempt at redirection didn't work.

In January of 1993 the first ever school shooting to make national headlines happened at the high school in our school district. School was called off for the entire week that incident occurred. After that, a law was put into place and students could no longer carry backpacks to school unless they were clear backpacks. I was worried that would be a challenge for me when I went to seventh grade the following school year. That was never an issue for me as none of the teachers at my Elementary School gave out major homework assignments that would require taking home any textbooks unless you were absent or needed to create a study guide for tests. Mom and Dad talked with the school principal of the junior high school as well as my caseworkers and counselors about me being able to carry a backpack if needed when in junior high school.

We were invited to a birthday party in February. It was my Dad's Great Aunt Martha's 90th birthday party. It was held at our local senior citizens center one Saturday in mid to late February of 1993. Mom was working that day and Dad happened to be off from work because it was on a Saturday. Mom often worked long hours at times, and she even worked some weekends when I was a kid. So, we went to the party in our family van. My Dad drove Mamaw, Nan, cousins Kristy and Clint, Me, and Lacey to the party.

The party itself went okay. I was happy to be eating birthday cake, one of my favorite foods and other birthday party treats. I brought my 35mm camera that I got for Christmas to take pictures of the event because mom and dad wanted me to. Toward the end of the party everyone wanted to take pictures for memories. It was at that minute that I noticed a window to the recreation room down the hall and it looked dark and scary.

"Girls, said Dad as he got out my camera, go over here and sit beside Aunt Martha so I can take your picture with her," said Dad.

"Dad, I yelled out of panic with tears filling my eyes. That room is scary looking. Can we just leave please.

"Lauren, please stay here and let me take your picture with Aunt Martha. She may not be around much longer. It won't hurt you," said

Dad as he motioned me to join Lacey and Aunt Martha in what I thought was the scary looking recreation room.

Dad handed Kristy the keys to our van and she and Nan went outside with me while He, Lacey, Mamaw, and Clint stayed inside the building to take pictures with Aunt Martha. About 10 minutes later Dad and everyone else came outside as I was still crying. When we left Dad expressed his concerns about the way I reacted and there was nothing to be afraid of.

I thought dad wanted to go inside the recreation room to have our picture taken with Aunt Martha. About a week later we got the pictures of the event developed and there was a picture of Aunt Martha alone and one where Lacey was sitting with her. By looking more closely at the pictures I discovered that the pictures were not taken in the recreation room that I perceived as scary. If I would have known that we would not be entering that room to have our pictures taken with Aunt Martha, I would have felt ok. I did not communicate it clear enough to Dad that I was scared of something I thought that I saw in the other room, and he thought that I was spooked about something in the main party room. This type of issue was an example of weird sensory fears that I had when I was younger that I was unable to explain and that no one else was able to guess the problem.

My friend Teccoa who was in my class started working with me on playing some basketball in the school gym to work on my coordination. Mrs. Pack felt like that would be a good idea. I liked it but it was difficult because I was still terrified to look at the picture of the Wildcat hanging on the wall in the school gymnasium. One day Mrs. Pack and I were walking to the gym for Teccoa to work with me on my coordination skills by shooting basketball and she could tell immediately that something was wrong. We waited on Teccoa to come to the gym, and I just felt the urge to run back outside because I was feeling an intense fear of the picture of the wildcat on the gymnasium wall. That type of fear feels like what a normal person would describe after watching a horror movie like the exorcist, a very eerie feeling. Yet at the same time you know that it is harmless.

"I feel like I need to go outside and get fresh air," I said, running fast back to the private classroom that we used.

As I ran back to our classroom Teccoa walked in the gym.

"Are you ready Lauren," Teccoa asked.

"Something is bothering Lauren today," said Mrs. Pack as she chased after me.

"Lauren, why did you run off like that? You never do that," Mrs. Pack asked out of curiosity and concerned about what may have been bothering me.

"I don't want to talk about it," I said not really wanting to admit the truth because I was worried what someone would say if I admitted what was going on and that someone other than Mrs. Pack would find out and I did not want to be pushed to face my fears.

"I know you are afraid of something in that gym. Please tell me what it is," said Mrs. Pack out of concern for me. Mrs. Pack had gotten to know how I had weird fears by that time, and she knew I had a fear of the owl picture hanging on our living room wall. It made sense to her that something in the gym would be bothering me.

"I can't. If I did it would only make things worse," I said, worn out and ready to go home, and not even feeling like even reading to the Preschool class, which I loved. I always told the truth about everything except for this because it made me feel more afraid to talk about the situation.

I noticed over the years that the worst of my problems always flared during stressful periods, major growth spurts or female hormone changes. The adolescent growth spurt with hormone changes can be hard on a person with High Functioning Autism and I believed that is part of the reason that I developed the strange fear of the picture of the owls in our living room and inability to tolerate the ticking of the clock in addition to the already existing fear of the picture of the wildcat hanging on the wall in the school gymnasium. I had been informed somewhat of starting my period before this time and what it would be like.

One month later in March of 1993 I started my period, and it was beyond painful. My mom had been educating me about the beginning of menses by talking to me and bought me several books about it. I read all of the books that she got me about starting my period and my interpretation of what I read about in those books about menstrual pain was that it was something that I could deal with. I was wrong. About two days before I started my period, I came home from school with abdominal pain that would not stop no matter what.

Mrs. Pack dropped me off at Nan's house after school just like she always did. Just as soon as I walked in the door, I suddenly felt a pain in my lower abdomen. I didn't think anything about it at first. I thought it would pass but the pain continued, and I mentioned it to Nan. When Mom arrived at Nan's house to get me Nan felt concerned about me and told Mom that I had a bad pain in my belly. Nan always worried about me and Lacey whenever one of us was sick in anyway.

My cousin and her husband and children were visiting Nan that week. Later that evening my uncle Melvin invited everyone to dinner at his house just like he always did whenever we have family visit. Just before we left to go to dinner Mom gave me some Tylenol to help control my belly ache, but it really didn't help much. The abdominal pain was still there but at least I could eat dinner and spend time with the family.

Later that evening after showering and going to bed the pain was still there and only getting worse with Mom giving me another Tylenol.

"My belly really hurts," I screamed out in pain while doubling over.

"Where does it hurt? Can you point to where it hurts the worst, please," Mom said concerned and using her nursing skills to examine me.

"Everywhere," I said, doubled over.

The first thing that popped into my head when I got this nightmarish abdominal pain was either a kidney stone or appendicitis. As the night wore on the pain continued and I did not sleep well. Mom took the day off from work and kept me out of school for the day just in case I needed to get checked out. The very next day I started my period, and I was a mess, emotionally and physically. I had monthly cramps from that time onward that were normal, occasionally experiencing severe pain, and from the start I always had severely heavy and long periods. During the days leading up to my period and sometimes during my periods my anxiety and moods were always worse and that resulted in worse meltdowns and stemming behaviors.

The day after I started my first period, we had a blizzard and it snowed at least two feet and no one could go anywhere. This was our Spring break week. My cousin and her husband were not able to make it back home and they had to call off from work an extra day because there was too much snow on the road for them to get back home.

One day before school was out that year, Mom took Lacey, our friend Donna, and me to the local Amusement Park one day. I was finally tall enough to ride the larger roller coaster without an adult and that was a relief for me. Riding roller coasters has always been a passion for me, and it has always been my dream to travel the globe to ride roller coasters.

June of that year was an exciting time, Mom and Dad got an above ground pool for Lacey and me. It was small but plenty room enough for my family and it was lots of fun. I loved to swim but I was also terrified at the thought of going underwater.

"Hey, said Lacey one evening while we were playing in our pool. Why don't you try going underwater. It's not as scary as you think."

"I'm nervous about drowning," I said.

"Come on Lauren, you can do it," said Lacey cheering me on and encouraging me.

"Wanna try it with goggles on," said Dad as he handed me a pair of goggles.

"Ok," I said as I stuck my face in the water and left the back of my head sticking out.

"Try it again, you almost got it," said Dad and Lacey."

I tried a second time to get my head fully immersed underwater and it worked. From that moment onward I was no longer afraid to stick my head underneath the water and learned how to swim that summer.

"Yay Lauren," said Lacey as I reemerged from under the water.

"Good Job, " Dad said, clapping his hands. I am very proud of you."

"Guess who learned how to go underwater without fear. I yelled at Mom as she passed by working on her flowers in her flower bed near our pool."

"Me," I said with excitement.

"Awesome," Mom yelled.

"Mommy, look at Lauren going underwater, '' said Lacey. Daddy and I helped her to get over her fear of it."

"Good Job Lacey and Larry and way to go Lauren," said Mom.

June came and went and soon it was time for our annual family reunion and fourth of July celebration. The out-of-town family came for the events. During that time everyone hung out at our place in our pool whenever we were not busy.

During the middle of July, it was time to start preparing for me to get braces. A week before I got my braces, I had two of my top teeth removed. When I got my braces a week later, I had a difficult time adjusting to the pain and it took about two weeks for me to get used to them. It was very frustrating to figure out how to floss my teeth even though the staff showed me and Mom how to floss before we left the dentist office. I was determined to do what the dental staff had instructed me to do.

This was my sixth grade fall picture

CHAPTER ELEVEN

Turn your worries over to the Lord. He will keep you going. He will never let godly people be shaken. (Psalm 55:22 NIrV)
Don't worry about anything. No matter what happens, tell God about everything. Ask and pray and give thanks to him. (Philippians 4:6 NIrV)

What happened when I turned 12 years old? President Bill Clinton had just completed his first full year as a president of the United States. I had braces on for one month and I had already gone back to the orthodontist for my first of my monthly appointments. I think that braces worsened my already existing hygiene type symptoms of obsessive-compulsive disorder because it requires patients to be vigilant about oral hygiene. The other symptoms of obsessive-compulsive disorder were starting to gradually emerge. I was already obsessed with taking care of my teeth anyway. Asperger Syndrome was introduced into the DSM-IV as a diagnosis under the category of Pervasive Developmental Disorders (PDD's) in Spring of 1994 along with Autism. Years later Mom told me that a psychologist diagnosed me with Asperger Syndrome and Julia my counselor followed up on the diagnosis.

I entered seventh grade in the fall of 1993. I made the difficult decision to place my beloved Papa Smurf in a box on the top shelf of my closet because I felt like I was too big to sleep with him and felt like if I had friends over at any time that would be the best thing to do. I was completely weaned off from taking haloperidol as a medicine. I continued to struggle with academics despite working hard.

Lacey started fourth grade that fall. She joined cheerleading on the Elementary School's cheerleading squad. Mrs. Pack was still my Aide for the first six weeks of school, and she was not able to continue being an Aide.

During the monthly meeting that was held in the school conference room at the junior high school in August before school started it was up to Mom and Dad as to who they felt would be the best for me as an Aide. One of Mom's cousins suggested a lady that had just moved in over the summer to be my Aide. I had Mrs. Pack for three years as my Aide at this point and she did not want to leave but I learned to be ok with it. The school could not rehire Bernice either.

"Hi Lauren, " said Mrs. Pack as she met me one morning in my first period class. I just wanted you to know that I have to quit soon, and you will be left with a new Aide." I was very anxious and told Ms. Pack I was. She was very kind and explained that she would be there next week to show the new aide our routine. As much as I dreaded it, I knew it was time for Mrs. Pack to move on and for someone else to be employed as an aide.

A week later I got off of the school bus to see my Aide standing with Mrs. Pack waiting for me. Mrs. Pack introduced her to me. I had to move on into the building to get to my first class, and she walked along with me making small talk. Mrs. Pack stayed for the rest of the week just so she could get to know Sue better and show her what to do. The following week Sue took over as an Aide for me. Sue tried to do her best to help me out at school.

I had PE the first nine weeks of seventh grade and for me being on the Autism spectrum it was difficult to handle being in a situation like that because I was awkward and uncoordinated unlike the other kids. My favorite exercise activities were always running and skating and I always felt more nervous to play in PE class, but I did my best to white knuckle it through nine weeks. I also had a painful problem with my left hip at the time, cause unknown and could not be identified. I had a normal bone scan of my left hip, but it showed a moderate sized cyst on my left ovary.

I still met once a week with Melanie and I really liked hanging out with her. Melanie continued to reinforce manners and social skills with me in a way that I could understand.

After a month or so of being in Junior High School I noticed that for some reason that some of the classes were bigger than other ones, meaning that there were more students than there were in some of the other classes. That was because the smaller classes were mostly special education courses.

I feel very blessed to have come from a supportive family environment with parents and a sister who truly cared for me and because of this I want people to know that just because a child has a disability such as an Autism Spectrum Condition, that does not always have anything to do with the family environment. Mom and Dad followed all of the teachers' recommendations for me. I continued to go to counseling on a weekly basis with Julia. She was still able to come to my school once a week to meet with me for one-on-one sessions. My parents and teachers as well as school administrative staff met with Julia and the caseworkers when they would come to my school on a monthly basis to reevaluate and adjust my treatment goals as needed.

One evening while Mom, Nan, and I were on the way home from grocery shopping we were discussing school and Mom explained to me why I was placed in special education and that it was ok to be placed in special education. Mom and Dad as well as my teachers felt like it would be best if I was placed in special education courses to catch up to my grade level because they felt like I missed out on important educational milestones due to my constant crying in school when I was younger and less stressful for me. I felt like I needed to be challenged more with academics even in Math courses and to take tutoring as needed. I always felt like special education courses needed to be tailored to each student's needs.

I was in Girl Scouts again. This time Girl Scouts met once a week in the school cafeteria during school hours. There were only about 10 girls in the whole school in Girl Scouts. These included girls from seventh, eighth, and ninth grades. I was the only seventh grader in the Girl

Scout club in my school. We didn't really do much in that particular Girl Scout group.

I was still able to go trick or treating that year despite having an outpatient procedure a few days before Halloween. I was a witch and Lacey was dressed as some kind of scary looking princess. This year the Halloween pictures turned out much better because we used my 35 mm camera that I got for Christmas the year before.

By the end of 1993 Sears no longer had catalogs of any type and the only way of picking out my gifts was from the JCPenney and Spiegel Christmas catalogs. Mom also had to tell me that year that Santa Claus was not real.

One night Mom came into my room before I went to sleep and wanted to tell me about the reality of Santa Claus.

"Sweetheart, said Mom I just wanted to make you aware of something about Santa Claus."

"What do you mean," I said.

"Are you aware that Santa Claus is not real and that it is just me and Dad getting you and Lacey your more expensive gifts."

"No, I said. I thought it was Santa Claus doing it," I said disappointed as I found out the reality of Santa Claus.

"No matter what happens I will always try to make Christmas magical for you and play Santa Claus for as long as you like," said Mom.

Kids on the Autism spectrum still believe in Santa Claus and the Easter bunny beyond the normal age of outgrowing those beliefs.

When Christmas of that year came Lacey and I both got school mascot Jackets with our names on them in addition to Barbie stuff, Polly pockets, and some other things. Polly pockets were a hot toy item that year, and they were easier to play with than Barbie dolls because you could easily pack them up to travel anywhere. I got a makeup compact and some red lipstick in my stocking and I wore them as much as I could.

The Winter of 1993 was one of the worst winters I had ever known in my life. Snow started the day of Christmas and Uncle Melvin and his family living close by ended up not being able to make it home and had to spend the night with us because the snow came on fast and was way too deep and slippery for them to safely go back home. It snowed constantly for the next three months. We missed nearly a month of school in January completely due to the snowstorm and I was worried that we would have to do makeup school in the summer. Back in the early 1990's we did not have the technology that we have today in order to allow kids to do makeup schooling online and the internet was not widely available yet. Dad had to drive Mom to work a couple of times in our four-wheel drive Jeep Cherokee or his old 1970's Ford F150 pickup truck. In the middle of January, the electricity went out. Whenever we lost our electricity, it was terrifying for me. Not only was it a change in routine but it was extremely difficult for me to handle it. During that winter our electricity went out several times and when it did it was out for more than one day.

I complained and cried every time that our electricity would go out. Mom and Dad did their best to help me to deal with things even though the situation was still very challenging and unpleasant for everyone. Mom told me that this is something that I just have to deal with for the time being and Dad told me that this happens sometimes and that we need to accept change even though it's unpleasant.

We had to stay with Nan Nan for a few days at one point during that winter because she had a kerosene heater that we used to stay warm, but she still did not have electricity.

Several days later we got a short break from the bad weather, and school started back for the Spring season. Students got their report cards from the previous semester. I was eager to show off my new school mascot Jacket that I got for Christmas. My new aide, Sue, was there when I went back to school.

During my third and fifth period classes of that year we had classes that would rotate every quarter of the school year. The first quarter of the school year I had PE and Kentucky History, 2nd quarter I had art and shop class (I did not do so well in shop class because I found the noises of the shop to be scary and alarming), 3rd quarter I had health and geography, and the fourth quarter I had music and home economics. The grading period that we had shop class the school arranged accommodations for me to go to the library. There was a guy that was in my fifth period class that I had a crush on since the beginning of the school year, and I was hoping that he would finally notice me. It had been long enough, and I just wanted to ask him if he would consider dating me. I finally got up the nerve to ask him in the five minutes before my fifth block class about two weeks after school started back for the Spring 1994 season.

Lunch ended and it was time for my fifth period class, and I told Sue I was going to ask my crush if he would consider dating me. There was no law that said I couldn't do it and what if he liked me but felt too shy to speak up about it.

"Hey," I finally said to my crush as I walked inside the classroom amidst a hallway full of students outside trying to get to their next class. I really think you are cute, and I was wondering if maybe you would consider dating me or hanging out with me.

He didn't say anything to me. He acted really shocked that I did that.

Sue disagreed about my decision to ask my crush about a relationship, and she told me. I had a meltdown over the issue and felt so hurt and embarrassed that I thought that I would never be able to date. I didn't mean to embarrass him; I had a crush on him since the beginning of the school year and I was hoping that he would notice me, and I felt that this was the only way for him to notice me. I have always been extremely honest and no filter. My mother has always said I was "honest to a fault," but that is a characteristic of autistic people.

It was then that I felt self-conscious about dating. I was so upset and embarrassed about the issue for a week that I didn't feel like doing anything. I thought I was never going to be good enough to date anyone because of my being too immature and having emotional control issues. I told my mom and dad about the issue, and both of them expressed their concerns. Dad and I had a conversation about the issue a few days later on the way home from Nan's house and he expressed his views about me expressing to my crush my interest in him.

"Why am I not able to date?" I said as I went to my room and laid down crying.

"Lauren said Mom. For one thing you are not old enough to date. You are only twelve years old. Just enjoy being a kid. You are very pretty, and the right guy will come along if it's meant to be."

Mom and dad grew up in an area and era where it was considered inappropriate for girls to ask boys out. Though I did not agree with these views on dating I did my best to respect Mom and Dad's opinions. Mom and Dad knew that whenever I wanted to achieve something, including a potential relationship I fixated on it so much that I got obsessed with it and if I could not achieve it, I would be devastated.

The weather got bad again. It was around the middle of February, and we had a major ice storm and flooding that caused even more school closures.

One night our house was the only house on our road that had electricity. That night Mamaw, Uncle Milt, Aunt Joyce, Kristy and Clint stayed at our house and went home when it was bedtime. The next morning our power went out too, and Mom had to go to work. She was able to drive to work that day. Dad was off from work that day since it was a Saturday. Dad was always off from work on weekends even though he and Uncle Milt farmed every day. Dad ended up taking Lacey and I to spend the day with Nan Nan because she had electricity.

Near the end of February, a local psychologist came to school and did another psychological evaluation on me. It was time for a periodic psychological test. The previous one was in fifth grade. This test took about half of the day to complete, and I ended up missing half of my first period class and all of second through fourth period class, but I got done in time for lunch. At the conclusion of that test the examiner determined that I had shown significant improvements since my last evaluation in October of 1991.

Following that psychological evaluation, it was time for my parents to come in and discuss the findings of the evaluation. The DSM-IV was released at that time and Asperger Syndrome was introduced as a diagnosis under the category of Pervasive Developmental Disorders. Julia told my parents (and me) that she found me to be much improved since the previous evaluation, two years prior. One of the symptoms of this disorder includes traits of obsessive-compulsive disorder (OCD). My Mom had been told before by a prior therapist that he thought I had Asperger's, and this rather confirmed it. Like most of the other conditions in this category it mostly affects boys. It is less common than other forms of Pervasive Developmental Disorder, but it is less severe, and she conveyed to my parents that she was impressed with the improvements shown in the two years that I had seen her as a patient. She gave my parents a booklet on Pervasive Developmental Disorder, which included a section on Asperger Syndrome and Autism.

"So, Mom, how did the meeting about me go," I asked as she walked in the door. Lacey and I already got home from school and like always Mom drove straight from work to the monthly meetings and Dad would meet her there.

"Julia thinks that you are improving but she thinks you have a condition called Asperger Syndrome and your teachers think you are doing well also, and they are very proud of you," said Mom. Mom gave me the booklet that Julia had given her to read.

Around the first week of March, it flooded and all of us ended up gathering at Mamaw's house, including Nan Nan because the intense raining and storming caused water overflows on the road and electricity outages. The end of our road was flooded and because of that Nan had to stay with us. A few days after our massive flooding and more power failures it was time once again to go back to school.

It was nearing the middle of the third quarter in my health and geography class. One day in my geography class our teacher had us doing an assignment and I was having trouble with it. The other kids in the class including my crush were almost finished with the assignment and I was still working on the first question.

"Come on Lauren, " said Sue. The other kids in the class are finishing up and you are still on the first question."

I tried to concentrate and felt like crying because I could not figure out how to get the assignment done and to make matters worse other stuff was clouding my mind like whether I was going to pass or fail geography and other classes. No one offered to help me complete the assignment.

I finally got the assignment done at the end of the class, but I did not get a good grade on it. My English teacher, Mrs Sanders picked up on the fact that I was struggling academically in school that quarter in most of my classes, including her class. One day in English class we were going over an assignment and I felt so worried over the assignment that I could not control my worry and belted out into a major meltdown in front of the whole class. Sue immediately escorted me outside the classroom and took matters into her own hands and told me what I needed to do when I calmed down.

The next day when I went to Mrs. Sanders' class, I felt better but still nervous. Mrs. Sanders was a caring teacher and truly cared about her students encouraging them to be their best. Before class started, I asked her if I would be punished for my meltdown. She assured me that I didn't do anything to require punishment. I was so relieved and grateful.

Springtime finally came and we got a break from the nightmarish winter of 1994 that left so many people in our area without electricity and water. The third quarter of the school semester ended, and it was time to start the fourth quarter. Spring Break fell in between the third and fourth quarters of the school year and Easter just happened to fall on Spring Break week of that year, and we enjoyed spending time with family for Easter.

Spring break ended and it was time for the fourth quarter of the school year. The music teacher for the seventh grade remembered me from elementary school and she felt like it would be a good idea for me to take her class without Sue and I was fine with that.

I continued to struggle in some classes, but it was a welcomed relief to take home economics and music class. I really liked home economics class. I ended up earning an A in home economics class and music and that boosted my grades and my ego a lot. In Home Economics class we learned basic life skills, cooking and even had to write an essay about something about our lives. In my essay I wrote about my life living with a developmental delay and how I managed to overcome a lot of challenges even though I was still slightly behind other kids.

Mom was curious about the assignment I was working on. I told her I was writing an essay for home economics class. Mom was accustomed to having to help me with a lot of my assignments, she told me that if I got stuck to let her know. It turns out that I did not need any help with the essay assignment, and I already had it completed by the time I went to bed that night.

I turned in the essay the next afternoon in Home Economics class and we got ready for the day's lesson and the next assignment. The following day we got our essays back and as I received my graded essay, I glanced at it and noticed that it said 100% A at the top of it. I was beyond excited.

I showed Sue my grade, she told me it was really good and that I should show it to Julia at my next counseling session. I was so excited to tell Mom and Dad my grade on that essay when I got home that evening. They were so happy with me and praised me for how well I had done.

At my next counseling session, I showed the graded essay to Julia, and she was very impressed with it.

"Lauren, this is awesome," said Julia. You have shown such improvement in the two years that I have been seeing you as a patient and you have worked really hard to do it. For most kids your age it takes them their whole lives to mature this much."

It was time for the annual end of the year assessment testing which I still struggled with. I did the bare minimum to get by on that test because it was not a test that students get graded on.

Most of our summer vacation Lacey and I spent swimming in the pool in our backyard in the afternoons whenever Mom and Dad would get home from work. We still stayed with Nan Nan on days that mom and Dad worked, and we would either ride bicycles if it were not too hot and I would read, and she would usually watch TV. I still went to regular counseling sessions with Julia in addition to monthly orthodontist visits. Mom was still working on her masters' degree plus she and Dad still had to pay for my counseling and orthodontist visits since a lot of it was not covered by insurance.

Aaron and Amber still came to see us on the weekends. By that time Amber had gotten her driver's license and she was able to drive Aaron to places that he needed or wanted to go to. Mom still took Lacey, Aaron, Rachel, Donna and me to the amusement park on a regular basis. One day that summer when we were at the local amusement Park, I told Mom and Dad that what I wanted more than anything for my thirteenth birthday was to go to a larger park about three hours from us. I was obsessed with riding roller coasters, and I was now tall enough to ride roller coasters.

Later on, in the summer before it was time for school to start back my uncle came back to Kentucky for a visit and this time, he brought his granddaughter Amanda to stay in Kentucky with us for a few weeks. She loved spending time with Lacey and I and we loved having her with us. While Amanda stayed with us my thirteenth birthday came and yes, we did go to another amusement park, and I loved every minute of it even though it was so crowded that I could not ride all of the roller coasters that were available. The only major roller coaster that we were able to ride that day was the Racing roller coaster and I loved it.

Dad told me how brave I was to do the big coaster, and I told him I wanted to do more. It was lots of fun and I wanted to go back but due to time constraints, we were not able to go back until the following year.

A week later it was time for school to start back. Mom had the annual back to school lecture with me about how to respect teachers because of how I treated Mrs Bentley that one day in fifth grade. Amanda was still here with us for another week and the week of Lacey's birthday her mom drove to Kentucky to get her to go back home. In Pennsylvania schools didn't usually start back until the end of August or after Labor Day.

As the time for school arrived Mom and Dad wondered whether a school aide would be approved. A few days before school started back Mom and Dad had the usual back to school meetings with my caseworkers, Julia, and the School Principal and Guidance counselor and other educators. Mom and Dad learned that an aide position had been budgeted for me and assumed that we would want Sue again. Mom told the group that she sincerely appreciated having an aide for me but expressed concern that she and I were not the best fit. It was determined in that session that Mom and Dad would still meet with my caseworkers, Julia, and the school staff on a regular basis and I would still go to weekly counseling with Julia.

CHAPTER TWELVE

Those who make fun of others will be judged. Foolish people will be punished. (Proverbs 19:29 NIrV)
We will be judged for what we do on earth. (2 Corinthians 5:10 NIrV)

"Well Lauren, said Mom as I got ready for bed the night before the first day of school. I guess you won't be with an Aide. You will be all by yourself just like the other kids. You will do great because you have improved so much."

"Good night, I love you," said Mom.

The next day Mom and Dad made sure that Lacey and I got ready for school on time as usual. It was her last year as a student in Elementary School. She was a fifth grader, and I was an eighth grader in Middle School.

So, what happened in my eighth-grade year. I still had braces on my teeth. It was my last year of middle school, and I entered the first of the teenage years. Ninth grade was moved back to the high school. In May of 1995 the building in Oklahoma City was bombed and it killed thousands of people. That was the major national event of the year. I was left without an aide for the first time since fourth grade and did good for the most part and gradually got weaned back into regular classroom settings from special education settings, but I had lingering anxiety from past experiences. I was able to function adequately for the most part without an aide with me. I still had uncontrollable meltdowns whenever I would get my feelings hurt, change in routine at school and if I had trouble mastering homework assignments. The low self-esteem continued and started to worsen. Melanie had to drop out of college and move back home for personal reasons even though she was almost ready to graduate. That left her unable to be employed by the big buddy program, but we still remained friends and kept in contact on a regular basis. My piano teacher got a full-time teaching job and had to quit teaching piano lessons. I still continued my weekly counseling sessions with Julia and Mom and Dad still had regular meetings with Julia, my caseworkers, my teachers, and the school administrative staff. My family started attending church on a regular basis. Prior to that we attended church irregularly.

As I walked inside the school building on the first day of school, I was surrounded by a sea of students crowding the main entrance of the school going to the different stations for each grade level to find their names and class schedule. I picked up my schedule and it said that I was in all four of the special education classes and two regular education level classes that would rotate every nine weeks of the school year just like it was in seventh grade.

I mentioned in previous chapters that I was bullied by kids in other classes when I was in elementary school. That came back with a vengeance in eighth grade. I thought the worst of the bullying was over, but it was not.

About two weeks into the school year, I had my first bad day of the year. It was a hot sunny day in late August and some kids in my last period class wanted to tease me about a hurricane coming and I was nervous about it but then logically I knew that hurricanes did not happen in our area. I knew that only happened in tropical areas and that it was a possibility that we could get effects from it but no actual damage. These kids figured out at some point that I had severe Anxiety over bad weather and thought it would be a good idea to see how I would react if they bullied me over the weather.

I walked into my last period class that afternoon after a bad day with tear-stained eyes from crying over other stuff that happened earlier that day and of course I felt very unwelcome by the other students.

"Did you know that there is going to be a hurricane," I heard one of the boys in my class whisper to another boy in the class.

"Hey Lauren, did you know that there will be a hurricane," said the boy, as I sat my stuff down at my seat.

"No, " I said, nervous about the impending hurricane and wondering whether I should go walk down to the school office and call someone to come and get me just in case. What time is it supposed to start," I asked.

"Anytime, " said the boys as they looked at each other. Both of them started laughing and then looked at me.

A day or so later those boys and some other students felt like it would be a good idea to persuade me into thinking that there would be an earthquake at the school, and I believed them.

"Lauren, said Courtney, one of the other students in my class. Don't listen to them. There is not going to be an earthquake."

I felt very blessed to have people like Courtney as friends. Courtney was a Cheerleader and athletic and she was one of the kindest people in the school.

"Thank goodness," I said, relieved that there was not going to be an earthquake and those kids were just trying to see how I would react if they said anything that would scare me.

I along with a few other students from all three grade levels got picked to go to a say no to drugs conference at Morehead State University in Morehead Kentucky. It was a blessing to be able to get to go with other students from the school and meet new friends. There were seven other students from the eighth-grade class that went, two seventh grade students, and two sixth grade students. I was surprised to know that I was one of the students that were picked to do this.

Like so many other females I liked shopping, makeup, and beauty for as long as I could remember. I liked beauty and fashion. Knowing that I was not athletic, I felt like it would be a good idea to learn what it was like to play sports. I thought that track and or Cross Country would be a good alternative to other sports, and it was. I was so desperate to be normal and successful that I would have done anything good to make myself feel more accepted.

The urge to be accepted by the kids that made straight A's was more important than ever and it nearly possessed me to the point where I worried about it obsessively. This was an irrational fixation of mine that

I felt like caused me an abnormal amount of worry as I have described multiple times in this book. For all of my non-special education courses I was in classes with all of the kids that were either athletic or made good grades or a combination of both and that made me feel even worse about myself.

One day in special education Social Studies class Mrs. Sanders asked if I would like to be moved into a regular education course because she felt like I was doing well in that particular class. The following week I was placed in a regular eighth grade History class.

I did okay in the regular education history class but like I did before I always got incredibly nervous on tests to the point where it would result in meltdowns and stemming behaviors even if I knew the material from the study guide and studied in advance. The first nine weeks of the school year, I did earn A's but after that I had a hard time keeping my grades up in that particular history class all because of my trouble with test taking.

I was dressed up as a ghost for Halloween. Mom had to work late on Halloween and Dad took me and Lacey trick or treating. Whenever we were trick or treating as young kids Mom and Dad always took Lacey and I trick or treating at our great aunt and uncle's houses that were close to where Nan lived, and we always came home with candy that would last us for a month.

During November of that year, I wanted to consider further weaning myself back into regular education class settings. I talked with Mrs. Sanders about getting moved into a regular education English class setting and she said that was fine by her. During the next meeting with meeting with Julia, the school guidance counselor, and my parents they approved and about the second week of November, I was placed in a regular education English class setting.

The chronic low self-esteem that I developed in elementary school continued and symptoms of obsessive-compulsive disorder (OCD) worsened. For the second quarter of the fall season, I took an art class as one of my rotating classes and I was normally very good at art. I sat at a table with three other girls. One day whenever we were working on art projects that required the use of colored pencils, I had forgotten mine. The three girls were sharing the same box of colored pencils, and I asked the girl that they belonged to if I could use hers since I was at her table. She told me she would rather I not use them. I felt hurt, very left out and embarrassed about that and immediately had a severe meltdown and I got so upset that I nearly messed up my art project and almost knocked her colored pencils off of the table. The art instructor was very concerned about me, and Courtney, who was sitting nearby went outside the room and got one of the school aides for me who went with me to the guidance counselor's office. I did not know how to tell anyone that this girl really hurt my feelings. I was on my period that week and fluctuations in my menstrual cycle always intensified and worsened meltdowns.

I had my first panic attack in November of that year after school one day. Lacey and I were outside playing while waiting for Mom to get home from work and all of a sudden, I got nauseous, dizzy, and extremely tired, and felt as if I could not breathe. My Dad's older brother (my uncle) from Ohio came for a visit and he and my dad helped me calm down.

"Are you ok honey," said My Uncle as I came into the house white as a ghost and feeling as though anything could happen.

"Just sit down and rest a few minutes," said Dad.

I did and within a few minutes I started to feel better.

Part of the obsessive-compulsive disorder caused me to develop fears that made me feel like I had somehow caused my mental illness/disability myself. Mom thinks it may have happened because I read a lot of her medical encyclopedias and child craft books. I feel like it was related to hypersensitivity of things happening within my own body that is also a sensory processing issue. I was acutely aware of sensations in my own body that other people would not notice about themselves, just as I have always been hypersensitive to things that I perceived as fearful. I think it was triggered and worsened by fluctuations in my menstrual cycle as everything else was in my life.

Throughout Christmas break I worked on getting ready for track season to start and could not wait to try to run track in the spring. Lacey got a Sega Genesis, and I ended up playing with it more than she did and on one game I got to the last level of it later in the year. We had a much milder winter that year than what we did the previous year, and I was thankful for that.

When school started back following Christmas break Students received grade reports for the previous semester. Looking back, I can see my irrational attitude over being disappointed over earning a B in a regular education History class. I took career development as part of one of my rotating classes for the third quarter of the school year. One day as part of our assignments we had to job shadow different area businesses. I got assigned to shadow the senior citizens center. That reminded me of the incident two years ago when I felt terrified to see what was inside their recreation room at Aunt Martha's 90th birthday party. All of the employees were extremely kind to me and instead of an assignment it ended up being fun. I went into the recreation room and discovered that it was not so scary as what it felt two years ago.

I learned during a conversation about religion and church with Mom and Nan what it would take to go to heaven when I died and about Jesus' second coming. This type of conversation and anything about bad weather always terrified me. We were coming home from grocery shopping one Saturday night in late January/February and on the way home I overheard Lacey ask Mom something about being a Christian.

"Mommy what does it mean to be a Christian," Lacey asked.

"It means asking forgiveness of your sins, asking Jesus into your heart, and that means you are saved, said Mom. Jesus wants us to grow as Christians, do what is right, and live for him. Getting saved and living a Christian life will allow us to go to heaven to be with Jesus when we die and someday Jesus will return to earth to take all of the Christians to heaven."

"When is Jesus coming back," Lacey and I both asked Mom.

"No one knows," said Mom.

"Mom, I asked. Will I get to go to heaven when I die? I have had so many problems in school and got in so much trouble. Will God forgive me for my problems at school?"

"I think so, said Mom. God knows you better than I know you because he made you and loves you very much. God only cares about what is on the inside and he knows that you mean well."

"Honey you will go right to heaven if you die because you are young and you are a very good girl, " said Nan.

A few days later, Dad, Mom, Lacey and I were sitting in a church service, and I heard our pastor talk about the end times and it scared me. Church sermons that are based on the end time can be scary and confusing to anyone on the Autism Spectrum. I was nervous about it and Mom tried to talk to me about it when we got home later that day.

A month later it was time to start preparing for track season and I was working hard and feeling excited yet nervous. Track practice started the first week of March and our coach made us run a lot.

The worst and most embarrassing incident of that year happened on a class trip to Virginia for three days the week before spring break. Mom went with me on this trip. It was in the middle of March of 1995. We left on a Wednesday around 6 in the morning and came back home late on a Saturday Night on a tour bus. I was beyond excited to go because at the end of the trip we would be going to Busch Gardens, a large amusement park. Being obsessed with roller coasters and amusement parks, I was most excited to go to Busch Gardens. We got up at 8am every day and had a full day of touring all of the major historical sites.

After hearing lectures from all of the teachers that went with us on that trip on both tour buses it was time to head to Virginia for two full days of sightseeing and a chance for students to get away from their parents and school. Not a lot of parents went on this trip, maybe because it was kind of expensive, but my mother did. (She also went on Lacey's school trips).

We got to our hotel that night and gathered our tour groups together, figured out which students would be allowed to swim in the hotel pool that night and who would be allowed to swim the next night. After dinner that night we took our first tour. When we got back from our first tour everyone wanted to go swimming at the hotel pool and the majority of the students went swimming that night. We had to raise our hand if we wanted to go swimming when the teacher asked us who wanted to swim. I must not have heard the teachers that night about raising my hand if I wanted to swim.

Later that night when we got back from our first tour, I walked outside of my hotel room to ask if I would be able to go swimming that night. When I saw one of the other girls coming back from the pool to her room, I started feeling like it was unfair that she was one of the students that got to go swimming and I didn't.

"Why did she get to go swimming and we didn't," I said to one of my roommates as we walked outside in the hotel hallway trying to control my frustration and keep from crying and saying mean things to the teachers.

"That's because she raised her hand when they asked, and you didn't. We will be in the group that will go swimming tomorrow night," said one of my roommates, trying to reason with me.

Mom, my roommates and I went shopping at the mall near our hotel for a little while the following night. Mom bought me a book about the ghosts of the area from the bookstore at that mall and they purchased souvenirs for their families. I was able to go swimming that night after about an hour or so of shopping at the mall across the road from our hotel and it helped me to relax. Swimming has always been relaxing, and it is recommended for anyone who suffers from chronic pain and psychological issues of any type.

While we were at the hotel during the evening during those three or so days that we went on the class trip to Virginia, mom stayed inside the room with my roommates and tried to redirect me towards trying to get to know them whenever we were not taking scheduled tours or doing other things near the hotel like shopping at the nearby mall or swimming at the hotel pool. I thought they were nice, but we had little in common and I felt concerned about who was going to ride coasters with me at Busch Gardens.

The day that we went to Busch Gardens everyone was on their own without any assigned groups. We got to the park at around noon, and we were scheduled to leave around six PM to head back home.

"Listen up kids, " said one of the teachers as we got to Busch Gardens. You guys have been a great group of students so far and as most of you know we will be heading back home tonight. Does anyone have any questions before I let you go? You are on your own here without a tour group. Please do not do anything wrong. Please be responsible and be safe and please meet near the front gate by 6 PM." The educational portion of the tour that involved touring everyone had to be in an assigned group of about 20 people.

Mom, the roommates and me headed off to sections of the park that didn't involve roller coasters because they already told me that they didn't want to ride any roller coasters. Regardless of the situation Mom would never ride a roller coaster because she is not only terrified of them, but she does not like them.

"Will you guys please ride the roller coasters with me," I asked as we walked around the park.

"I really want to ride that roller coaster," I said looking at the roller coaster going down its first drop and through its two loops.

"Lauren, do you really want to ride that roller coaster," asked Mom even though she knew I was a huge roller coaster fan.

"Yes, Mom please, '' I said, asking her to let me on the roller coaster.

"Alright Lauren let's go ask and see if we can find someone that will ride the roller coasters with you," Mom said.

I felt too embarrassed to ask Mom about letting me get on the coaster by myself but looking back I probably should have ridden it alone. I felt frustrated with no luck, and I ended up getting lost. I was lost in that huge park trying to find someone that would ride the coaster with me, without any money, for what seemed like an eternity. I tried to stay calm and I found a Lost and Found Center and stayed there until Mom or someone from school found me. I was trying to keep from crying and feeling disappointed that I could not find someone to ride the roller coaster with me.

All of a sudden Mom turned around and she noticed that I was gone. It was a nightmare for both her and me. She was terrified about something happening to me because of my special needs. Mom prayed silently as she walked around the park looking for me and while trying to contain her severe anxiety about me and frustration. Every time that she saw someone from our school she stopped and asked them if they had seen me. Many people had seen me, so it gave her some reassurance. Mom passed the Lost and Found station for kids. She thought to herself, "I have always taught my girls to go to one of those if they got lost," but was very doubtful of me being there.

Mom walked over to the lost and found station and there I was. I had just walked in there less than five minutes before Mom arrived. Back in 1995 there were no cell phones, and no one could easily call and text each other when they got lost. She was so relieved.

As we walked back outside, I happened to not only see Mrs. Sanders but at that time one of my roommates volunteered to ride one of the other less thrilling roller coasters at the park and a water-log ride that was open. We were able to ride the log ride and smaller roller coaster twice. Normally I had fun at amusement parks because I am a true roller coaster fan but not in this case because I got lost in the process of finding a partner to ride coasters with and it was a school trip. Based on my experience with this I would highly encourage teachers to assign a buddy for students with any form of special needs based on their interests. I am sure they didn't because my Mother was present. I feel like it is important for young people to learn to be supportive of those with any form of special need including High Functioning Autism.

The remainder of Spring break Dad drove our family and Nan to visit with family. I was exhausted from the school trip and disappointed from not getting to ride the looping coaster at Busch Gardens and wanted at least two days of rest before traveling again. When we got there, I had a good time visiting with my family and ended up with an Easter dress from the new outlet mall that just opened up.

Whenever we went back to school after the class trip and spring break it was time for the fourth quarter of the school semester and exactly one week later it was time for our first track meet of the season. All of the students and teachers that went on the eighth-grade trip was talking about the highlights of the trip. I told one of the other students at school that I got lost while at the amusement park while on the trip, unaware that they would tell everyone in the school that I got lost. Soon the majority of the students in the 8th grade class knew that I got lost at

Busch Gardens while we were on the class trip to Virginia. They teased me unmercifully.

I was excited but nervous about our first track meet. I ran the 100-meter dash and came in fourth place if I am not mistaken. Dad drove from work to meet me there while I rode the bus with the rest of the team. Track season lasted from the first week of April through the end of May. We had about one meet per week at schools in nearby counties and it was nice to get to meet kids from other schools while waiting for my part of the event.

The pressure to keep up with the other girls on the track team worsened my anxiety over failure so much that I frequently experienced meltdowns at practice and after my event at one of our meets. One day during practice one of the other girls on the team was having a bad day and whenever I asked her a question about something she reacted unkindly at me and that caused me to have a major meltdown. Track helped me to deal with some of the sensory issues associated with my disorder yet at the same time I felt the constant pressure to keep up with the other girls on the team. Whenever I did not feel pressured to keep up with the other girls on the team I felt as if running were not only a good exercise, but it also felt very therapeutic. If we had smartphones, tablets, and Bluetooth headphones back in those days I would have been constantly running and listening to my music which may have made me a better track athlete because when I run or walk, I find that listening to music with my headphones makes it fun. Despite feeling defeated and having meltdowns when I didn't succeed, I would recommend sports like track, cross country, and swimming as an alternative to other more aggressive sports for children on the autism spectrum.

As the fourth quarter of the school semester progressed, I continued to succeed in my regular education 8th grade history and English classes and felt like I should take a regular education Science course with my two regular education courses that were rotated every nine weeks of the school year.

At the Spring meeting between my parents, teachers, counselors, and the school administrative staff it was determined that I would be okay to proceed with a regular education Science class for the remainder of the school year. Math was the only special education class I was enrolled in. When I got admitted into the regular education Science class, I was able to keep up with everyone else and I earned an A in the class.

Kids started prank calling my house and my Nan's house saying really mean things to me. This was a major issue that frustrated my whole family, even my dad who is calm about stuff like that. They would call late at night and wake my parents up.

One day it got so bad that I was getting prank calls right and left at Nan's house. I was sitting outside on the porch working on homework and Lacey was sitting inside watching cartoons. I heard the phone ring and Nan answered it.

"Hello," said Nan as she picked up the phone. A male voice asked for me, and she asked who was calling. He said mean things about me and used bad language which really upset Nan and she firmly told him to never call there again.

We were never able to find out who made those prank calls because the person who called me had their numbers blocked. I received prank calls in the middle of the night from both males and females and this angered Dad very much when he was very calm about telling the people to stop the prank calling. My Mom became very fearful for me to go to any school event alone for my safety. Mom and Dad spent many sleepless nights over me receiving prank phone calls. The people that prank called me were so bold and fearless that they talked back to my dad who was very stern but spoke calmly to them. My teachers, the school counselor, and principal, and all of the Middle School staff were very supportive of me and my family and bent over backward to help us in whatever way possible, but there was nothing they could do about that problem.

That year everyone had to write essays for all of the answers to the questions on the Year-end assessment testing and that was very hard. On awards night I got my picture taken with several other students for earning honor roll status for the entire year and a certificate.

Summer for my family went on as normal and we did the things that we normally do every summer. We were not able to go on a beach vacation due to Mom still working on her master's degree. Lacey and I spent time in our small above ground pool in our backyard whenever we were not staying with Nan Nan on days that mom and Dad worked. Lacey joined a summer league softball team for the first time, and she loved it. She was one of the best on her team. I always liked to stay at home and swim while Mom and Dad watched Lacey play softball at her games, but I supported her even though I did not show it. I still continued to attend regular counseling sessions with Julia.

I got invited to two summer birthday parties by some kids in my class and that was nice. My out-of-town family came home for our annual family reunion and of course we had lots of fun. Amanda and her younger sister Richelle spent a month with us from near the end of July toward the middle of August and whenever they would spend time with Lacey and I it was so much fun. Toward the end of the summer, I asked Mom and Dad to take me to the nearest amusement parks multiple times. Mom and Dad took Lacey, Amanda, Aaron, and me to the closest large amusement park one day and we spent the night in a nearby hotel the night before. On that particular trip with my sister and my two closest cousins we rode all of the roller coasters.

The day before my birthday of that year I got my braces off and had to wear a retainer to keep my teeth in place. I was excited to get my braces off, but I disliked wearing the retainer. I wore it faithfully as I was instructed to do. I was advised to wear it full time except when eating and brushing my teeth until my wisdom teeth came in.

Me and Lacey on Easter Sunday 1994 and
my spring school picture 1994

CHAPTER THIRTEEN

James 2:8-10 and Leviticus 19:18 NIrV Love your neighbor as you love yourself. If you really keep this law, you are doing what is right. But you sin if you don't treat everyone the same. The law judges you because you have broken it. Suppose you keep the whole law but trip over just one part of it. Then you are guilty of breaking all of it.

What happened that year? President Clinton got reelected for the second term. My dad started working with me on learning how to drive because I was fourteen years old and in two years I would be old enough to drive.

A few days before school started Mom called her friend, who was a teacher at the local high school to get an idea of what my teachers would be like. A day or so later while Dad was at work Mom and I went to another meeting with my caseworkers, the chairman of special education at the High School, Julia, and the school principal. This time I was brought in for a portion of the meeting while Mom stayed the whole time.

I kind of had an idea of what High School would be like and what my classes would be like after having a couple of tours of the High School and Mom getting my school schedule ahead of time. The night before school, Lacey and I got ready for bed, and Mom and Dad hugged us like they always did. We were all a little excited.

Mom insisted on getting our pictures, but she always did. This year was special, the first day of middle school for Lacey and first day of high school for me. Mom said she really felt like we were growing up, neither of her girls in elementary school. She took pictures of us together and individually. She wished us a great day, told us she couldn't wait to hear about our day, and we headed out to the bus.

I got to school that morning with all of my classmates from Elementary school through middle school. I went to the station where the freshman schedules were, picked up my copy, glancing at it, and headed to my first period class of the day. I heard an announcement on the school intercom for all incoming freshman students to go to the gymnasium for an orientation session. A couple of the teachers and the school guidance counselor talked to the students about school rules and the dress code. Then it was time to head back to the second half of the first period class. I still had special education math class near the end of the day. The bullying started back immediately and even people that I never expected to bully me started bullying me.

Mom and Dad asked Lacey and me about how school went for both of us and both of us had a good first day back to school.

After reading the school announcements the next morning I found out that Cross Country Tryouts would be the following week and since I ran track last spring, I thought that Cross Country would be a good idea to keep in shape for track and it would be a good alternative to other more time-consuming sports such as Cheerleading, Basketball, Softball, and Soccer.

When I got home from school that afternoon Dad was already home, and I asked him about trying out for cross country. Dad told me no. He said I had problems last spring and felt that this was definitely too hard for me. He did not want me to feel any more pressure to keep up with my teammates nor did he want me to experience any of the added emotional stress that I felt while competing. When Mom walked in the door after work, I asked her what she thought about me doing Cross Country and she felt the same way as Dad.

A day or so later I came home from school crying because I had a stressful day at school. I was tired and frustrated of feeling different, being bullied, having a disorder that I was beginning to understand that I would never get over. Why didn't the kids like me? Why did they tease and taunt me unmercifully?

Mom tried to reason with me. She tried to tell me that the kids who had grown up with me crying all the time didn't understand me and didn't know how to deal with me. Her advice was to ignore those people who teased me, and they would quit bothering me. She assured me that there were lots of kids who had problems that I was just not aware of. She assured me that I was very pretty and a good girl. She praised me for my progress.

I continued to do fine without an aide, but I still had my anxiety issues that upset me with a meltdown at least once every two weeks and especially at certain times of the month. The prank phone calls also continued. The pressure to be on top of everything got to me and I developed worsening of obsessive-compulsive disorder symptoms, continuing panic attacks and very low self-esteem. My abnormal fixations that I experienced of trying to be the best at everything and feeling like I would not amount to anything coincided with my obsessive-compulsive disorder symptoms and this made all things worse. Whenever I had a bad day, I still could not control my emotions. During the fall I went through a phase of feeling so tired that I could not function and for one week I was so exhausted and stressed that I did not want anyone to sit with me at lunch. That particular week I noticed that some of the girls that had previously shied away from me asked me to come and eat lunch with them. I did not know what to say. I just did not say anything. I did not know how to tell those girls that I felt so fatigued that I did not feel like having anyone around me. This hurt their feelings.

I switched my English class to first period class so I could have a study hall class the last period of the day in order to complete all of my homework assignments before going home for the day. One of the Special Education teachers needed some more students for her special education Math class, which was offered at the same time as my special education Math class, and I volunteered to be one of her students. At that time Math was the only special education course that I was enrolled in. She was a really nice person but at the same time she refused to let me outside of class whenever I had a meltdown or needed to go to the bathroom even though she was highly aware of my condition. Restroom access and allowing kids to leave the room to calm down is important in managing symptoms of High Functioning Autism. Restroom access allows them to control bladder and bowel issues and letting them leave the room to release their feelings is one of the healthiest ways of handling meltdowns for people on the Autism spectrum. Trying to suppress or control emotions for people on the spectrum does not work. Allowing students with Autism to release their emotions by crying and stemming as long as long as they are not being mean to anyone else or endangering the safety and wellbeing of themselves or others is the best way of dealing with meltdowns. Gently redirecting them also helps too.

Dad wanted to work on teaching me how to drive to give me a break from the stress of school. One Saturday about two weeks after school started Dad left Lacey at the house watching TV and drove me in our Jeep Cherokee to the hay field across the road from our house. I didn't know what we were going to do.

Dad allowed me to practice driving in our Jeep Cherokee for about two hours in the field. I was glad to start working on learning how to drive yet tired at the end of the session. The rest of the fall passed, and Dad continued teaching me how to drive on the weekends in our hay field.

One September Friday, Lacey and I were out of school, and we stayed with Nan Nan while Mom and Dad were both working. I had homework to do, and Lacey did too. I took a break from homework and while Lacey was watching TV and Nan was making our lunch, I peeked through Lacey's Math book. As I looked through Lacey's Math book, I came upon a picture of a roller coaster at a park near Chicago. I loved reading about coasters.

Two weeks later toward the end of September I stayed with Nan on a Friday night. The phone rang and I answered, it was Uncle Melvin. He was working away and just calling to check on Nan. I knew that he was working close to where that park and coaster were located in Chicago. After chatting with him for a few minutes, I had to ask! I mentioned the name and location of the coaster and asked if he was anywhere near the park or if he had seen or heard of it. He told me that he was staying across the road from the park and that he could see their roller coasters from his motel window. I handed the phone to Nan for her to talk and she and Uncle Melvin were amazed that I knew about a coaster and amusement park near Chicago. A few minutes later Nan picked up the phone and called Mom to tell her the story of my knowing about the roller coaster.

The following month, around the middle of October, Mom had to fly to Chicago for a mandatory business trip for her job and Dad went with her. They stayed for two days while Nan Nan stayed at our house with Lacey and I to help get us ready for school in the mornings. I was homesick for Mom and Dad, and it only made a bad two days at school worse.

While Mom was gone to Chicago, I had a very bad day at school, and it turned into a bad two days at school. I confronted one of the girls that I tried to be friends with since seventh grade about her attitude about being friends with outsiders and that I still wanted to be friends with her no matter what. This made her really mad at me and caused me to feel super hurt and embarrassed. At that point I felt like my reputation at school was ruined and that things would get worse. By the time I got home from school that day I was so fatigued and exhausted from crying and worrying about my reputation that I did not feel like doing anything but reading. I worried obsessively about the incident and what others would think of me for years.

After dinner that night Mom called from her hotel in Chicago. She asked about my day and of course I told her about what happened at school earlier that day. Mom advised me to take an Atarax that night and talked to Nan about it. I took Atarax on an as needed basis during particularly stressful times.

Nan did not hear well, so Lacey set an alarm clock for me and her to to help us get up. Because I had taken the Atarax, I slept so soundly that I missed my alarm clock and Lacey had to wake me up for school the next morning. I was always a sound sleeper when I slept, and this was only intensified by me taking Atarax that morning. When I went to school that morning, I still felt worried and cried continuously most of the day. After spending an hour in the counselor's office crying, I apologized to my friend, and she forgave me but one of her friends was still upset with me.

Mom and I were sitting at the kitchen table on a Saturday afternoon that fall and not knowing much about my condition I asked her if she knew anyone that had the same emotional and school issues as me. She told me that two of her cousins cried in school when they were younger like I did and another one of her cousins suffered from a mental illness. What Mom described to me about her cousins sounded very similar to what I experienced, and I wondered if they may have experienced the same problems that I had as a child.

I chose not to go trick or treating because I thought that I was too old to do it. I just went to Nan Nan's house to help her pass out candy to trick or treaters. The fall passed and it was soon time for the holiday season. My panic attacks continued to worsen, and I continued to feel like I may have done something to cause my emotional control disorders. Aunt Sylvia and Uncle Dewey arrived at Nan's house on Christmas Eve and Dad took Me and Lacey to see them that evening because Mom was working late. That very evening, I had back-to-back Panic Attacks that I just could not control including one that happened when Aunt Sylvia told a hilarious joke. I was in the midst of laughing at the joke when all of a sudden, I felt as if I were suffocating and ran outside in the cold air to catch some fresh air without a coat on screaming and crying.

I continued to experience ongoing panic attacks all night and at one point my heart was beating so fast that it actually felt uncomfortable against my chest. I was always the first in my family to go to bed at night and the last one to wake up in the mornings whenever I slept well, excluding Christmas. I woke everyone up early that morning at the crack of dawn to open gifts. Dad got the video camera and videoed us opening gifts.

Midway through my stack of presents I came across a slightly smaller gift. I shook it before opening it and I knew it was not clothes. When I unwrapped that gift and opened the box, I was beyond excited at what I saw. It was a 3D roller coaster movie that showed 14 different roller coasters at 8 different amusement parks in the United States and a book about all of the major amusement parks in the United States and Canada. I had no clue that I was getting this and had never even seen books or movies about roller coasters. I was beyond excited.

I could not wait to watch my 3D roller coaster video. Lacey popped it in the VCR for us to watch. Feeling exhausted from poor sleep related to too much holiday excitement and panic attacks the night before, I watched the roller coaster movie multiple times that day and even when we had company, they watched part of it with me while Mom and Aunt Sylvia were finishing up the Christmas Dinner preparations. I considered that particular Christmas the best Christmas I had so far because I received a Roller Coaster movie and book although I constantly used my camera, I got three years earlier. When we exchanged gifts after the meal, I opened the gift from Aunt Yvette and Uncle Melvin. It was a huge makeup kit for me and Lacey to share. I wore the makeup in that kit whenever I had time in the mornings and if I felt like it.

By the time that New Years of that year arrived I watched my 3D roller coaster movie so much that I memorized all of the roller coasters that were in it and the order they were in. I saw that there was another roller coaster video in a catalog that Mom got on a regular basis that had roller coasters from other countries and of course I wanted it and showed it to Mom. Once again that year we had another winter snowstorm and school was out for about half of January but thankfully the electricity did not go out like it did two years earlier.

School started back for the second half of the semester, and I was glad to get to go back to school so I would not have to miss much summer for the year. I joined FHA (Future Homemakers of America) in the fall and was working on earning my Junior Degree in FHA and preparing to compete in the STAR events competition in February of that year. I didn't like that I was not able to run track like I wanted to and that is one of the reasons that I joined FHA. In February of that year, I competed in STAR events for FHA and was a winner in my division. I had unrealistic expectations of being the best of the best at everything intensifying OCD, and Panic Attacks. I developed an irrational idea that because I had a developmental disorder and an anxiety disorder that I would be at high risk for unhealthy habits such as drugs and drinking, unwanted pregnancies if I were to even date at all, developing adult-onset health problems, less likely to go to college and get a good paying job, and so on. I felt that other people would see me this way too; I never denied any of my problems. I think that these worries may have also been part of my obsessive-compulsive disorder and the abnormal fixations of my Asperger Syndrome.

On the morning of Valentines Day of 1996 Lacey and I got ready for school like we normally did and as we entered the kitchen to eat breakfast Mom had our Valentine gifts and candy laid out. "Happy Valentine's Day girls," said Mom as she handed us our Valentine gifts.

I got the other roller coaster video that I wanted, and Lacey got another movie.

When I got home from school that afternoon, I noticed that Lacey was watching my new roller coaster video. That day some of Lacey's friends brought her home early when school was dismissed that day. We rewound the tape and watched it together.

My Panic Attacks were getting worse, and it felt like I was having them constantly. Traditional panic attacks are similar in ways to the weird sensory fears that I had when I was younger even though I still experienced them from time to time as I got older. Both can make your heart to beat faster than normal, have irrational fears, dilated pupils, happen for no apparent reason, uncontrollable screaming and crying, and make you feel exhausted. Sensory fears happen as a result of being overstimulated by a certain situation and not being able to filter out things in the external environment. With sensory processing disorders from autism spectrum disorders a person can be overstimulated or under stimulated. In the case of my irrational fears of certain things in the environment I was experiencing overstimulation. Panic attacks can come on suddenly and for no apparent reason and can cause physical symptoms too such as feeling like you may be dying or having a heart attack. Sensory fears for me always caused the feeling of tingling on my head down my back and my through my arms in addition to some of the physical symptoms caused by panic attacks, feeling as if I saw or heard something that I perceived as eerie whether anyone else noticed it or not, as in the case of me being spooked by the picture of the wildcat hanging up inside the school gymnasium, and me feeling like I noticed stuff in the darkened recreation room at my aunt Martha's 90th birthday party. My weird sensory fears were getting much better; they were always worsened by fluctuations in my menstrual cycle as were my panic attacks, and mood swings.

Mom talked to Dr. Singh about prescribing me some Xanax to be taken as needed until I could get an appointment with a psychiatrist. I took the Xanax as recommended and Mom feels like it may have worsened my Panic Attacks. Mom heard about a really good Psychiatrist, Dr. Stanley from one of her nurse friends at the hospital whose son was a patient of Dr. Stanley. She got the referral from Dr. Singh and gathered my records in April and got an appointment with Dr. Stanley in early May that year.

Mom never told me early about the upcoming appointment because I always worried and fixated on upcoming appointments, trips or anything. She never told me about the appointment until the evening before. The next morning, we left around 8:30 so we could get to my 10 o'clock appointment with Dr. Stanley, we left early to figure out how to get there and to fill out the necessary paperwork before my appointment. When we got there, Mom filled out all of the paperwork and handed the receptionists my medical records and insurance cards.

After introductions, Dr. Stanley led us into her office. Mom and I both described all of the symptoms that I had experienced my entire life to Dr. Stanley. I told Dr. Stanley about the bullying issues at school, my Panic Attacks, and all of the other symptoms that I experienced.

"This is what I would like for you to do, " said Dr. Stanley. I would like for Lauren to be placed on Haloperidol again, Luvox, and Prozac. I do feel like Lauren has obsessive compulsive disorder (OCD) and Anxiety Disorder Not Otherwise Specified, (Anxiety NOS), as well as a history of Pervasive Developmental Disorder symptoms. I would like for Lauren to get some further psychological testing done along with a Thyroid panel lab work and an EEG (electroencephalogram) of her brain to rule out seizure activity." Staring spells are common in some types of seizure disorders and autism spectrum disorders; I used to have episodes of where I would just stare, and it would seem as if I was not aware of what was going on. Dr. Stanley caught me in an episode that day in the office while I described to her some migraine aura symptoms that I had all of my life in addition to my other symptoms.

After my appointment with Dr. Stanley, I went back to school for my afternoon classes and to get my assignments that I missed from the morning classes. Mom took the remainder of the day off from work. I had a bad day once I got back to school and when I got home from school that afternoon, it was obvious to Mom about what kind of afternoon I had. After dinner that night Mom gave me my first dose of medication.

The next afternoon as Lacey and I got home from school the phone happened to ring as we walked inside the house and Lacey answered it. It was Mom, she told Lacey to tell me not to take my medicine. She explained that I would be getting an EEG of the brain and some blood work the next day and the EEG required me to be sleep deprived.

The next morning Dad drove Mom and me to the hospital where Mom worked as a nurse to have my testing done that was ordered by Dr. Stanley. Lacey went to school as usual and after I got back home from my testing Dad brought Nan to the house. Mom and Dad had to leave to go out of town for a couple of days for some kind of training for Mom's nursing job.

I went back to an appointment the following week with Dr. Stanley for a psychological test. Based on the results of that test it was confirmed that I had obsessive compulsive disorder (OCD). The results of the EEG were normal, meaning that there was no evidence of seizure activity, and the thyroid panel blood test was borderline on the low end of the normal scale.

Dr. Stanley at least made sure that I had access to medication, and he always worked me in his schedule for appointments whenever I needed to be seen. The first week I started on those medications I experienced horrible side effects. Luvox and Haloperidol taken together caused me to vomit them back up whenever I would take them regardless of whether I took them with food or on an empty stomach. I went back to school the following week after starting to take my medication and the side effects were so strong that I could not function.

Because the side effects of my medications were so strong my mom elected to remove me from school for the last two weeks of school that year. She went through the school counselors and administration. I completed all of my remaining assignments and turned them in and me being removed from school for the last two weeks of school did not affect my grades. During this period when my side effects worsened my actual illness, I experienced worsening of my anxiety. I developed fears of being poisoned by certain chemicals and this resulted from me not being able to shake the fact that I may have accidentally ingested or gotten exposed to something that may have caused my emotional control disorders. Mom attributed these feelings to me reading too many World Book medical encyclopedias and she had to hide them from me.

During the second week of June, we traveled traveled out of town for my cousin's wedding reception. It was Dad, Mom, Nan Nan, Lacey and Me, that went. Midway through the week Dad and Mom took Lacey and me to an Amusement Park and I did not feel well at all. That was one of the few times that I went to an amusement park and did not feel well. I felt more nervous than what I normally feel, and a lot of the reason was caused by side effects from the many medications that I was taking at the time.

This was the start of a summer of frustration for me which included multiple trips to Dr. Stanley for medication adjustments and Mom and I were both worried that I would need to be hospitalized due to emotional control issues. It took me several months to get stabilized on my medications. These medications gave me nausea and vomiting, constipation, visual hallucinations at night, pain in various parts of the body for no reason, bladder control problems and urinary tract infections, alternating between insomnia and sleeping a lot, and tremors. The worst side effect that I experienced that summer was weakness in both arms from my elbows to my fingertips. That started the week that we went to the wedding reception. With the weakness in my lower arms, I had no strength to move that part of my arms. They were temporarily paralyzed. I could not write, brush my teeth, or eat without making a huge mess. I had to do some work to get my lower arms and hands back functional again even after I stopped the medication that caused damage to them.

Aunt Sylvia and Uncle Dewey came to Kentucky in July of that year for our annual Family Reunion. One day Lacey and I were at Nan's house while Mom and Dad were working. Aunt Sylvia was there, and she asked me if she could try to help me work on getting the strength back in my lower arms and hands and I was glad to have her help me with that. I decided to work on my hands and lower arms to get my strength back and that did help. I found out that it was Haloperidol and Luvox together causing me those side effects plus nausea. I was given another medication to control the side effects of those three medications. The medication that was used to control side effects from Haloperidol, Luvox, and Prozac also gave me side effects. I was taken off of Luvox, Haloperidol, and that other medication and switched to Tegretol instead, along with Prozac. Tegretol helped somewhat to stabilize my moods; I had to get routine blood and urine tests to check my liver function because Tegretol can cause liver problems as a side effect, and I did not like that.

One side effect of my medications that I experienced that summer that did not go away regardless of switching medications was recurrent bedwetting. I never had bedwetting prior to that. I felt frustrated and annoyed with my bedwetting. My bedwetting was an inconvenience because it was a nightly occurrence.

One morning Mom woke me up early and had me to give a urine sample so she could take it to the lab at her hospital to check for the presence of a urinary tract infection. I hated being woke up so early, but I would do anything to figure out the cause of bedwetting. I didn't even wet the bed when I was little, I was given antibiotics to treat the UTI, but my symptoms continued.

Summer continued on and I started feeling better and a bit more stabilized with my medication. I would swim in our backyard above ground pool with Lacey. Lacey still continued to play summer softball and she was getting very good at it. My birthday it was simple with cake and ice cream and a trip to an amusement park.

CHAPTER FOURTEEN

Agree with one another. Don't be proud. Be willing to be a friend to people who aren't considered important. Don't think that you are better than others. (Romans 12:16 NIrV)

I turned 15 years old and entered my sophomore year of high school. I was almost old enough to learn how to drive. I was very active in FHA since I was not able to run track and cross country due to my severe anxiety with competition. Julia, my counselor got a new job and I had to see other counselors. Mom and Dad still met with my caseworkers and my teachers on a regular basis to evaluate my goals and to make sure that I was continuing to make progress. My Dad continued working with me on driving lessons in our hay field on the weekends whenever the weather was nice.

About a day or so before school started, I met with the director of special education to review my school schedule. I noticed that she was writing down my class schedule from classes that I signed up for last spring. I signed up for classes that I knew that I would like and would be beneficial for me in the future. I still had to be enrolled in special education Math class. Besides the mandatory Math, English, and Science, I enrolled in cooking class, typing class, career development course, and a parenting class.

School started back about mid-August or earlier. From the first day of school onward I applied makeup every morning and reapplied it often during the day regardless of how I felt. Mom did not agree with me wearing bright colored lipstick and dark eye liner, but I always liked to coordinate my makeup with my outfit and my moods. Like most teenagers, I loved trendy, fashionable clothes and the make-up.

For Lacey's 12th birthday about a week after school started, she had a sleepover with some of her friends from softball and friends that she met while in 6th grade. I still experienced the same problems as before including worrying about my grades, yet my worries about my grades were not quite as severe thanks to being on medication. Kids still continued to bully me over being different. By the time that school started I continued to take Prozac and Tegretol for my moods and Desmopressin Nose Spray for my bedwetting. I still continued my regular visits with Dr. Stanley. In addition to joining FHA, I also joined Future Business Leaders of America (FBLA), but I was not as active in that as I was in FHA.

The annual blood mobile was held in the school gymnasium and was held in the middle of September of that year. FHA members usually helped out. I wanted to work at the bloodmobile for the first time. I thought I already signed up, but I forgot. Instead of asking why my name was not on the list to work at the bloodmobile I got upset and started complaining that I was not allowed to work at the bloodmobile. The teacher who was responsible for the bloodmobile felt like I just forgot and that she would gladly sign me up, which made me feel better that time. When I got home that evening and told mom what happened she felt like I could have suppressed my feelings better and felt as if I should not work at the bloodmobile because I burst out into tears before asking to be signed up when I found that my name was not on the list.

The whole evening, I worried about the issue and only cried more, which smeared off my makeup that I precisely applied earlier in the day. Instead of punishing Autistic people for meltdowns or teaching them to suppress their emotions allow them to cry, vent their feelings, and stem if needed as long as they are not in danger of harming themselves or others and allow a recovery period to happen. Whenever they have recovered from their meltdown, talk about the incident with them and how to avoid it in the future without judging them or criticizing them.

For Halloween that year I went with the FBLA group to deliver candy to the kids on the pediatric ward of the local hospital. I was dressed up as a witch, some of the other kids were dressed up as Flintstones characters, and a couple of girls dressed up as princess type characters. It was fun getting to pass out candy to kids that were not able to go trick or treating because they were in the hospital.

During the week of Thanksgiving, I had to have my wisdom teeth removed and I was only able to eat soft foods whenever we had our Thanksgiving meal. Mom took off from work on the week of Thanksgiving to help take care of me during my recovery from getting my wisdom teeth removed.

The company that produced the 3D Roller coaster videos that I got the previous year came out with another video in the series. I wanted it as a Christmas gift and asked Mom to put that on my Christmas gift list. For Christmas of that year, it was the first time that I did not receive any toys as gifts yet at the same time I still played with my Barbie dolls and Polly pockets on a regular basis. I got the new roller coaster video that I asked for, and Lacey got the holiday collector Barbies that she asked for.

New Years passed and soon it was time to go back to school for the second semester of the school year. We got our report cards from the previous semester, and it turns out that I failed the final exam in my science class but got an A average in the class because I worked hard. I struggled in most of my classes that year except for my cooking classes and my parenting class. It was time to start working on my FHA STAR event and second level of degree in FHA called the regional degree. The FHA regional STAR events competition was held in February, and I won in my event category for the second year in a row.

A few days after Easter of that year was our Spring Break. For Spring Break My whole family was getting ready to go to Orlando, Florida with the Middle School and High School band to march in a Parade at Universal Studios. Lacey was in the Middle School band at the time, so we went to support her and all of the other students on the trip. She played the clarinet. If there was one lesson that Mom learned while we went on my 8th grade trip to Virginia two years earlier, it was figuring out that I could easily get lost. On this particular trip we were scheduled to go out to eat at a Dinner Theater on our first night there, go to the Disney Magic Kingdom on the first full day, Universal Studios on the second full day of the trip to march in the parade, and Sea World on the day that we were to come back home. It was a 24-hour long road trip on a tour bus and three full days of doing stuff.

When we got to our hotel, we went out to eat at the Dinner Theater about an hour later. It was a bit too cold to go swimming that night and we did not have time on the whole trip to swim in the indoor pool. Lacey did not stay in the room with Mom, Dad and me. She stayed in a room with her friends on a different floor. The next morning Mom woke up with a stomach virus of sorts and was not able to go to Disney Magic Kingdom with us. Memories of me getting lost on my 8th grade trip to Virginia two years earlier haunted her. Before we left for Disney Magic Kingdom Mom called Lacey's room and asked her to come up and talk to her just to make sure she knew to keep an eye on me no matter what. We are typical sisters that argue and fight once in a while; Lacey has always been my best sidekick and has always stuck up for me even in tough situations. Lacey assured Mom that she would help Dad keep an eye on me. Mom also advised Dad to make sure I kept money in case I got separated from him. Dad gave me twenty dollars and advised me to put it in my pocket and make sure I didn't lose it.

I didn't get lost that day. I stuck with Lacey and her friends or Dad and some other parents on the day that we went to Disney Magic Kingdom. All of the parents and kids in our group stuck together and whenever we kids were on a ride the parents in our group usually waited on us at the ride exit if they did not ride with us. After the day at Magic Kingdom the band group from the Middle School and High School played miniature golf and I was able to play with them. The following day Mom felt better and was able to go to Universal Studios with us and watch the high school and middle school band march in the parade among bands from several other schools. The middle school and high school band were combined as one group for competition. After we spent the day at Universal Studios, we went to a Waterpark that evening and that is where the awards ceremony was held. Luckily at the awards ceremony our band group got a first-place award, and I got a trophy for winning third place in miniature golf the night we played miniature golf. (Win, win). The following day we went to Sea World before heading back home that evening.

By the time that spring of that year came around things started to look up for me at school. I applied to be an FHA officer for the following school year since I loved FHA so much and I got nominated to be an FHA reporter. I was excited about that. My grades improved, and I almost got straight A's one term. By the end of the school season for the year I was already thinking about which amusement parks that I wanted to go to for the summer. One Park close to where my cousins lived was on my bucket list because I had never been there, and it was in a close driving distance of where they lived.

Around the first and second week of May of that year the school took a group of students on a field trip that I knew I would like. I signed up to go one day while another group of students went another day. The day that students in my class and some other classes were given permission slips for the trip I knew that I wanted to go.

I showed Mom the permission slip that evening and told her and Dad about the trip, telling them how much I wanted to go. Mom was concerned about me going without someone with me. Dad suggested that Lacey go with me, and they approached her about it. Lacey really didn't want to go but consented to do it. I was so thankful that she was kind enough to go with me.

The end of the school year brought assessment testing requiring students to write essays for answers which was very hard for me. I disliked that. The following week, awards day was held during one of the morning class periods. It was hard for me not to feel jealous of other girls that earned awards, and this worsened my feelings of self-worth. These insecurities about myself resulted in a meltdown and stemming behaviors. I continued to have so many unrealistic expectations and felt myself suffering from severe jealousy toward girls that appeared as if they had it all together in the way of grades, athleticism, and outlook for the future. It took twenty years for me to learn that grades and being athletic does not always equal success later in life. Courtney tried to help calm me down that day and she gave me a friendship ring. I was so appreciative of that kind gesture.

When school ended that year things were much brighter for me than what they were the previous year because the medication side effects were not as strong. I still continued regular checkups with Dr. Stanley. Dr. Stanley was concerned about my obsession with roller coasters, and he felt that it was a result of my OCD and wanted me to try to either develop new interests or reduce my interest in roller coasters to help me to be more average. I still continued taking my medication as directed yet at the same time I felt like it was not good to try to suppress my abnormal obsession with roller coasters if it made me happy.

Around the second week of June of that year we went on a family vacation to the beach. Nan Nan and Mamaw went with the four of us to the Beach and it was a nice trip. Dad took Lacey and I out shopping or to amusement parks in the evenings. I got so fixated on wearing makeup that I even had to wear it to the amusement park knowing that I would smear it off if I rode a water-log flume. When we got back home from vacation Lacey continued to play softball and later in the summer, she was chosen for the all-star's softball team. We swam in our pool as usual that summer. As usual in the summer Lacey and I swam in our above ground pool. We stayed at home more during the day because we were old enough to take care of ourselves now. Many people on the autism spectrum cannot be left alone and I felt blessed to have matured enough to be left at home alone at times during the day while Mom and Dad worked even though Lacey and I still stayed with Nan on a regular basis.

I still wanted to go to the amusement park that was near where my family in Pennsylvania lived. The park had three roller coasters that were on two of my roller coaster movies. Two of them were wooden roller coasters and the other one was a Steel Coaster that was the tallest and fastest roller coaster in the United States at that time. One day around the second week of July that year as we were on our way to a party at a friend's house, I asked Dad if he would consider taking me to my uncle and Aunt's house to visit, so we could go to the amusement park that was nearby because I was determined to ride the roller coaster that was considered the fastest in the US. He surprised me with his answer, they were already planning to go at the end of the month.

A few days later we were picking green beans in my Nan's Garden to can for the winter. My cousin, Aaron was with us that day because Aunt Yevette and Uncle Melvin were out of town that day. Aaron asked me if I was getting excited about our trip, I told him I couldn't wait. Mom had already asked his parents if Aaron could go with us. He told me he was excited too. Aaron was always so much fun just to hang out with.

A week and a half later we left on our trip to visit with family and go to the amusement park. Once we got to our family's house we had a good time visiting and discussed which would be the best day to go to the park. Two days later all of cousins happened to be off from work and they were all happy to go to the park with me along with their children. It happened to be my 16th birthday and what better way to spend my 16th birthday than at an amusement park that housed one of the world's fastest roller coasters. I got up early, excited for a super fun day and color coordinated a bright pink lipstick to match my fairly comfortable outfit. It was a fun day! Toward the end of the day, all of us rode the biggest and fastest coaster twice in a row and all of the other roller coasters only once the whole day. I screamed with the excitement of adrenaline pumping through me after the first ride and couldn't wait to ride again.

People with High Functioning Autism/Asperger Syndrome usually have an intense special interest and mine happens to be roller coasters. Not only is riding roller coasters my special interest, but it has boosted my self-confidence and makes me feel a sense of accomplishment when I walk down the exit ramp. Based on this experience as well as others I would for sure encourage those with High Functioning Autism/ Asperger Syndrome to pursue their special interest and connect with others that may have similar interests.

I enjoyed this particular trip and getting to spend the day with my family and visiting with them on the other days. At the end of the trip, my cousins' husband told me that he would send me information about joining a roller coaster fan club since they had internet on their computers at the time and we still did not have it yet.

CHAPTER FIFTEEN

Strengthen the hands of those who are weak. Help those whose knees give away. (Isaiah 35:3 NIrV) Those with strong faith should help the weak. (Romans 15:1 NIrV)

What happened during my junior year of high school? President Clinton got impeached. Princess Diana died in a car accident near the end of August 1997. TY beanie babies were a hot collector's item. Nan turned 80 years old on January 26th, 1998, and we had her a surprise birthday party at our church fellowship hall. I got my driver's permit. Mom completed her master's degree in nursing in the Spring of 1998. There were several school shootings at various schools across the United States.

I had just turned 16 years old and had been studying on and off for my drivers permit all summer. School was split into block courses, meaning that instead of taking six or seven classes a day we took four classes a day per semester and many of the elective classes were split into nine-week sessions. My first quarter semester of my junior year I took a Science class, Business Management (which I disliked), and two home economics classes which I earned an A in. The second quarter of my first semester I can remember continuing Science class and Business management, taking a global issues/geography class, and Psychology class.

About a week after school started back, I went to the mailbox after getting off of the school bus and found an envelope addressed to me from my cousin. I was excited and opened it because I knew what it was. Whenever I opened the envelope, it contained information about a fan club for roller coaster enthusiasts. I knew I wanted to join the fan club right away. Our church was taking some of the young people to a weekend church camp about two hours away and homecoming night at School was coming up, so we had to think about that.

At that point we had already bought my homecoming dress and paid to go to church camp, and I already knew that I was going to attend both homecoming and church camp. It was already planned out that I would only stay one night at church camp so I could come back to go to the homecoming dance. What more was there to do? Nothing other than continuing studying for my driver's permit test and taking it later that week and my homework that was due that week.

I took my drivers permit test for the first time the week of the homecoming dance and church camp and failed it. I had to study hard for the drivers permit test.

The homecoming dance for that year happened to be on the same weekend that we went to Church camp. Because of this, Mom and I only stayed one night at church camp and Lacey stayed with the rest of the church group for the full two nights.

Mom and I had to drive back home around noon the first full day of Church camp and I was so disappointed that Church camp coincided with the school Homecoming Dance. When we got back home, I got dressed in my homecoming dress and Mom drove me to Uncle Melvin's house for Aunt Yvette to do my hair and makeup.

"Oh my gosh Lauren, said Mom when Aunt Yvette was finished with my hair and makeup. You look beautiful."

Our class was looking for parent volunteers to work at the Homecoming Dance, so I asked Mom to volunteer. Aaron went to homecoming that night too and he rode with me and Mom to the dance. Within minutes of arriving at the dance, trouble started for me. I felt like I was one of the few girls coming in without a date or a group of friends (or so I thought). I felt insecure and disturbed.

I immediately ran upstairs on the balcony overlooking the entire gymnasium to where Mom was sitting and cried uncontrollably.

"Lauren, what happened," Mom said.

"This is not fair, " I said, crying and wringing my hands. I'm one of the few people in here without a date. All of the guys like other girls better than me, those that don't have any types of mental illness, who are smarter, and more athletic than me. This is so embarrassing and hurtful."

Mom tried to reassure me and encourage me to enjoy the activities, She finally told me that I was messing up my beautiful hair and makeup. After a lot of encouraging words and coaxing, my Mom finally gave up and we just left and went home. Mom made arrangements for someone else to pick Aaron up after the dance. It was at that point that I felt nervous about ever attending a school formal dance such as homecoming or prom again.

Church camp was still going on that weekend, but they still had services at our church on Sunday. The following morning Mom and I went even though I still felt messed up from what I perceived as a bad experience at the Homecoming Dance.

A day or so later I asked Mom if I could please join the roller coaster fan club," She consented and wrote a fifty dollar check for me to join. It was mailed out the next day. I was so happy and relieved to finally be joining a roller coaster fan club.

Three weeks later I went to the mailbox after getting off the school bus to find an envelope addressed to me from the coaster fan club, it was full of pamphlets and brochures. I could not wait to get inside the house and open it and when I did there was all kinds of cool information and a newsletter consisting of several pages, which I read from front to cover.

School progressed and soon it was time for the second quarter of class rotations for the semester. Along with Science and Business Management I was enrolled in Global Issues and Psychology class. I was not interested in business, so I just couldn't do well in that class. Later during that quarter of the semester, I tried to get my driver's permit for the second time and still failed the test. I was devastated about failing the test.

Again, it was my friend Courtney who asked what was wrong when I cried after coming back to school. I told her that I had failed my permit test for the second time. "You're not the only one that failed it, " said

Courtney. One of my friends failed it twice before taking it. Courtney was always supportive and encouraging to me.

That year for Christmas was the first time in two years that I did not receive any roller coaster videos or anything else coaster related. TY beanie babies became very popular in 1997 and Lacey wanted Ty beanie babies. I didn't sleep and woke everyone up because I wanted to see my new stuff.

I have a hard time getting motivated to do stuff that I dislike, and we had to clean the house while Mom cooked Christmas dinner. We were having guests at our house to celebrate Christmas. Because I had to help clean up, I had a meltdown. That caused me to have a meltdown even though I did my best to help.

Near the beginning of the Spring 1998 school semester Dad took me back to try once again to get my driver's permit. When I was taking my driver's permit for the third time the policeman that was in the room at the time had seen me the other two times that I tried to take my permit test, He decided to give me a different version of the test. I got frustrated and cried of course because I was stressed and worried that I would fail it again. I passed it. When I found out that I passed the permit test I was so happy, relieved and ready to start working on getting my license six months later.

In the Spring semester I took US History, English, Algebra, Sociology one nine weeks, and for the last nine weeks of the school year I was signed up for Drivers Education.

In January Mom and Aunt Sylvia started planning a surprise birthday party for Nan's 80th birthday party at the end of the month. The month of January went by fast, and suddenly it was time for Nan's surprise 80th birthday. Aunt Sylvia came to our house a day before Nan's surprise birthday party to help Mom with all of the cooking and preparations for the party. Mom and Aunt Sylvia invited all of their siblings and their children and grandchildren to Nan's birthday party. Most of the out-of-town family stayed in a motel nearby the night before the party. The rest of the out-of-town guests stayed with Uncle Melvin and Aunt Yevette. Mom also invited all of Nan's siblings that were still living plus all of their families to the party, close friends and neighbors.

On the day of Nan's birthday party, we had to be at the church fellowship hall by around 12 noon and the party started at around 1pm. Everyone already got to the party before Nan got there. When it was time to get Nan, Uncle Jack from out of town went to get her and helped her inside the building. Mom and Aunt Sylvia went to the church early to get stuff set up and I came later with Dad so I would have time to shower, find a decent looking outfit and apply makeup. I wore a dark purple lipstick that I got for Christmas because I felt like it coordinated with my outfit.

"Surprise," everyone yelled as Nan walked inside. Nan was very shocked that everyone threw her a surprise birthday party.

I helped with the cleanup at the party since I did nothing to help with the preparations. I enjoyed all of the good food and fellowship with all of my family while at the party. Since the party was on a Saturday all of the out-of-town family and friends drove in on Friday and left on Sunday.

For the last week of January and the first week of February we had another major snowstorm in our area that left many people in our area without water and electricity for two weeks, including me and my family. Once again, I did not deal with that well at all. I had a lot of meltdowns over having our electricity out. When the electricity came back on, I was more than thrilled to have the light back on.

Near the end of February, I went back to Dr. Stanley for my bimonthly checkup with him. I asked him about weaning back on some of my medications because I felt like I did just as good with taking one medication as what I did with more than one medication. He did not want me to wean back on any of my medications or just drop down to taking one of them.

He wanted to add another medication to my list, and I refused because I did not feel like it was healthy to take that much medication. I felt like I was on enough medication already and the Desmopressin medication that he prescribed me for bedwetting was not working. He told me I should stay right where I was, and if I quit my medication, it could make me much worse that what I was before.

Soon it was time once again for the annual FHA regional events and for me to compete in STAR events for the third year in a row. I competed in the Job Interview event for the second time in a row and earned my state degree, the highest level of degree in FHA. Because of this I was eligible to advance to the state FHA event in March of that year. I finally decided to go to the FHA state meet that year even though I disliked missing school. Mom took off from work and drove me to the state meeting on the same day that the other students left on the bus. Mom picked me up at school a few minutes before school let out for the day and we drove the three-hour drive to the state FHA event. While we were at the state FHA meeting, I won in my division of STAR events category.

On the last day of the event, Mom and I left the state FHA meeting a little early. As we were walking out the door to leave a news reporter just randomly asked me about how I would treat someone in a wheelchair. There was a girl at that FHA state meeting that got paralyzed in a school shooting a few months earlier.

"Excuse me mam, " said the interviewer." I would like to ask you what you would do if you were to encounter someone in a wheelchair.

"I would treat her the same as I would anyone else, I said. Just because she suffered an injury that paralyzed her does not mean that she should be treated differently than other students."

Mom was surprised and thrilled that a local TV news reporter just randomly interviewed me. I knew the importance of treating others with respect, even those with disabilities. Growing up in a Christian based environment and learning basic social skills in therapy sessions taught me the importance of treating others with kindness. The interview was televised in that city that evening, but we were not there to see it.

After we got back from the state FHA event it was almost time for Spring Break and Lacey's 8th grade class trip. Lacey's 8th grade trip was on our Spring Break week. Mom and I went with Lacey on her 8th grade class trip. Lacey's class went to Washington, DC instead of Virginia. That trip was a great trip and no one on that trip got lost (especially me).

It was time for the fourth quarter of the school year to begin and for me to start my driver's education class and to go shopping for my prom dress. I started working on getting ready for Prom by going to a nearby tanning bed and I picked out my prom dress. The theme of our prom was Titanic, and I wanted a dress that would match the theme yet at the same time look good on me. My prom dress was a perfect fit for me and the theme.

The day of Prom arrived, and Aunt Yvette did my hair in her shop just like she did for Homecoming, and one of her friends that was there helping her with Prom makeup, did my makeup for Prom.

"Oh my gosh Lauren, " said Mom as I got finished with getting my hair and makeup done for prom. You look beautiful. I hope you will have fun tonight and not worry about anything."

When it was almost time for me to leave to go and get my pictures taken for prom before heading to prom anxiety and excitement ran through me. My late picture appointment made me late getting to prom. Mom and Dad dropped me off. Mom walked me inside and she happened to see two of the teachers that I had in the previous year and told them to keep an eye on me should I start to get upset like I did before. She told them to call her. They thought they should come and get me at any time. I was all alone going into prom without a group of friends or a date and whenever guys would ask me to dance, I would always ask permission from their date. Many of the popular guys asked me to dance with them and whenever they did, I was beyond thrilled yet very nervous about angering their dates. None of the other girls got mad at me for dancing with their dates.

Mom and Dad couldn't wait to hear how things went whenever they came to pick me up after prom. I told them it was good, that I didn't get upset this time and I got to dance with some hot guys. I know my parents were pleased to finally have some happy news from me.

The month of May continued and soon it was time for school to be out for the summer. Dad continued to work with me on learning how to drive and I was hoping to have my driver's license by the time that school started for my senior year. Dad felt that I needed some more practice before taking the test to get my actual driver's license.

I really wanted to be an active member of the roller coaster fan club since I was a huge roller coaster fan. The club was planning to go to the same Amusement Park I went to last year for their annual convention in June 1998 that was near where my family lived. I wanted to start attending events on a regular basis with the coaster club. We went to visit family in the area for most of the week of the coaster club convention and Dad took all of the children with us to the park. We ended up going there just as regular customers for only one day because Dad had other ideas and it was still lots of fun. Whenever we got back home from the trip Lacey continued to play softball and when the regular summer softball season ended, she again was selected for the all-stars team for the second year in a row.

In the evenings whenever Lacey would have softball practice, or a home game Mom would watch her play ball while Dad would usually take me out to practice driving for about two hours. Those arduous two hours of driving often resulted in meltdowns and frustrations about not being good enough, especially at the end of the session whenever I would get tired. I am very thankful for those long arduous driving lessons with my dad. Had it not been for my dad working with me like this I may not have ever gotten a driver's license.

As the summer went on, we had a trip to Virginia planned near the end of July. It was a trip for Mom's nursing job. Dad, Lacey and I went with her. I wanted to go because there was an amusement park that I wanted to go to in the area about two hours away and our hotel was attached to a huge mall. We stayed in Arlington Virginia, within the Washington DC area and we were able to take the subway to Washington DC. Most of the time while Mom was at her conference, Lacey and I went to the mall that was attached to our hotel. I was able to buy some new clothes for the school year at that mall. One day while we were there Dad took Lacey and I to the Smithsonian Museum, the aquarium, and a restaurant in downtown Washington DC via the subway. While we were at the restaurant eating lunch after our visit at the Smithsonian Museum, we noticed that there were several police cars following a line of traffic outside the window of the restaurant.

"Dad, what do you think is going on outside with all of those police cars and the line of traffic," I asked while continuing to keep my eye on what was going on outside and eat my lunch at the same time.

"I don't know, said Dad. Something is going on."

Later that evening, we found out what that line of traffic and bunch of police cars was all about. Two policemen were shot on the capitol steps. That event made national news. The remainder of our trip went on and when the trip was over Dad drove us to the amusement park that I wanted to go to. We stayed for two nights at a hotel on the premises of the park and while at that park I was able to get all of their roller coasters added to my list of roller coasters. After that we headed back home.

I was hoping to be able to take the driver's license test and hopefully get my license by the time that my birthday arrived and at least before it was time to start back to school. I had not yet tried for my driver's license because Dad still felt like I needed more practice on driving.

My spring picture of my junior year
I was 16 years old

CHAPTER SIXTEEN

Children obey your parents as believers in the lord. (Ephesians 6:1 NIrV)
Fathers don't make your children angry. Instead instruct them the ways of
the Lord as you raise them. (Ephesians 6:4 NIrV)

I started back to school in August of that year about a week after
my seventeenth birthday and about a week before Lacey's fourteenth
birthday. It was my senior year and Lacey was an incoming freshman.
For most people their senior year is their best year of high school but
for me it was stressful. I dreaded it all along because seniors had to
do a portfolio of writings for English classes that were required for all
students in order to graduate. The portfolio assignments were very
stressful and hard just as I expected. During the first semester of my
senior year Dr. Stanley put me on Luvox again to handle the stress
associated with having to do a portfolio series of writings for my
English class. I was on four different medications: Prozac, Tegretol,
Luvox, and Desmopressin nose spray. All of those medications mixed
together in my body made me so sleepy every day that I could not
stay awake regardless of how much I slept at night. The bedwetting
was worse than what it ever was, and I could not even take a nap
without urinating in my sleep. Some of the other side effects from
medication that I experienced were irritable bowel syndrome issues,
tremors, drooling of my mouth, heavy menstrual periods, urinary
hesitancy and frequency, and joint pain.

When school started that year for the first semester of the school
year, I was enrolled in contemporary health issues for my first block

class, I was a school office aide for the second block, culinary arts during my third block, and English class as my last class of the day. My favorite class that semester was being an office aide because it was relaxing, and it gave me something to do that I liked. When I worked as an office aide, I was able to get away from all of the kids who were mean to me because I was different and was able to get restroom access when needed. Culinary Arts class was a fun class, yet it was a bit stressful at times too and English was a struggle to keep a C average. I was still active in FHA and had the role as an FHA reporter. Lacey tried out for the junior varsity cheerleading squad and made the team.

One day on the bus heading home for the day, a girl in Lacey's class just happened to be sitting next to me. She asked me how old I was. I told her that I was a senior.

"Are you excited about being a senior," she asked.

"No, I said. We have to work on portfolios for English class and those are really hard. That's the worst part of being a senior." Because of the stress I felt related to having to work on portfolio assignments for English class I developed flares of my stemming behaviors and worsening of irritability. When I mentioned this to Dr. Stanley, he told me that I needed to take Luvox again Mom and Dad agreed to it.

Homecoming was approaching and I went to the homecoming football game, but I did not feel like going to the homecoming dance. I did not have a date plus I was worried about having another bad experience. I was burned out from feeling chronic school and social stress because of my anxiety and being developmentally delayed compared to other teenagers, fatigued from my medications, and even though I still wanted to do well academically I did not perform as well in school as what I did when I was on less medication. Lacey went to homecoming, and she had a date.

One day during the late fall of that year I had a really bad day. We had a guest speaker for our contemporary health issues class, and she handed out some forms to fill out. One student had a question and I answered it. Another girl in the class, bragged on me for helping out the other student and playfully teased me but I misunderstood her intentions and what she said. Misunderstandings with people have always caused me to experience hurt feelings that lead to meltdowns and stemming.

I sat back down at my desk and struggled not to cry but I ended up crying anyway. The contemporary health issues teacher who was also my special education Math teacher three years earlier, still refused to let me leave the room whenever I was upset despite seeing that I was so upset and worried. That only made things worse for me on that day. When I told her about how I felt she told me that I just needed to lighten up and learn how to accept playful teasing which is very difficult for those with any form of Autism. The girl that accidentally hurt my feelings did not realize the extent of my problems. She was one of the students that were well liked by teachers, she had a good reputation among other students in the school.

The day went on and continued to be an upsetting day for me. I was so upset by the end of the day that Mom had to get me an appointment with Dr. Stanley the following week. This bad day was on a Friday, and I had the weekend to recover and rest. On Monday morning as I walked into class, I saw the girl who hurt my feelings talking with her best friend and she did apologize for hurting my feelings.

It was not a Christmas gift but one day after Christmas of that year Nan bought me a huge stuffed animal cookie monster that I absolutely loved. She got Lacey one for Christmas and she saw that I loved Lacey's Cookie Monster a lot. That's when she decided to get me one. I ended up sleeping with it every night.

When I went back to school for the second semester I took Another Science class, another global issues/history type class, Public Speaking and I continued taking Culinary Arts class. The annual bloodmobile was in January of that year, and I signed up to work at it. I worked most of the day at the bloodmobile. Everyone in FHA had the chance to sign up and work at the bloodmobile.

The day of the bloodmobile was the day that I got my driver's license. Dad took off from work to go with me to take the test to get my driver's license.

"How did I do," I asked the policeman as I finished taking my driver's license test.

"You passed," said the policeman as he reviewed the exam.

"*Thank you, Lord,*" I thought to myself as I breathed a sigh of relief. Dad was pleased with me and told me I did a good job. Dad told me he would take me for ice cream after school as a celebration.

Dad dropped me off at school and went back home. I headed straight to my section of the bloodmobile. The social conflicts started back again. Two girls got annoyed with me for coming back and checking on them when they were about to pass out after giving blood. Some of the other kids that were working at the bloodmobile teased me in a negative way and I had a meltdown over it. Being able to work at the school bloodmobile was normally a treat for me because I liked anything dealing with healthcare and medicine.

Dad immediately noticed that I had been crying when he picked me up after school to go for ice cream. My makeup was smeared and my eyes red and swollen, tears started up again. Dad couldn't understand after getting my operators permit and going out to celebrate, why I was upset. I told him about my experiences, trying to explain why I felt as I did.

"When Mom got home that evening, she was very concerned when she discovered why I was crying when I should have been rejoicing over getting my driver's license. I told her that two girls got angry with me when I kept constantly checking on them when they almost passed out after giving blood, and that other people were mean to me again. I felt I just couldn't do anything good enough for anyone. The only person that said anything good about me was Mom's friend who was a teacher. She at least said I did a good job working at the bloodmobile. I was exhausted from all the crying. If something goes wrong for someone on the spectrum, regardless of what else happens, their day can be badly ruined.

I wanted an Elmo to match my stuffed Cookie Monster and Mom got me one as a Valentine's Day gift. I put it on my bed with my stuffed Cookie Monster and slept with both of them every night from that day forward.

In February one day I happened to sit next to one of the girls at lunch who was very athletic and earned good grades. I had trouble opening a packet of ketchup and asked her if she would help me open it. She was applying lipstick with her makeup compact at the lunch table and did not hear me when I asked her the question. She mistakenly thought that I said something mean about her, and she started to respond back to me in an unkind way. I did my best to tell her that all I wanted from her was help in opening a packet of ketchup and that I did not mean to cause her any distress.

I got detention for using bad language one day when I was working on a project in culinary arts class; I was feeling frustrated and trying not to have a meltdown. The detention was only for two days, and it was only for one hour after school. While enduring my detention sessions I read a book and worked on homework assignments that were due that week.

Nationwide school shootings continued, and Columbine High School in Colorado had the worst school shooting ever in March of 1999 year killing several students. The week before Easter and Spring break of that year someone posted a note in the window of the guidance counselor's office that scared a lot of students into thinking that there could be another school attack. I was so focused on my grades, getting into college, picking up a prom dress if I were to even go at all and feeling too worried about kids bullying me to even worry about what a note said. On Good Friday a lot of the students checked out of school without parent permission because they were worried about a potential school attack. It was unknown as to who wrote that note and posted it.

The morning of the potential shooting attack, I drove to school just like I had every day since I got my license three months earlier, with Lacey riding to school with me of course. I checked into my first block science class and got out my stuff for class. As class started and roll was called, I was called down to the office via the intercom in the science classroom and the teacher answered the call on the intercom.

"Can you please send Lauren Ratcliff down to the office please. Her grandmother called to check her out," said the intercom voice.

I knew that something was going on, but I was not aware of how serious the situation was at school until I got downstairs to the school office and noticed Lacey waiting by the door for me and already checked out while several students were waiting in line to check out and one of the teachers was consoling a student who was crying. I felt concerned about getting into trouble for skipping school but yet I knew at the same time that safety at this time was way more important than getting detention. Nan was really worried, and I did not want to worry her anymore.

"Here Lauren, '' said the secretary as she handed me the phone. Your grandmother wants to talk to you."

"Lauren, '' said Nan, filled with anxiety in her voice. Please come on home, I have already checked you out."

I drove home with Lacey riding with me, and we headed to Nan's house and spent the rest of the day there until Mom and Dad got home from work. Thoughts ran through my head that it could be anyone that got killed in the planned attack on the school even though there was a list of students that the attacker planned to kill. Uncle Melvin had already come and got Aaron and had taken him home, so I didn't need to worry about him. Since it was Good Friday, my out-of-town family would be coming to Kentucky that day. Despite all of the issues with the note that stated that there would be an attack on the school with a planned list of students to kill, Lacey still had a softball game that evening. Lacey was a member of the High School softball team as well as the Junior varsity cheerleading team, and summer league softball teams.

Spring break of that year, we stayed home, and I went to a local tanning bed to use up the sessions that Mom paid for as a way of looking the part for my senior prom.

A week after Spring break of that year the Junior varsity cheerleaders went to a state competition five hours away and Dad, Mom and I went with them. They lost the competition. On the way back from that trip I got the craving to go on an amusement park outing with the roller coaster fan club on the same weekend as my prom. I disliked the idea of missing prom, but I was so tired of being around kids that I felt bullied me.

"Mom, I said as we got home. I think I would rather go to this amusement park outing than go to prom. I cannot stand kids making fun of me, I just don't want to go. I just need to get away for a day.

"Ok, said Mom. That's fine by me."

I immediately got out my checkbook and wrote the check to the coaster club and stamped it for Dad to mail out the next day. Mom and Dad opened me up a checking account shortly after my seventeenth birthday and I felt very thankful at that point to have a checking account.

On the date of the amusement park outing with the coaster club I was excited to go and thought about all of the kids going to prom at the High School and how I just could not mentally take going to prom without the potential of having a meltdown. I also did not have a date or a group of friends to go with. I would have been alone. When I got back home that night, I was glad I went on that coaster club outing but felt guilty that I chose not to go to prom out of worry that kids would bully me.

Just a few weeks later it was time for me to graduate from High School and start the next chapter of my life. As I sat there at my seat at our graduation ceremony, I thought about all of the students from Columbine High School who were killed in the shooting and how it was unfair that they would not be able to graduate and move on to adulthood. My graduation party was held at our church. It was a party consisting of all of my aunts and uncles and cousins from both sides of the family.

The whole summer I did not do much. I bought a pool pass for our local public swimming pool and drove there by myself every day. Lacey played summer league softball and a lot of times her friends' parents would come and get her and drive them to softball practice together. I had taken the ACT twice, and in June of that year I took it my second time and didn't do so well the second time either.

The one thing that I regret about what I did in high school is skipping prom and homecoming during my senior year because I was so worried about the kids continuing to pick on me and not having a date. I now feel as though I should have gone to both events anyway and not worried about having a date or anything else.

My family and I took a beach vacation in June that year, but this time we went with my dad's sister and her family. Nan Nan and

Mamaw usually went on vacation with us but from that time forward they decided not to go on vacation with us. The trip was nice, and I was able to get one new roller coaster added to my list. After we got back from vacation it was time for our annual family reunion and fourth of July celebration and of course my family came for a visit as usual. It was nice as always.

The summer passed and soon it was time for me to start thinking about what to do for my 18th birthday and getting ready to get admitted as a student into Ashland Community College, the local community college.

High school graduation, May 1999

CHAPTER SEVENTEEN

Everyone has sinned. No one measures up to God's glory. (Romans 3:23 NIrV)

About two days before my 18th birthday, I went to one of my bimonthly checkups with Dr. Stanley. During the visit he asked if my obsession with roller coasters had decreased at all in addition to the typical psychiatric exam questions that he asked me. Dad went with me to that appointment instead of Mom and he went inside the room with me to talk to Dr. Stanley.

"Has Lauren's obsession with roller coasters decreased any," Dr. Stanley asked Dad out of concern.

"No, said Dad. We are taking her to another park in a few days." It never made sense to me that having an intense interest would be wrong unless it was impacting my health or the health and safety of others. We did go to another amusement park, and it was nice.

Lacey went back to school as a sophomore. She tried out for the Junior Varsity Cheerleading squad and made the team for the second year. It felt weird not to go to school in the mornings and have Lacey go to school without riding with me.

About a week after Lacey started back to school it was time for me to register as a first-time college freshman. Mom took off from work to go with me to register for classes, attend orientation and take the admission test. After a full day of orientation and preparing for my Community College admission I was ready to take on my next chapter of life. A week after orientation and registration it was time for me to start college classes. Mom and Dad were very supportive all around in helping me with my educational goals. I had to play catch up with Math due to my math learning disability associated with Asperger Syndrome and of the fact that I was in special education Math courses since Middle School.

It was always a dream of mine to go to college and obtain a professional career. I was still on three different medicines and continued my regular checkups with Dr. Stanley. At that time Dr. Stanley tapered me off of Tegretol and just gave me Luvox, Prozac, and Desmopressin nose spray instead.

In the past I learned that I would get fired over not being able to control my emotions in a job setting but I knew that I could not control my emotions when I got upset. Therefore, I felt hesitant to apply for a job at that time even though I seriously considered doing so.

I really liked the atmosphere of Kentucky Christian University because it was Christian based and bible classes were required by all students at the school to graduate. I did some research on the college and consulted with some advisors about getting in there as a student. I decided to wait and earn my associate degree before transferring there.

One month later and after starting my college courses Mom and Dad purchased a desktop computer with internet access. Dad's friend who worked with computers set the computer up for us and connected it to a router. I was glad to have a computer with internet access, but we had to use dial up back in 1999 if we were to get on the internet. We had to limit internet access because we needed the phone lines to be available for Nan or Mamaw in case one of them needed one of us for something. I spent a lot of time researching stuff on the internet and learning how to use it. I knew a little bit about the computer system that we got at the time because we used that type of system in the library at my High School and for typing class my sophomore year of high school.

During my first semester of college, I enrolled in two remedial classes (the first level of developmental Math classes and a writing class), Introduction to college, and a reading class. I was so focused on passing Math that I did not focus as much on the other classes. I ended up failing my math course.

I went through a slump, and I think it may have been related to side effects of the medication I was taking at the time. I still did not feel well half of the time and I was super fatigued; I could not stay awake. The medications affected my ability to function. I knew what I wanted to do for a major and I went through a period of time where I almost did not care how my grades were. I had a fascination with the medical field but knew a medical program would be very challenging, so my next best option was to try a social work type field that involved counseling young kids with problems similar to what I had. I was not planning to give up on any of my educational or employment goals, but I was weak in my study skills and homework habits.

I considered taking a holiday job to pay for school for the following semester, but I felt like I needed to relax, and I was worried about getting fired over having a meltdown on the job if I did get a job. I got Roller Coaster Tycoon computer game as a Christmas present and loved it. As the last Christmas of the century ended everyone started getting prepared for the dreaded Y2K disaster that could happen on January 1st, 2000.

I was very nervous about the Y2K and Mom tried to calm me down and told me what it would be like if it happened. The deal was that the computers would have to be updated in order for people to buy stuff at all. If computers were not updated, then people would not be able to buy stuff for a long time. I thought there was a possibility that we would have to figure out how to survive on minimal things and not be able to do stuff that I like. I thought we would suffer from some sort of major catastrophe.

I confessed to Mom that I was worried about Y2K, and that I didn't want anything to happen. Mom, always the optimist, assured me everything was alright. She said, "we are country people, and we know how to survive." So, what happened? New Year's Day of 2000 was another day, and nothing happened. It was just another day. I was relieved.

Lacey went back to school the week after New Years, and I had already pre-registered for classes and I did not take any Math courses for the semester. All of my classes were off campus. I was enrolled in

College English 101, Speech, and Medical Terminology. I signed up for the second level of developmental Math, but I had to drop it because I needed to repeat the first level of developmental math. I was only taking nine credits instead of the 12 credits that were considered to be full time.

Near the end of January of 2000, Dad, Mom and I flew on an airplane with Lacey and her Cheerleading squad to New Orleans for competition. It was my first time flying on an airplane. We stayed in New Orleans for about three days and the second full day there the cheerleading competition was held. Lacey's squad lost the competition to the other squads that were there, but they all had a great time.

When we got back from New Orleans Lacey went back to school and Mom and Dad went back to work. My college classes continued to go on without any Math classes. This is one thing I feel like should be said whether it is related to my High Functioning Autism or not. I had a lot of problems with my Speech Professor that semester that affected my ability to succeed in the class. He was a very rude and obnoxious person, in my opinion, and I felt a bit insecure around him.

I did not have the courage to tell anyone that this professor was doing things that I felt like were wrong. Looking back on the situation I should have stepped up and told someone about the situation when I realized that there was an issue. I was able to obtain a C in my English class and a B in my Medical Terminology class. I still wanted to earn my associate degree from the local Community College and go on to to obtain a degree in helping children with conditions similar to mine. Near the end of April of 2000, it was time to pre-register for fall classes and I registered for all of my fall classes.

One Evening that Spring while I was at my Nan's house a family friend happened to be there visiting. She playfully teased me about something that we were talking about, and I misunderstood her that she was teasing me. I still had problems understanding when certain people were playfully teasing and others, I could easily detect playful teasing. That evening, I responded unkindly to her because I misunderstood her. She is a kind person and is fun to be around and I usually enjoy talking to her. When Mom found out about my reactions, she felt disappointed and considered issuing consequences.

The semester seemed to fly by. Spring went on and I received academic probation because I failed my really hard remedial Math class from the previous semester and earned a D average in my speech class. If I had a different speech professor, I felt like I would have earned a much better grade. I was unaware about applying for student disability services. I grew up with the misconception that if you had a disability that it was better not to go to college and that if you earned poor grades in college courses then college was not the best option. If I was confident enough to step up and ask about disability services, I believe that I would have earned better grades for the semester. I was trying to save time and money by taking all of my classes off campus and trying to stay safe in bad weather situations during the winter months.

Mom mentioned a place for students with disabilities, Perkins Vocational Rehabilitation Center, about an hour from where we lived. The place is a vocational school for students with any type of disability. One day that spring I researched all day on the internet for the Center and could not find any information about it. They did not have a website at the time.

As spring turned into summer 2000, I spent most of my summer going to the local public pool, taking Lacey to and from softball practice, playing my roller coaster tycoon game on our computer, and reading a lot. I knew that I was not able to have a job, so I felt like I had to do something to entertain myself. Mom was concerned that I was showing signs of depression because I spent a lot of time in the house playing roller coaster tycoon and reading and she even mentioned it to Dr. Stanley. I didn't feel depressed. I really liked playing roller coaster tycoon because some of the medications that I was on made me feel very tired. Mom gave away our doll house because she thought that I was too old to play with it and worried about what people would think if they saw me playing with Barbies at age 18 going on 19. She told me that she now regrets giving it away.

"Mom, I said whenever she got home from work that afternoon. I researched on the internet all day and found nothing on the Vocational

Rehabilitation Center that you mentioned. The Center did in fact have a Cosmetology program that I wanted to enroll in. How am I going to get any information on it? If you think I should attend beauty school, I should just apply at one of the places around here and I like makeup and skin care better than doing hair."

"Well, if you don't care, would you please sit down with me at the table and we will pray about it," said Mom. We prayed about what to do. We discussed what I should do in the way of education often.

One day that summer as we were driving back home from going out to eat, I was complaining about my grades in college and Mom and Dad both suggested that I go to beauty school instead because I liked working with hair and I was good at applying makeup and taking care of my skin. I told them I would rather get a professional degree but would consider beauty school.

We were not able to take a vacation that year because Mom and Dad spent a lot of money on my college education and Dr. Stanley wanted me to see one of the counselors in his practice. Our insurance at the time was not covering counseling sessions with the counselor in Dr. Stanley's practice and Mom and Dad had to pay out of pocket for those counseling sessions. Lacey still played school softball and summer league softball as well as cheerleading. Summer progressed and due to Lacey's full sports schedule and my school and medical expenses I was only able to go to one amusement park that summer. My out-of-town family came to Kentucky for the annual family reunion and the Fourth of July to celebrate.

My cousin Amanda spent a month in Kentucky with us. Lacey played on the all-star's softball team for the third year and was still one of the best players on her team, in my opinion. I finally decided to enroll in a a local cosmetology program. Mom took off from work one day to go with me to sign me up for cosmetology school at the local vocational school and pay the tuition and book fees.

Orientation day for incoming Cosmetology students was scheduled and Dad took off from work to go with me to orientation and to tour the cosmetology school with a group of other students. Afterward Dad wanted to go around to various businesses including a place where his friend's wife worked that helped people find jobs. Dad at the time was also determined to help me find a good job with good pay and benefits should college or cosmetology school not work out for me.

A week after my 19th birthday I was getting ready to start cosmetology school. That was the only other program that I was interested in at the time if I felt like I was not able to pursue a college education. I preferred to enroll in Cosmetology at Perkins Vocational Center (PVC) but was not able to because I did not have enough information on the school. I got asked out by a guy that I had a crush on that worked at the hospital where Mom worked at as a nurse. He was a valedictorian of his class and at the time studying to be a pharmacist, but he later changed his major. I was downright shocked and extremely nervous when he asked me out. I enjoyed talking to him on the phone. Based on my experiences with being bullied constantly in school, being developmentally delayed and suffering from mental illness, I felt very worried that he would dump me when he figured out that I had problems. Having Asperger Syndrome does give me the ability to remember pleasant and unpleasant moments for years that most people would not remember. This makes me feel great anxiety about the recurrence of a social situation that has worried me that others would not remember, thus causing me to feel very insecure about dating relationships and some social interactions. For about six months after high school graduation, I had a crush on my cousin Aaron's best friend which did not go well either.

A couple of days later I sent the boy a rude email saying that I was no longer interested in him and that he was not good enough for me. None of this was true. This really hurt his feelings and I did not want to do this. This was one of the few times that I can remember of me being mean to someone on purpose to protect myself against getting hurt and acting as if I were too cool for someone. As much as I preferred to date guys like this because of their values I chose to decline his interest out of my insecurity about my developmental delays and mental illness. I convinced myself that I was not good enough to date this amazing boy. I truly regret the way that I reacted about this situation. When Mom found out that I sent the mean email she was shocked and angry at me that I reacted like that toward the boy.

CHAPTER EIGHTEEN

Our troubles are small. They last only for a short time. But they are earning us a glory that will last forever. It is greater than all our troubles. So, we don't spend all our time looking at what we can't see. That's because what's seen lasts only a short time. (2 Corinthians 4:17-18 NIrV)

What happened in the year 2000-Spring through summer of 2002? Y2K was not the big deal that everyone thought it was. President George W. Bush got elected as the new President of the United States. On September 11th, 2001, terrorists destroyed the World Trade Center, and it changed our nation forever. To avoid terrorism, security was strengthened at federal buildings and airports. Terrorists turned Anthrax into a deadly bacterium and anything powdery in an envelope in the mail was to be reported because of being suspicious for agents that may contain the Anthrax bacteria. The war in Afghanistan began. There was still not enough research about the different types of autism spectrum disorders. A new elementary school building was built which housed students and staff from my former elementary school and a nearby elementary school.

I was excited and nervous to begin my journey as a Cosmetology student. On my first day of class I noticed Jenny, a girl that I had gone to school with all of my life sitting next to another student in the cosmetology lab section.

"Hey Jenny," I said as I walked inside.

"Hi Lauren, said Jenny. You can just set your stuff inside the classroom and then come back outside.

"Ok, thank you," I said as I walked toward the back of the cosmetology department to the classroom.

Mrs. Preston was the chairman of the cosmetology department and head cosmetology professor. "Good morning class," said Mrs. Preston as she walked inside the classroom and handed out guidelines for the program and our syllabus. I am Mrs. Preston, the dean of the Cosmetology program."

After Mrs. Preston went over our rules and introduction to the class, we had our first assignment immediately. It was to work on some mannequin heads. From that day forward I worked really hard in Cosmetology School. I thought that I was good at working with hair, skin, and makeup and that it would not be as stressful as other professions. I was wrong.

I had my first bad day with a meltdown about a month after the class started. I struggled greatly on that day not to cry about anything. Everything went ok until the end of the day. I had a hard time finishing an assignment where we once again had to roll the hair on a mannequin head and that took me all day. Not long after that I had another bad day with the same thing happening. On the second bad day I had an appointment with Dr. Stanley. Since students were not able to run off copies of any reports of anything I had to ask Mrs. Preston to run off copies of my midterm grade report to give to Dr. Stanley. It happened to be midterm week on the week of my second major bad day. On that day I discovered that my grades were not as good as I hoped, and I was very upset about that.

Mom still liked to go with me to all of my doctor appointments even though I had my driver's license for two full years at the time and I was nineteen years old. I met Mom at the nearby Walmart and parked my car there while we drove to my doctor appointment. Mom noticed that I been crying and asked me why I was upset; I told her that I was very disappointed in my lab grade average. Mom told me that she felt like that I needed to practice more on the mannequin head that came in my lab kit when I entered beauty school yet at the same time, she told me it is ok if I earn a C average. C's earn degrees, she always told me.

I did not know how to tell Mom that I felt like I needed a break whenever I got home from class every day. People on the spectrum need frequent rest breaks from anything they do in order to function at maximum capacity and back then I felt like I had zero energy to do the slightest thing whenever I would get home from class in the evenings. I felt so tired and fatigued that I could not take the time to apply makeup like I wanted to in the mornings before leaving for class. Much of this was a side effect of my medications. The first thing that I would do whenever I got home from school was lay on the couch and watch TV until Mom and Dad got home from work so we could go to Nan's house and eat dinner or eat dinner at home. Nan still wanted to cook supper for us daily.

Whenever I got to my appointment, I handed a copy of my midterm grade report to Dr. Stanley. I told him about everything that was happening in beauty school and how I felt concerned about my grades. He wanted me to stay on the same dose of medication that I was currently taking and to come back in about two to three months like I usually did. In addition to being prescribed Prozac and Luvox for my OCD, panic attacks, and constant crying I was prescribed Tofranil instead of Nose Spray for my bedwetting and urinary frequency.

Cosmetology students are required to work on live clients as part of the curriculum when they achieve so many hours of lab class. Mrs. Preston felt concerned with my emotional control problems and how that would affect my ability to work on clients. She wanted to help me succeed but did not know how because of my emotional control issues. I continued to work hard to keep my grades up in cosmetology school but once again it was very hard. As the semester progressed, I earned a C in the lab class which frustrated me. I mainly got upset over my grades.

During my winter appointment Dr. Stanley prescribed me a fourth medication and when he found that new medication gave me severe side effects, he switched me to another one in the same category that also gave me severe side effects. One of those two medications made me cry constantly and the other one caused me to have tremors in my hand that were so intense that it was hard for me to control the steering wheel when driving.

One day on my way to school in the winter of 2001 I lost control of the steering wheel when I dozed off and accidentally bumped into another car in front of me at a red light. The accident just bruised the front end of our car and the back of the car in front of me. Feeling frustrated with the side effects of my medication and about being late for class I had a meltdown that resulted in stemming. I got my first cell phone ever as a Christmas gift and it came in handy for that accident. With that cell phone I was able to call my mom at work and tell her what happened while I was crying hysterically. One of the other girls in my class had seen my incident as she was passing me from another direction and told Mrs. Preston what happened. Jenny came to the scene of the accident to check on me. She arrived around the same time as the police did and told them about my condition. The police were kind to me and helped me to calm down and I appreciated their efforts. If I were able to calm down, I would have not missed much class and would have been like a half hour late maybe but because I was so hysterical it caused me to miss the morning class session.

Mom asked Dr. Singh about placing me on birth control pills in addition to my other medications for my uncontrollable moods and stemming behaviors which were horrible anyway, and much worse during fluctuations in my menstrual cycle. Both of them agreed and against my wishes I went ahead and took the birth control pills. I had two weeklong menstrual periods that were so inconvenient that it was hard to control, and my chronic hip pain returned with a vengeance. When the hip pain came back it was the same type of pain that I had when I was much younger.

Spring of 2001 passed by and soon it was time for Spring break week for the area colleges. We did not do anything for Spring Break, and I was ok with that. Mom contacted Perkins Vocational Center and scheduled a tour for me one day in April of 2001. It was an excused absence because I told Mrs. Preston, that I would be taking a tour there because I was considering transferring there. Mrs. Preston approved with that thank goodness and she thought it would be a good option for me.

On the day that I was scheduled for the tour of Perkins Vocational Center Mom took the day off from work to go with me. We lived only about an hour away from there and it was about 30 minutes away from where Mom worked as a nurse at the time. Whenever we got there for the tour a friendly lady in a wheelchair greeted us as we entered the front doors.

"Can I help you," said the lady.

"Yes, we are here for a tour," said Mom.

"What's the name," said the lady.

"Lauren Ratcliff," said Mom.

"Ok, said the lady. Someone will be with you shortly, Have a seat."

A few minutes later I noticed another lady in a wheelchair coming down the hallway toward the entrance toward me and Mom.

"Hello, I am Mrs. Blanton, said the the lady in the wheelchair, "and you must be Lauren."

"Yes. Nice to meet you," I said, shaking Mrs. Blanton's hand.

"I will be taking you on your tour of the facility, " said Mrs. Blanton. Are you ready?"

"Yes," Mom and I both said.

Mrs. Blanton then took Mom and I on a tour of every part of the Center. I was mainly interested in their Cosmetology Program because I had previous experience and was still interested in the beauty industry at the time if traditional college did not work out for me. While we were there, we talked with one of the Cosmetology instructors and she explained everything to us about Perkins' Cosmetology program. Whenever we were done touring the center Mrs. Blanton took us to the evaluation room to talk with Mrs. Ross, the evaluation coordinator to see what I would need to do to get admitted into the center. I had to get all of my school and medical records plus I had to make an appointment with the vocational rehabilitation counselor in our area. Mrs. Ross told me that she sent an email to the vocational Rehabilitation Counselor in our area and for me to be expecting a call from that office to be seen soon.

"Well ladies, " said Mrs. Blanton as Mom and I finished talking with Mrs. Ross, "That concludes your tour. Do you have any questions?"

"No, Mom and I both said. Thank you for the tour."

After the tour of the center Mom and I went out to eat at a nearby restaurant and went back home. When the semester ended for my current cosmetology program, I drove there a few days later to sign a release to have my transcript faxed to Perkins Vocational Center (PVC). When I got finished, I went to the mall to grab some lunch. As I arrived at the mall, I had great difficulty finding a parking spot and because I had issues with controlling the shaking of my hands, I ended up bumping into another car and at that point my mom took me off of the medication that was causing my hands to shake so much. I am so glad that I was able to stop taking that stuff. I still continued to take the Prozac, Luvox, Tofranil, and the birth control pill and I felt as if I saw no improvement in taking three psychiatric medications and a birth control pill over taking just one medication daily and another one as needed.

A few days later I had an appointment to meet with the vocational rehabilitation counselor for our area. Dad took off from work to go with me there. I immediately applied for vocational rehabilitation services with their instruction. The counselor told Dad and me that I should hear from PVC within about two weeks. I waited to hear from PVC as to when I would be admitted for evaluation to the center.

We went on vacation during the third week of June to the beach and it was lots of fun. Whenever we returned from our vacation, I got our mail and in our stash of mail was a letter from PVC and the Kentucky Department of Vocational Rehabilitation. I immediately opened the letter and read it. It stated that I got admitted to PVC for the 3rd week of July 2001 for evaluation. I was relieved to know that I would soon be admitted to PVC but the week before I got admitted for evaluation, I was very nervous about going away from home.

About two weeks or so before I went to PVC, I suffered from a flare of my Anxiety that resulted in worry that caused meltdowns so severe that Mom considered taking me to the hospital. I am so thankful that I was able to calm down enough that I did not need to be seen at a hospital. We had family in that week that were visiting and my jealousy toward one of my cousins was in full swing. She was so pretty and so smart, but

I don't know why I was so obsessed with her talents, instead of admiring and enjoying her, I felt extreme jealousy. I perceived her as going to find great success later in life because I thought she was going to achieve goals that I wanted badly to achieve but felt I would not be able to achieve due to my disability. This caused the severe flare of my anxiety.

On the day that I went for evaluation at PVC I woke up full of anxiety and crying uncontrollably. Mom normally took pictures of me and Lacey on our first days of school, but she chose not to this time because I was crying so hard. Mom, Dad, and Lacey were all trying to calm me down and they helped me pack my stuff for the week. I thought that I would get admitted immediately after evaluation and start classes the following week, but I didn't.

On the one-hour drive to PVC Dad drove me there and Mom and Lacey rode with me to help me get situated. The whole way there, Mom described her experience as a student feeling very homesick throughout her first couple of weeks in college, and Dad told me how homesick he was in Germany in the Army. They were encouraging me, telling me that each day and each week would get better. We also talked about the importance of learning to live away from home, get a good education and to become independent. I was reassured for the moment, but it was just like what I experienced during my early elementary education. When we arrived at PVC, Mom, Dad, and Lacey helped me to settle into my dorm room for the week.

They stayed a couple of hours with me, helping me to get settled in, making my bed and making my room comfortable. Then it was time for my family to leave. Mom, Dad and Lacey gave me hugs and still offering reassurance. I began screaming and crying uncontrollably and several other students tried their best to calm me down.

Struggling through constant tear-stained eyes I pushed myself to overcome my intense homesickness. I stuck the week out. I went to the arts and crafts department every evening that it was open in order to redirect my separation anxiety and homesickness. Tuesday through Friday of that week from 8am until 4pm were full of testing and it was exhausting and boring. I met some friends whom I remain friends with to this day.

At the end of the day on Thursday of that week, Mrs. Ross met with me to discuss what she felt would be best for me. Based on my problems with emotional control and of the fact that I had never been employed she felt like I would be best suited for the Work Adjustment Program (WAP) at PVC prior to entering the cosmetology program even with cosmetology experience.

Some students at PVC started work adjustment immediately and others like me waited for two weeks after evaluation to start the program. The majority of students who attended PVC had some type of disability including local students who commuted daily. I went home and celebrated my 20th birthday with my family, and it was a small party with just my immediate family. That year Mom gave me a birthday cake that had a picture of a roller coaster on it from one of my magazines that said, "*Happy birthday roller coaster queen!*"

I began the (WAP) program at PVC on the second week of August of 2001. If Cosmetology did not work out, I wanted to enroll in PVC child day care program because I loved children. I only needed the (WAP) program and weekly counseling sessions with one of the mental health counselors at the Center. Many of the other students at PVC have to take Occupational/Physical Therapy, Drivers Education, and Life Skills Programs in addition to a training program. The (WAP) program is about a two-to-three-month program based on each student's individual needs and training program goals. I stayed on campus in the student dorm and white knuckled my way through my homesickness that caused me to cry a lot like I did when I was much younger. For the first full semester that I stayed at PVC I brought my huge stuffed Cookie Monster and Elmo to sleep with me in my room at night and sometimes I took them home with me on the weekends.

Throughout my duration in the (WAP) program at PVC I worked really hard for three months and two weeks. I stayed in the (WAP) program longer than most of the other students do because I needed to work on some Math skills that were recommended for all Cosmetology students. Cosmetology reopened in the spring semester. The PVC Cosmetology program was closed for the fall semester and reopened in

January of 2002. I was excited to get enrolled in Cosmetology at PVC because I so wanted to be enrolled in that program all along.

During the evening hours at PVC, I spent most of the time in the Arts and Crafts department painting. During the late evening hours, I would exercise in the recreation room and someone from the recreation staff would pop in a Tai Bo or yoga tape for students. By doing these tapes with the recreation staff I discovered that I really liked Yoga and considered it one of my favorite ways to get exercise. I always participated in those sessions and sometimes the physical therapy room was open in the evenings for students to use for exercise and I went there to exercise too.

During the fall season at PVC, I ended up meeting some more friends and a couple of guys wanted to ask me out. One of them really liked me and I had feelings for him too; I just did not want to show it. I pushed myself not to have them out of worry about how he would feel about me when he discovered that I was developmentally delayed and about my lifestyle compared to that of other girls my age. I read a lot and learned that psychological disorders of any type can strain relationships. Though I knew I was socially and emotionally developmentally delayed I was taught the importance a of a strong work ethic, achieving educational and career goals, and living a healthy lifestyle and preferred dating guys that shared the same values. I was also hoping for someone that would support my fascination with riding roller coasters. I never told anyone that I wanted a relationship with this guy and just continued to focus on my educational and career goals as well as nurturing my Christian faith.

I officially completed the WAP program on December 14th, 2001, and went home for Christmas break. I enjoyed taking a month long break off from school and felt excited to get started in PVC Cosmetology program. One day I when I was looking for something in our kitchen drawers, I noticed that Mom filled out a job application for me to work at our local Walmart, but we forgot to submit it. Lacey and I got money for Christmas as one of our main gifts. She spent hers on getting her car windows tinted and I spent part of mine on beauty supplies to practice on for school and saved the rest of it.

Soon it was time for Cosmetology to reopen at PVC. It reopened the second week of January of 2002. PVC Cosmetology students spent half of the day in lab class and the other half of the day in lecture or vice versa for some students. I still continued my weekly counseling sessions, daily painting in the arts and crafts room and exercise sessions. When school started back, I took my beloved papa Smurf and the other Smurf's to school with me to stay in my dorm room because Cookie and Elmo were too big, and I felt like I still needed the comforts of stuffed animals. Students at the Center were required to commit to following steps to achieving their individual goals and following rules that were implemented by the center. If any of these rules or goals were broken the students' faced consequences. Since I had more time in the mornings, I wore makeup again on a regular basis and all I had to do when I finished getting dressed in the mornings was to walk downstairs to the Cosmetology department. After eating my breakfast in the school cafeteria, I always brushed my teeth and applied my makeup in the public bathrooms near the Cosmetology department. My makeup application always included bright red lipstick and one of my professors also loved bright red lipstick.

Lacey graduated from High school in May of 2002 and on the evening of her graduation I was able to attend the ceremony. Since I was not allowed to have my own vehicle at PVC without special permission, Mom had to come and get me after work and drive me home to go to Lacey's graduation and drove me back to school at PVC the following day on her way to work. Most of the students that stayed on campus at PVC did not yet have their licenses and for those that did, they had to obtain special permits from the school to drive. Most students that stayed on campus used PVC transportation services. Since PVC was only 30 or 40 minutes from where she worked it was more convenient for Mom to drop me off on Mondays and pick me up on Fridays instead of me driving there myself. I did not attend Lacey's graduation party because PVC took a group of students to an amusement park on the day of her party. Anytime there was an amusement park trip I always signed up because I was a roller coaster fanatic and it felt good to hang out with my fellow students from PVC.

I was scheduled to graduate in September of 2002 from PVC Cosmetology Program and take my Cosmetology license exam in October of 2002. I finished with my lecture portion of the program near the end of May 2002 and had to take a series of written exams, in the time period of the day that I would normally have my lecture class. It took about a couple of days to finish them and fortunately I passed all of them. When I passed my written exams, I took the lab only portion of the class until I finished in mid-September of 2002. Since I was due to graduate in September of 2002, I was eligible to participate in the PVC annual graduation ceremony that was held in June.

Mom, Dad, Nan, and Aunt Sylvia came to watch me march through the graduation ceremony at PVC. Graduation there was really nice, the staff worked really hard on making it nice. There was a two-week summer break after graduation. During the two-week summer break, I practiced on getting ready for my series of lab exams and state board examinations for Cosmetology. Mom and Dad took me to an amusement park in Ohio that I had never been to and that was fun. It was part of my graduation present and when we were finished, we stopped to visit with family for a day or so. My family also celebrated the summer in the typical fashion that we always did in the short break.

Whenever I went back to school after the summer break I went through a really stressful time near the end of July and in the first week of August. That consisted of meltdowns that nearly resulted in consequences. The root cause of those meltdowns was being stressed out over my grades. At PVC students were issued a privilege card or honor student status that can be used for recreational trips with the school and if they broke any school rules within a certain time period privilege and honor statuses were affected.

One day when I was having a really bad day at school, I called Nan on the pay phone after class crying uncontrollably. Crying and screaming I expressed to her my frustration about my grades, and other stuff going on in class that week that bothered me. Back in 2002 most people did not have cell phones and the few cell phones that were available back then were not as fancy as the iPhones that we have today and were very expensive, so that pay phone was my contact with the outside world.

While I was on the phone with Nan two students came over to console me. One of them was a boy, who just noticed me and immediately had a crush on me. He saw that I was so upset that I could not control myself and he wanted to help calm me down. He did help calm me down and talking to him helped me to feel better. I started having feelings for him even though I did not show it the way I should have.

"Are you ok," said the boy.

"Crying and screaming uncontrollably I told him everything and he tried to help me talk through my frustrations.

"What is your name," asked the boy.

"I'm Lauren," I said feeling way too upset to be polite but thankful to have someone to console me.

"What's your name," I asked the boy.

"I'm Chris," said the boy.

From that day forward Chris and I were best friends and he called me daily at home whenever I was home, and we would talk for hours. I always ate dinner with Chris in the school cafeteria. He lived about four hours away from me.

I turned 21 years old on August 2, 2002, and was now old enough to buy alcohol, but I would never do such a thing because I cared about my health and religious faith. The students in the Cosmetology Department decided to throw me a surprise birthday party and that made me really happy. It happened during our morning break period on the date of my 21st birthday. One of the other girls asked me to walk outside with her and when we got back to the cosmetology lab department, I noticed the surprise birthday party.

"Surprise! Happy Birthday," yelled all of the other students and one of the other professors as they gathered around me with a birthday cake and gifts. I thanked the other students in class for the birthday party and it helped to me to feel a bit better while facing a tough two weeks. Having friends that care may not cure a person's situation, but it can make a difference in how they feel.

Mom came to pick me up on her way home from work that Friday as usual. She knew that I had a bad week even though the other students threw me a birthday party for my 21st birthday and that I got asked out by one of the boys at the school.

"Mom, it's not fair that I am not doing well in Cosmetology school. I just know that I am not going to pass the state board exam. I did not do well in college. I'm just so frustrated about having an emotional disability that I can't control," I said venting out my feelings.

"Lauren, please do not say that '' said Mom. You have worked very hard to get through cosmetology school and you are almost finished. You should be proud of yourself. You are beautiful and well loved."

My Dad bought me a 2000 black ford escort, my first ever car as a birthday and graduation from cosmetology school gift. Mom dropped me off at PVC for one of the last times ever following that weekend. Also, that week Mom and Dad helped Lacey move into her college dorm room to begin her freshman year of college.

One day in August of that year I just cleaned up my dorm room to get ready to move out and focused on preparing for my lab practical exam in cosmetology. While taking a break from getting ready to move out and from working hard on my cosmetology lab exam I decided to go town shopping one evening for one of the last times ever as a student at PVC. Twice a week recreation staff at PVC took students shopping at the local shopping center district which included Walmart, a few clothing stores, a shoe store on one end, and on the other end a discounted bookstore, and a a few restraunts. Being the avid reader that I was, I decided to go to the bookstore. While I was at the bookstore, I purchased a book about Autism and Pervasive Developmental Disorders. This was the first time that I ever saw a book about this spectrum of disorders. I read several books about obsessive-compulsive disorder, and I was glad to read a book about Autism/PDD. It was a book written by a man who was at one time a nonverbal autistic and he was able to overcome a lot of his Autism. Knowing my disability, I felt like I could overcome my problems if this man was able to do it.

When I came home from PVC, I decided that I would keep both my Smurfs and my Cookie Monster and Elmo on my bed to cuddle with at night. I didn't care any more about being too old to sleep with my stuffed animals. They brought me comfort and made me feel better.

I passed my cosmetology lab practical exam around the first week of September of 2002. It was then that I was finished as a student at PVC. I was not able to take the October Cosmetology board exam for several reasons and had to wait to take the November board exam. The practical part of the cosmetology required that we bring a live model with us to work on. My Aunt Sylvia went with me as my model to test on, and I passed. The very next week I took my first job ever.

Beauty school graduation

CHAPTER NINETEEN

And do everything you can to live a quiet life. You should mind your own business, and work with your hands, just as we told you to do. (I Thessalonians 4:11 NIrV)

One week after I earned my Cosmetology license, I started working at a full-service salon that just opened up in my hometown. My family knew the person that owned the salon, and she knew about my history of being a special needs person. I had my first meltdown two days after I started the job and my boss felt that I should just leave immediately for the day instead of trying to redirect my feelings to feel better. Business was slow at first because it was a brand-new business. I worked very hard to be a good employee for my boss and to always treat the other employees and customers with respect. From the first day that I started working there I felt so worried about getting fired that it caused me intense anxiety that led to regular meltdowns.

Whenever I got my first paycheck a week after starting my job, I immediately signed the check and took it to the bank to deposit a portion of it into my savings account and another portion of it into my checking account. We got paid weekly and the other employees earned a percentage of what they made by working on clients. Despite me working really hard and with overtime hours the check was only $50. I was very disappointed with only earning $50 yet determined to work harder hoping that I would get paid a lot more, at least what it would be to earn minimum wage after taxes. I noticed that as the other employees started working there many of them already had customers and I wondered when my boss would ever start letting me work on customers to build my skills up.

I worked consistently trying to build up my skills and to impress my boss, but it did not work out and after the holidays I cut back to part time work with the same amount of pay that I was earning while working overtime prior to Christmas 2002. The fear of being fired on any job for being socially unacceptable and not being mature enough worried me so much that I could not function on the job and medication did little to alleviate those worries. Mom and Dad always taught me that you have to be able to control your emotions on the job and you have to be socially acceptable. I learned the same thing in counseling when I was younger and at PVC.

I started going back to Dr Stanley as a patient. While I was at PVC, I saw the psychiatrist that came there about every two months just like I did with Dr. Stanley. I was turned over to Dad's insurance when I turned 21 years old and my checkups with Dr. Stanley were not covered under his insurance plan. Therefore, Mom and Dad had to pay completely out of pocket for me to be seen by him. That was very expensive. Prior to that I was on mom's insurance plan. Mom's insurance plan at the time covered for dependent children up until the age of 21 years old whereas Dad's insurance plan covered dependent children up until the age of 24 years old. As Mom and I walked up to the receptionist desk to schedule my next appointment on my first trip back to Dr. Stanley in a year and a half and to pay for my appointment we were told that the insurance would not cover it. The receptionist told us that it would cost $125. Mom wrote her a check.

I had to go back to Dr. Stanley a month later because he prescribed me two new medications. Dr. Stanley switched my medications constantly during that time period and one night during February of 2003 something very scary happened to me. On the night before my appointment, I wanted Mom to sleep with me to help me to fall asleep and she did. I fell asleep that night and as I fell asleep, I fell into a deep sleep that scared Mom really bad. Mom had trouble sleeping that night and it was hard for her not to notice any abnormalities about me that night.

All of a sudden Mom noticed that the bed was soaking wet as if I had urinated in the bed, but it was from sweat. I was very pale, cold to touch, and my breathing was extremely shallow. Mom checked my heart rate, and it was so faint that she could barely find it. Her nursing instincts told her that this was a concerning effect. That incident with me scared Mom out of her mind and she mentioned what happened to me the next morning before we left for my doctor appointment. It was clearly visible to her that one of my new medications was causing me some dangerous side effects.

When we got to my appointment with Dr. Stanley the next morning Mom mentioned to him about the concerning incident the previous night where I sweated an abnormal amount and had a faint heartbeat and very low blood pressure. Dr. Stanley thought I had a virus but none of my family was sick.

My boss felt like I needed to go back to more counseling, and it was at that time that Mom made an appointment for me to start going back to the same mental health clinic that I went to when I was younger to see one of their counselors and Psychiatrist. Dr. Singh at the time gave me Zoloft to take and I felt a lot better after taking just Zoloft than what I did taking a bunch of other medications but the only thing that happened was the stemming behaviors worsened after I dropped down to one medication only. Mom and I went to my appointment and at that time I started back seeing their psychiatrist and counselors. On the day that I went to see their psychiatrist she reconfirmed that I had two different problems, Pervasive Developmental Disorder/Asperger Syndrome and Obsessive-Compulsive Disorder (OCD) and told me what she felt like I should do about it. It was still very expensive for me to be seen once again as a patient at this place and insurance only covered a minimal amount.

In Spring of 2003, I was continuing to look for work and find ways to earn a living for myself. I thought I had gotten fired from my job at the salon, but Mom told me that she took me out of working at that salon. I collected job applications from nearly every major business in the area and drove all over town asking for applications. I even purchased $300 of beauty supplies at a local beauty supply store to practice on and build my business. That was the first time that I made a huge purchase on a credit card and normally I would have never used credit cards at that time.

Easter of 2003 came and went, and my family came for a visit like they normally do. While they were here, I gave my aunt a haircut and I practiced putting artificial nails on her young granddaughter. I was thankful for that opportunity. After Easter was over with that year, I continued to gather up more applications and researched for more open interviews for area businesses with no luck. I made an appointment with the vocational rehabilitation counselor for our area to discuss more options. I opted for a program for people with disabilities called Preparing Adults for Competitive Employment (PACE).

PACE is a six-week program where people get paid to work in addition to what they are getting paid as a regular employee and you have to meet with your PACE advisor on a regular basis. I considered taking PACE at the salon that I worked at before Christmas of 2002, but I felt like it would be better if I took it with my mom's cousin who owned a much slower paced salon and in a kind and loving atmosphere. Our family went on a beach vacation in the middle of May of 2003 because that was when Lacey's college classes ended for the semester. After we got back from our beach vacation, I began my PACE program with my mom's cousin. I went to work three days per week at my PACE program worksite during the summer of 2003 and since it was close to where Nan lived, I went to her house for lunch during my lunch hour.

I really enjoyed taking PACE with my mom's cousin at her salon and wanted to continue working with her, but I had to quit near the end of July. The week before my PACE program ended Lacey went with me looking for job applications at all of the various salons in both of the shopping malls in our area. When I got home that evening someone called me from JC Penney to ask about an interview for a nail technician at their salon a week later. The week before that interview was my 22nd birthday and for my 22nd birthday present Mom and Dad took me back to the amusement park that we went to five years earlier and we visited with family too. I was nervous about my upcoming interview at JCPenney salon but excited to give it a try. When we got back home Lacey had not gone back to school yet and she went with me to my interview. I did not get the job and I was disappointed. Lacey felt very proud of me for stepping up and applying for a job.

As the month of August went on, I prepared for my second Cosmetology license exam. This time I only had to take the practical exam. Back in 2003 hairdressers had to take two exams after graduating from Cosmetology school. The first exam was taken one month after graduation from Cosmetology school and was an apprentice exam where you earned an apprentice License. The second exam was taken six months later and once you passed this exam you were considered a fully licensed Cosmetologist. I took my second Cosmetology license exam in September of 2003 and passed it.

Whenever I completed my full Cosmetology license, I got a job for a month as a nail technician at a small nail salon in my area. I liked my boss, but business was slow for both of us and there were times where I was lucky enough to earn $20 per week. A month later I started looking for jobs again and this time I interviewed for a job at a national chain business beauty salon in the area because I had seen an ad in the local newspaper that they were looking for a hairstylist.

A few weeks into the new year one day while Lacey was in the bathroom getting ready to leave to go back to school, I was peering through the advertisement section for jobs in our local newspaper. I happened to see the same advertisement for a hairdresser at the same salon. I had not heard back from them about my interview, so I decided to call them and see if I got the job or not. I still did not get a job there. They were still just running the ad.

Lacey was in the bathroom getting ready and at the time I made the phone call I didn't think she would be able to hear me. I try to make phone calls in private and in this case, Lacey overheard me when she was in the bathroom getting ready. When I hung up the phone Lacey came back in the room and asked who I was talking to and why. Lacey felt concerned about me getting upset if I did not get the job, and she communicated her feelings about the situation. I misunderstood her and that caused me to experience a meltdown and to stem.

By Spring of 2004 I considered going back to school to earn a degree that would enable me to work with people that have something similar to me or earning a career in a that was not nursing. I called the local adult education center and applied to start taking math courses to get me re enrolled in school at the Community College for the following year. I applied for two more Cosmetology jobs and got one that I applied for.

During April of 2004 I got a job at a Hair salon at one of the two malls in Ashland Kentucky as a part time employee. I worked one weekend there and because of my social misunderstandings related to having Asperger Syndrome I was terminated from that job. There was a man who came in and was teasing me about getting a burr haircut. I gave him one and he was only teasing me. Two days later the salon manager called me at home to discuss her concerns about me. She along with the other employees picked up on the fact that I was having difficulty interacting with clients and recommended I find a salon that was slower paced. I felt disappointed but determined to keep going.

A week later I interviewed for a job at a daycare center in the area because my dad felt that I would be good at that job because I liked young children. My Dad knew one of the people that worked at the daycare center, and he called them and set me up an appointment for an interview. I went to the interview at the daycare center and applied for the job. As part of the job interview process, I had to get tested for Tuberculosis via a skin prick in my arm at the local health department and wait for the results of the test to come back. It took about two days for the results of the test to come back, since it was negative, I was able to hang out with the kids at the daycare center for a day and learn the rules of working at that particular day care center. About two days later after spending a day with the children at the day care center the owner called me back to let me know whether I could get the job or not. I did not get the job at the daycare center either because the owner felt that I was too shy and timid.

I felt very depressed and felt worthless. I was fed up with trying to find jobs and felt really frustrated that people did not understand my disability. I cried uncontrollably the entire day as I do whenever something does not go right for me. When Dad came home from work that evening, he was shocked to hear that I did not get the job at the daycare center because he thought I was really good with kids. Mom and Lacey were very disappointed for me also.

I talked with the Vocational rehabilitation counselor for our area, and she suggested that I continue looking for jobs and to consider getting a job coach. Job coaching is also one of the services offered by vocational rehabilitation that provides persons with disabilities someone that will go out to the job site with the person and be there for emotional support when needed regardless of the type of job that the client works for. What I wanted more than anything at the time was a boss and fellow employee that were patient enough to understand my disability and to see that I wanted to work and achieve my goals. I had concerns about being judged if I got a coach, I wish that I would have searched for a job and gotten a job coach anyway. At the time I did not agree with the fact that vocational rehabilitation hired job coaches only for emotional support regardless of whether they were educated in the client's job field or not. If smartphones were available back, then I would have agreed to having a job coach because I could have just FaceTimed and texted them daily and did so in a private place whenever I experienced a meltdown.

Sometime in May of that year I was just randomly surfing the internet while checking my email and I researched what it would be like to sell Avon and Mary Kay. I loved makeup and skin care, and I knew that I would like to sell either one of them. I sent information to be mailed to me about selling Avon. About two weeks later I got a phone call from the local Avon district sales leader. During the first week of June of that year I signed up to become an Avon representative and I was excited to start selling Avon because I liked their stuff.

It was only $10 to sell Avon because the kit only contained a few catalogs to pass out to customers and your contract for Avon. Selling Avon helped me to improve on my math skills and allowed me to interact with other people while I delivered my orders to customers. I was able to get easy access to all of my own personal beauty products. Avon has a lot of lipsticks that are very bright, and I felt thankful to have access to bright lipstick and other amazing products.

Summer of 2004 went on and I had no job offers despite still looking. It was hard not to feel jealous of Lacey who had no trouble finding a summer job and she got admitted to a four-year nursing program. Chris still continued to call me on a regular basis even though we were never able to visit each other. I went swimming at the local public pool every time that it was hot outside.

We visited family near the end of July of that year and about three weeks after that on the week of August 14th, 2004, Dad drove me back to the area for an event at a small amusement park with a waterpark near my family. Dad had just recently retired from his job as a mine inspector, and he was able to travel with us easier. The place where my uncle and his family worked held their annual company picnic at that amusement park. My Aunt had already purchased my ticket and because of that I wanted to go. We stayed with them for about three days and on the day before the picnic at the park I had a meltdown. I tried my best to suppress it, but it did not work. I was feeling a bit bored and homesick, and it was different traveling without Mom and Lacey. I was full of excitement on the day that we went to the park. I was excited to add two new roller coasters to my list. While I was at the park, I did not have a meltdown, but I felt frustrated about other things such as my camera tearing up completely, me coming off of the waterslide at the waterpark the wrong way and causing my chronic hip pain to flare up bad and feeling emotionally insecure about myself.

When we got back from the park my family asked me how the day at the park was. I gave them the idea that I had a meltdown at the park when actually i had the meltdown the day before. I told them about the social stuff that I was worried about. They reassured me that everything was fine, which helped to relieve my worries somewhat. I was still jealous of one of my cousins that I perceived as smart because I got the idea that they were an honor student in school and that this person would likely go to college and earn a good paying job. There is a philosophy that people on the spectrum only understand something in a black and white thinking mindset. This means that they can understand what is going on but not understand the big picture of a person or a situation. I understood people that was I jealous of in a black and white thinking mindset whereas a normal person would have seen the person or situation in a colorful picture, meaning that things are not always what they seem, and they can see the real situation before it is widely known. I was out of high school for almost five years and still had the misconception that good grades equaled success and fewer regrets later in life.

The next day as Dad and I drove back home he gave me the idea that he thought I had an actual meltdown at the park, but I didn't. I did not tell Dad or anyone else this, but I was on my period that week and hormonal fluctuations in my menstrual cycle always worsened my symptoms of Asperger Syndrome. Most of the time when we traveled when I was younger it seemed as if I was always ready to start my period or on my period. Since high school my periods were often longer than normal and were unpredictable at times, which often made for constant mood swings, Anxiety, and worry all of which worsened stemming and meltdowns.

Dad asked me why I reacted the way that I did on this trip, and I told him the reason as best that I could explain.

"Lauren, you have no reason whatsoever to be unhappy with yourself," said Dad. You are way too smart and too pretty to react like that."

As the fall of 2004 rolled around, I continued to sell Avon and worked really hard at selling it and bought makeup and other products. In between times I earned money from selling aluminum pop cans at the local recycling center. With every bit of money that I earned from Avon and selling pop cans at the local recycling center, I would deposit half of it in my checking account and the other half in my savings account.

Five years of being out of High School, submitting applications for many businesses and hair salons around our area and six months of being an Avon representative I felt like I needed to go back to my original goal, which was to go back to college and obtain a degree working with young children who have something similar to me. I decided to reapply as a student at our local Community College. I felt determined to change the way that people with Autism are viewed by the general population.

Autism Speaks was formed in 2005, and I am very thankful that it was formed. Autism Speaks is one of the largest organizations that provides research and awareness about Autism worldwide. Bob and Suzanne Wright founded Autism Speaks. Their grandson was diagnosed with Autism in the early 2000's. One in one two hundred and fifty children were diagnosed with Autism according to Autism Speaks in 2005, and that number has grown significantly since then. The symbol for Autism awareness is a puzzle piece that often consists of other puzzle pieces on it. The primary colors of Autism awareness are Red, Blue, Light Blue, Yellow, and sometimes Purple but the main color of Autism awareness is blue because more boys are diagnosed with the condition than girls are. The puzzle piece and the varied colors represent the mystery and complexity of autism spectrum disorders. Maybe that's another reason why I like to wear bright red lipstick. During that year April was designated as national Autism awareness month and April 2nd was declared as global Autism awareness day.

I enrolled in college again in spring 2005 and I took my second English class, College English II. Our main assignment for the whole class was to write a ten-page research paper that was due at the end of the semester. I chose to write mine on Asperger Syndrome because at the time there was still not a lot of research about the condition as compared to other forms of autism spectrum disorders. One day in class I was struggling and felt stressed out. The professor of that class asked me if I thought about talking to someone in disability services at the college and I didn't know that disability services existed. I earned an A on the research project as well as a B average in the class.

During the summer of 2005 I continued to work hard at selling Avon to earn my personal beauty products and to pay for gas. I went to one amusement park that summer and I wanted to go to more parks, but it did not work out even though Dad had more freedom. Mamaw had to be placed in a nursing home at the end of May of 2005 because it took two people to get her out of bed and it was impossible to care for her. Mom and Dad bought a camper for the first time, and they went camping quite a bit that summer all in local places because Dad needed to be nearby for Mamaw. Because they went camping at our local campground, I would visit them but not stay with them. Whenever I went to see them, I would ride my bicycle around the campground selling Avon's bug repellant.

I brought some Avon catalogs to our family reunion in July that year and sold some Avon and enjoyed my family and good food. The end of the summer of that year Mom and Dad were thinking about health insurance options for me because I showed great difficulty in holding down jobs due to my emotional instability from High Functioning Autism/Asperger Syndrome. There were not a lot of job options available that would have been beneficial for me.

One day near the end of August of 2005 I had a really bad day. It was on a weekend which meant that Mom was off from work, and she wanted me to go with her to get out of the house. I went with her despite my bad mood. Mom had several errands to run, including getting her hair cut at a local salon. It did not take long for her to get her hair cut and I was feeling upset. The entire day I was frustrated because at that point I knew that I was never going to be able to hold down a good job with benefits because of my misunderstood disability. While Mom was finishing up getting her hair done, I felt very upset and frustrated to the point that I stemmed so severely that I accidentally kicked the windshield in the car and made a large crack in it.

Mom was shocked at the windshield; I know she was disturbed about it. I apologized, but continued to scream, cry and stem. Mom and I talked about the situation and how I felt that day. She tried to reason with me and reassure me. She explained to me about how she felt like I needed to deal with my emotions.

I continued to feel misunderstood because of my Asperger Syndrome and this has caused me to experience social miscommunication and hurt feelings. With the help of my parents, I applied for disability in September of 2005 at the age of 24 years old for my diagnosis of Asperger Syndrome and I had no plans of staying on disability because I was determined to achieve my goals. I took an off-campus psychology class in the fall semester from the local community college.

During the fall of that year, I decided to take a one-year break from my antidepressant and just take medications when needed. I learned that medication made little difference in my symptoms of Autism and that taking one 100mg antidepressant daily and or as needed and another one for insomnia or chronic pain as needed worked well for me.

For the Christmas season of 2005 I purchased gifts for everyone in my family from Avon. Christmas of that year was spent at Aunt Sylvia's house and Dad brought Mamaw there to eat dinner with us and took her back to the nursing home after our Christmas dinner. Mamaw seemed to enjoy herself, and all our family were happy to have her. It was Mamaw's last Christmas with us.

In the Spring of 2006, I returned back to college as a full-time student at Ashland Community College. My career plans were the same as they were six years earlier. I worked hard and continued to sell Avon to try to make enough money to buy my personal stuff with it and gasoline to go to class every week. I continued to struggle very hard to get through school and worked really hard to control meltdowns at school. In the Spring Semester I took a repeat of the first level of developmental Math class that I failed six years earlier, Biology class with a lab, and a Nutrition class. I signed up to take all of my history classes that summer and for the fall term I signed up for a repeat Speech class, Anatomy and Physiology, and a second level developmental Math course.

I sold enough Avon in April of 2006 to earn the president's club sales level. I was excited to find out that I earned president's club sales level. That was a great achievement to me.

Mamaw's health continued to decline, and we were unable to bring her home from the nursing home to celebrate Easter with us. Mamaw passed away at age 88 near Mother's Day of 2006, actually her funeral was held on Mother's Day.

A week or so after that it was time to start the first History class of the summer session. I was busy with my Summer History classes during the summer of 2006, both of which were hard and for the first class I earned a C despite working hard and completing all of the extra credit work possible in the class. I received a B average in my second history class. Dad wanted us to take a family vacation that year, but we were not able to do much because I was in school all summer, but I was able to go to two amusement parks and got four new coasters added to my list.

I finally decided to apply for financial aid in that summer, and I got it. Speech class was much better than how it was six years earlier, all due to the difference in the instructor, in my opinion. Despite working hard in Anatomy/Physiology and Math I ended up failing both classes and had to drop them.

I had my first bad day of school ever where I got desperately upset about my classes about a month into the semester. It was close to midterm week. We had an assignment in Anatomy and Physiology lab class that I found incredibly hard and ended up failing despite the professor trying to help me. I picked the most difficult class at the college for Anatomy and Physiology because of scheduling (and trying to avoid night driving and driving in bad weather). The better options for Anatomy and Physiology for me would have been night classes and none of those felt convenient for me. The day that I had my first bad day I held it together until class was over with and went in the bathroom and locked myself in the stall and started crying and stemming with my hands uncontrollably. My math class started immediately after Anatomy and Physiology, and I was late for my math class that day because I was crying uncontrollably about failing Anatomy and Physiology.

When class was over, I asked my math professor if she knew how I could get tutoring and if she would be willing to help me with my math homework and at least bring my grades up in Math class. She advised me to go to the tutoring center. Immediately afterward I went to the tutoring center and applied to tutoring and student disability services. Two days later I met with the director of tutoring services and student disability services. When I met with the director of the program, I handed her my medical records that included my diagnosis of Asperger Syndrome and immediately applied for the program. When I applied, I got accepted into the program. A week later I started tutoring services for my Math class and Anatomy and Physiology class. I should have never taken two such challenging courses together, but I wanted to show Mom and Dad that I could get tutoring and earn a college degree despite a learning disorder and Asperger Syndrome.

One day I was studying for another test in Anatomy and Physiology while I was at home, and I was very stressed out about it. I had a meltdown that involved stemming by twisting my hands and screaming and crying. Mom heard me walk into the living room venting how frustrated I was about passing my class and complaining about having Asperger Syndrome. She followed me into the living room and tried to reason with me about dealing with the stress of school.

In the 80s and 90s a college education was highly encouraged despite the lack of resources that were available back in those days. I had been out of high school for seven years and had still not gotten over the idea that success equaled good grades in high school and a college degree. I also believed the idea that good grades and a college degree meant less marital issues if I were to get married, less likely to make poor choices, better financial stability, and better health habits. These ideas that I had grown up with worsened my anxiety over failure. All of this worry affected my ability to live a normal life and to hold down any job. This was one of my major symptoms of both obsessive-compulsive disorder and Autism and of course this always worsened meltdown and stemming behaviors. I learned over the years based on my own research that knowledge is powerful and if you have the knowledge, you should use it. I always had the idea that I would regret all of my social issues and meltdowns. As I have gotten older, I still regret some of the choices that I have made as a result of my fixations about my Autism. I have learned that I need to always do what is best for me and if anyone feels insecure about dealing with a person on the Autism spectrum that we need to speak up by educating about Autism and how to help those on the Autism spectrum in ways that works best for them.

I signed up for all off-campus classes and my first ever online class in the spring of 2007. I took a repeat of the second level of developmental Math course, Developmental Psychology, Sociology, and World Religions. My math professor understood my disability and was willing to help me because her son also had Asperger Syndrome. She helped me before and after class as needed to help me pass the class so,

I did not use the tutoring services that semester. I earned good grades in my other classes and that helped me a lot. I started back on taking my antidepressant daily and Atarax as needed to help me sleep at night.

I signed up for the last level of developmental Math classes for June 2007 and college Algebra for July of 2007 but had to drop my College Algebra class and switch to a non-Math class because the dean of student disability services and tutoring advised me to do that. The second half of May and most of the month of June I took the last level of developmental Math courses. The class was offered every day in the mornings for about two hours. When class ended for the day, I went to lunch and came back to tutoring for my math class at the tutoring center from around 1-3pm every afternoon.

Near the end of May 2007 Lacey graduated from nursing school with her bachelor's degree. Mom, Dad Lacey's boyfriend Dustin, and her best friend Amy went to both the nursing pinning ceremony and the graduation ceremony. I later went to her nursing pinning ceremony with Uncle Melvin and his family and Nan Nan because I wanted to study more for my math class. Amy and her family threw Lacey a surprise graduation party after the nursing pinning ceremony. After that Lacey moved back home and she continued to work full time as a certified nursing assistant (CNA) until she could get her nursing license. While she was in nursing school, she worked part time as a CNA to pay for her extracurricular activities in college.

One day while I was taking one of our three major tests for my math class at the tutoring center I got frustrated and had a meltdown. I got up to take a break from the test and as I walked outside Megan, the dean of tutoring and disability services handed me something.

"Hold on a minute, said Megan as I got up to walk outside for a break. I have something for you I have been meaning to give this to you and did not know when I would be able to give it to you."

"Cool, I said, as she handed me a certificate of sorts. What is this?"

"It's the student perseverance award for student disability services, " said Megan. You earned it this year at the awards banquet for students who receive disability services. Since you did not come to the banquet, I decided to hold onto it until I was able to meet with you again."

I was excited to show Mom and Dad that I earned a perseverance award from the college disability services and told them about it and showed it to them as soon as I got home. They were both excited for me and told me so when I came home from class that evening.

Since I had paid for my College Algebra class during the second summer session and was not able to take it, I signed up for an online Human Biology class and earned a high B in the class. Until I was able to get financial aid at school, I paid for all of my tuition with my disability money and money that I earned while selling Avon. The worst thing about me having to drop my College Algebra course that was offered in July was that I was not able to get any refunds for dropping the class and financial aid did not cover for off season classes at the community college. The June Math class ended near the end of June, and I passed the class with a C average. I was relieved to have passed the class and took a break for a week. During the break that I had I went swimming at my Uncle Melvin's pool.

Sometime near the first week of July my online Human Biology class started. We still had our annual family reunion near July 4th, and my out-of-town family came home. Even though I was taking an online class I still had enough time to swim in the summertime. I studied for my tests in Human Biology while lounging at the pool. I was able to go to the closest major amusement park, about two and a half hours away from us. The park got a new roller coaster for the 2007 season, and I added it to my list of roller coasters. We spent the night at a nearby hotel the night before going to the park. On the way to the hotel the night before and on the way home the next day I studied for my online Human Biology class. Lacey drove me there. Our midterm and final exams had to be taken in person at the main college campus. I took my midterm exam sometime near the middle of July and my final exam for the class around the end of July. I took my exams privately with one of the other people that worked in disability services at the college. A week after the summer season classes ended it was time for the fall term semester to begin.

For the fall semester of 2007 I enrolled as a full-time student taking College Algebra, Ecology, and Philosophy. I failed both College Algebra and Philosophy and ended up having to drop them despite taking tutoring for College Algebra. All three courses were online only courses but for College Algebra I had to take an in-person midterm exam and final exam at the college. I did not need Philosophy, so I just dropped that class, but I had to repeat College Algebra during the Spring of 2008 term.

Along with repeating College Algebra as an in person regular class I took an online Kentucky History course in the Spring of 2008 term. Just as I did when taking the last level of the developmental Math courses the previous year, I took tutoring for half of the day and for the other half of the day I took the actual Math class. I worked constantly on my College Algebra class so much that I barely had time for anything else even my history class. Having Autism/Asperger Syndrome makes it difficult to focus on more than one thing at a time; for that reason, I was not able to work and go to school at the same time unlike so many other college students. I am very grateful that Mom and Dad were able to help me with school during the times that I was not eligible for financial aid and to help with stuff that was not covered by financial aid. My sales with Avon slacked and I got behind schedule at times in my history class due to spending so much time on College Algebra homework and studying hard to pass the class.

Nan turned ninety years old on January 26th, 2008, and I nearly missed her birthday party completely due to having so much homework from my history class that I was unable to complete earlier in the week due to having to study so much for college Algebra and go to tutoring for it. I disliked that I nearly missed her party completely because of having to turn in an assignment for my history class that was due that evening to be turned in via email. I was lucky enough to be at her party about half an hour before it was time for the party to be over. When I got there it was time for everyone to take pictures with Nan and all of the grandchildren were able to take pictures with her just as they had ten years earlier at her 80th birthday party.

A week before midterm week I decided to take a break from studying really hard to pass College Algebra and made reservations for an indoor waterpark resort. The indoor waterpark resort opened about a year or so prior and is about three hours away from us. I paid for two nights to stay at the indoor waterpark resort. Lacey went with me and while we were there, we were only able to stay one night there and had to leave the very next day because the weather service issued a major snowstorm warning for the area. We only spent one hour or less in the water park and I felt very disappointed about that. We left just in time before the worst of the snowstorm hit the area. It took everything in me not to have a meltdown. Whenever we got back home, I worked on studying for my College Algebra midterm exam.

At the end of February, it was time for midterm week, and I had to take my College Algebra midterm exam. I took the midterm exam with one of the people from the disabilities department alone in a private room just like I did with all of my other in person exams. I got frustrated and had a meltdown because I did not know much of the material on the test. Much of the information that we had covered in class was not listed on the exam. I was slow getting the test completed and despite studying really hard for the test I failed it. I was devastated because I knew that there was a possibility that I would fail College Algebra again.

When Easter of that year came, I was so busy with working hard on my College Algebra class that I felt lucky enough to be able to even spend time with my family and celebrate Easter. Soon it was time to start studying for the College Algebra final which really stressed me out.

As the first week of May came it was time for finals week. I was very worried about failing the College Algebra final. Failing any Math final in any Math course at our local community college meant having to repeat the entire course. On the day of our final I walked in the disabilities office ready to take my exam. I started having the same feeling as I did while taking the midterm exam. I failed the final exam too. If you fail the final exam in their math courses, you can repeat the exam a second time the same week which I did. I failed the test the second time. I ended up failing College Algebra the second time too and I was devastated about that. I had to graduate with an associate degree with a failing grade in College Algebra that would not transfer.

"No No No," I cried while stemming and crying uncontrollably when I found out that I failed College Algebra a second time.

"Honey, it's ok, '' said Megan as she tried to console me. You have worked very hard and have earned good grades in all of your other classes and you will be able to earn a write off since you were not able to pass College Algebra. You will still be able to graduate with your Associate of Arts degree and work on a bachelor's degree. You should be very proud of yourself."

A few days later it was time for the community college graduation ceremony. It was held at a nearby theater. Mom, Dad, Nan, and Lacey attended the ceremony. After the ceremony they took me out to eat at the Golden Corral buffet restaurant. Chris still called me on a regular basis, and he wanted so badly to come to my graduation but that did not happen. I got admitted to a local Christian college for the fall semester of 2008 and I was disappointed that my College Algebra would not transfer because I failed it, but I was thrilled to hear that my third level of developmental Math course counted as my math credit for my bachelor's degree.

A month after my graduation with my general associate degree Lacey and I went on a cousin's vacation with our cousins Amber and her daughter, and Aunt Sylvia's daughter Tara and her two children to the beach. I felt like it was well deserved after working hard to get that associate degree. Lacey completed her first full year as a registered nurse with her bachelor's degree. The weekend of my birthday there happened to be a concert that I wanted to attend, and Lacey went with me to that concert. The following day we went to a waterpark.

As the summer moved on it was time for me to start my next chapter of my educational journey. New student orientation for all incoming students was quickly approaching and I was nervous yet excited to begin my journey toward a bachelor's degree.

CHAPTER TWENTY

If you are afraid of people, it will trap you, but if you trust in the lord, he will keep you safe. (Proverbs 29:25 NIrV)

Orientation weekend for students at the college was near the end of August of 2008 and school started the following Monday. Most of the classes that I had taken at the community college for my associate degree transferred. I entered as a counseling psychology major and for that major we had to have a statistics class, a specific computer class, and a literature class. One of the rules that was laid out in the student handbook was being able to control emotions and I misinterpreted that. I thought that it meant that constant crying and meltdowns were not allowed. I did my best to control my emotions and consulted with all of my professors, the dean of counseling psychology, and the tutoring center about how to help me when it came to schoolwork and dealing best with my Asperger Syndrome. The statistics professor, Dr. Coates, helped me before every class period on the days that we had class and that boosted my grades in Statistics a lot. I took the statistics course, a one-credit Intro to College course, Old Testament Overview, Introduction to the Bible class, and Acts. Students also had to attend a chapel service twice a week in the school's chapel. I somehow managed to do ok in the chapel services. I have trouble sitting through a church service at our church and am constantly fidgeting or drawing in church. Sitting through a church service can be challenging for persons with any form of Autism.

My first major meltdown happened near midterm week whenever we had to take a test for Statistics. The test was an open book test, yet we were not allowed to have any help from the professor. *"If it is an open book test, I will be ok,"* I thought to myself as I began working on my test. An hour passed and I was only halfway done with the test, and I started to get frustrated and started crying. A few minutes later a staff came into the room and checked on me and tried to console me. One lady suggested I go downstairs and speak with Dr. Coates about the issue. She even offered to go with me.

I went downstairs and talked to Dr. Coates about what to do since I was having a problem with getting the test completed. I happened to run across the president of the college, Out of genuine concern he asked me what was wrong. I told him I was failing this test and I just knew I was going to get kicked out for getting so upset. I told him that I had read in the student handbook that emotional control issues can get students kicked out of school. He assured me that was not what that meant. I went home later that day feeling rough after a meltdown and stemming over my statistics test that I thought would take all day for me to complete.

My grade report came in the mail in December of 2008 for the fall 2008 term. My grades for the semester were good!

During Christmas of 2008 Lacey started planning her wedding and everyone was excited and participating. I felt jealous and left out because I felt like this was something I couldn't share with her. I had never really dated anyone even though Chris still called me on a regular basis and wanted to be with me more.

After the holidays I took an off-season literature class that was a week long, The assignments and had to be turned in a week later when the regular school season started back for the Spring semester. The Spring 2009 semester was very hard for me. I nearly failed two classes and failed one class. I enrolled in a one credit Microsoft Excel Computer class, a one credit Microsoft powerpoint computer class, two counseling psychology classes, and one Bible class for the semester and the entire semester was tough. The Microsoft Excel class lasted the entire month of January, and the PowerPoint class lasted the entire month of February. I literally could not take a break from school. I spent so much time working on my classes that even going out to eat by myself felt like a treat.

I continued to work with student disability and tutoring services. It was much easier for me to work with the professors than it was to work with disability services and tutoring services. I continued to talk with my professors and the dean of the Counseling Psychology program about my diagnosis of Asperger Syndrome and what would be the best way for me to succeed in the program.

Ever since I was old enough to understand my disability and researched Autism Spectrum Disorders, I did not agree with how people on the Autism Spectrum were viewed by society. I wanted to learn how to make changes in the way that the world sees people on the Autism Spectrum regardless of which major that I chose while as an undergraduate college student. As Christians the Bible teaches us that we need to be patient with others and nonjudgmental. If you know or work with someone with an autism spectrum disorder, take time out of your stressful day to seek solitude and practice some form of mindfulness or do something that is healthy such as exercise. If you are able to do that it helps you to feel better and when you feel better, it's much easier to appreciate all of the small blessings about yourself or your loved ones with autism spectrum disorders.

A good lesson that I learned that fall is how to tame a stray cat and how this can apply to dealing with individuals with Autism. A little black kitten with white feet came to our house that fall, and it was very wild. I wanted to tame it and tried very hard to catch it. One day Nan was with me at the house, and I told her that I was frustrated that I could not catch the kitten to get it tamed. She suggested offering the kitten some toys, treats, and food and just sitting near it without trying to catch it. I tried that technique for the next month, and it worked. I was able to get the kitten tamed and I named him Tommy. Whenever something was pushed on me, I would push back if I felt uncomfortable just like Tommy did. Whenever people were patient with me and did not push me to do something when I was not ready or just encouraged me in any way, I was more likely to comply.

The dean of counseling psychology taught most of the courses for the Counseling Psychology program and I had him for two of my classes during the Spring 2009 semester. One day in particular during one of those classes I had a meltdown. I had a stressful week and had little sleep that week due to having so many homework assignments due that week and a test to study for. It finally caught up with me during that particular class period. That class was offered in the evenings. When I got to class that evening, I turned in my weekly assignment along with everyone else in the class and after we turned in our assignments, we took a quiz.

I had issues with taking a quiz and did not receive a good grade on the quiz. When everyone finished taking the quiz and reviewed the answers it was time for the lecture portion of the class. I was struggling to keep from crying, I ended up crying anyway. I just sat there and did my best to hide the fact that I was crying but it did not work.

"Lauren, are you going to be, ok? '' asked the professor. You have cried this whole class period."

I did not answer him until after the class period ended.

"Lauren, can I please talk to you after class," asked the professor.

I stayed for a few minutes after class to talk to the professor and he expressed his concerns for me if he admitted me into the counseling psychology program, but he stated that students were allowed to take all of the counseling psychology classes that they wanted if they were a University Studies major or a bible major. Some counseling psychology classes were required for some of the Bible majors at the college. I was disappointed; however, this later turned into a blessing.

I had to drop the other psychology class that I was enrolled in, because I had a D average in the class despite working hard in the class. I failed my Microsoft powerpoint computer class that I took that semester and had to wait to take it a full year later. My Bible professor that I had that semester was very lenient with me and understood my Asperger Syndrome because he said that he had family members with the condition. During the Easter season that year my Bible professor for that semester offered us an extra credit assignment for attending a Passover meal offered in the school's community center, which I thought was a really neat thing to attend.

Soon it was time to pre-register for fall classes and I registered for Bible classes and counseling psychology courses since I was told that I could take as many of the counseling psychology classes that I wanted to take based on my major. I felt determined to prove to all of my professors that I felt capable of succeeding in whatever program that I chose. As the semester continued, I was able to pull up my grade in the two remaining psychology courses that I took and when the semester ended, I took a two-week-Old Testament class in May which was very interesting.

Soon it was time for summer to begin. Lacey and I went to the beach with our cousins, Amber and Tara and their families and that was a lot of fun even though I had a meltdown one day. When we returned from our cousin's beach vacation, I went to my first ever New Kids on The Block concert in Ohio. New Kids on The Block were split as a group for about fifteen years prior to getting back together as a group the previous year. Since I was a huge New Kids on The Block fan, I was beyond excited to be going to my first concert. Lacey went with me to the concert and the following day we went to the Amusement Park that was near the concert venue to ride their newest roller coaster. A few days after the concert and amusement park trip I had a laparoscopic surgical procedure done to check my female parts for any abnormalities. That surgery confirmed the reason why I had menstrual problems and mood swings that worsened my Autism/Asperger Syndrome during certain points in my menstrual cycle. During my laparoscopy the surgeon confirmed that I did indeed have Stage IV Endometriosis, which was treated by burning it off and clearing it with a laser in addition to finding a slightly abnormal shaped uterus. Endometriosis is a disorder of the female reproductive tract where tissue from the lining of the uterus grows in other parts of the abdomen and causes painful periods, heavy bleeding, infertility, and in some cases severe hormonal mood swings.

The doctor told my mom that I had stage four endometriosis, and that they wanted to start me on Lupron shots after my followup appointment. She recommended that I take Lupron. Lupron is a series of shots that contain hormones that stop women from menstruating, which slows the growth of Endometriosis and treats the disorder.

I was not able to go swimming until I went back to my doctor for my surgery follow up appointment. I dealt fine with that, and I just focused on visiting with my family that came home for the Fourth of July holiday and Uncle Milt and Aunt Joyce's daughter Kristy came home with her new baby.

A month later I went back to my final checkup with my surgeon that did my laparoscopy. I chose not to take Lupron until I was finished with school. My 10th year high school reunion was approaching, which was near the end of July of 2009, about a week before my 28th birthday. I enjoyed my visit with students that graduated with me, and most of the people that attended that high school reunion was married and had children. The rest of the summer my mom and Dad continued to prepare and help with Lacey's upcoming wedding in October.

The month of August passed, and it was time to get ready to go back to school for the 2009-10 school year. I took two counseling psychology classes and one Bible class. One day after class I had a disagreement with one of my professors because I was concerned about some stuff. Try as I might I struggled not to have a meltdown which did not work. When I got home that night Mom tried to reason with me about the incident like she always does.

Lacey got married to her husband, Dustin on October 10, 2009, at a larger church in town and the pastor of our church married them. I was maid of honor in the wedding and three of Lacey's friends from college were bridesmaids in the wedding. Dustin's niece was the flower girl. It was a nice wedding, and I took lots of pictures at the reception. Most of my family from out of town came to the wedding as well as all of our local friends and family. Most of Dustin's family and friends came to the wedding too.

The day following their wedding Lacey and Dustin left on their honeymoon for a week. While they were gone on their honeymoon school stress, emotional stress from Autism/Asperger Syndrome and the pain from Endometriosis wreaked havoc on my immune system. I came down with a moderately intense respiratory tract virus that made me feel sick for about a week and left me with coughing and wheezing that lasted for about six weeks. Mom was sick with a similar respiratory virus. I thought it was the Swine Flu at first because it was going around at the time. A girl in one of my classes that sat next to me had the Swine Flu. After about six weeks Mom felt like I should get checked out. I went with Nan to one of her appointments with Dr. Singh and he ordered me a chest X-ray and some basic lab work but no specific tests for any particular microbe. I just had a slightly elevated white blood cell count meaning that I did have some type of viral infection going on even though I was starting to recover.

Soon it was time to register for Spring classes and I needed to figure out which classes that I needed to take for the Spring semester if I were to switch to a bible major because I considered one of the bible majors at the college. I met with the dean of Bible and Ministry, and we went over what classes from earning my associate degree would transfer and when I would be able to graduate. I figured out that only thirty of my credits would transfer for a bible major and that it would take me another five years to graduate. I told the dean of Bible and ministry that I wanted to switch immediately to a University Studies major. I went ahead and signed up for Spring courses at the same time, an online Bible class that was only offered in December, and an online summer literature class.

I walked over to the registrar's office immediately and told them that I wanted to switch to a University Studies major. The secretary at the registrar's office told me that if I switched to a University Studies major that all of my credits would transfer, and I would be able to graduate in the Spring of 2011. I was excited to switch to a University Studies major and realized that a prayer was answered.

When I got home after class that evening, I could not wait to tell my family that I would be able to graduate in the Spring of 2011. My family was as happy as I was that I was going to graduate.

"Lauren I am so proud of you," said Lacey as she got ready for her night shift at the hospital that she worked at as a nurse. Lacey lived with us for about six months after they got married because Dustin was still working out of state (Florida).

I finished out the fall semester and prepared for the 2009 holiday season. Mom and Dad bought Lacey stuff for a potential new house since she and Dustin were planning on buying a house at the time.

Lacey bought me a 16G iPhone 3GS as her Christmas present for me and I loved it. I had two outpatient surgical procedures done, including one on my left hand to remove a ganglion cyst. That affected my ability to get some assignments for my online class turned in timely.

The 2010 spring season began, and I continued to take psychology classes. For that semester I took two psychology classes, the one credit powerpoint computer class that I failed the previous year, and an Ethics class. Ethics was a very hard class, I got a C in the class. The professor of the class helped me with the assignments and coached me on how to study for the tests in the class which later boosted my grade average. Everyone that graduated from the college at that time had to take Ethics. I took social psychology and adolescent psychology class as my two psychology classes for the semester.

The Spring 2010 semester moved on and soon it was time for Easter. Easter season of that year arrived and students were encouraged to bring 30 coins of any denomination in a money bag for the chapel service on Holy Week as a representation of what Judas was paid to participate in the crucifixion of Jesus as described in Luke 22. I thought that was a great idea.

The remainder of April passed quickly and soon it was time to end the semester and register for the fall semester. I was preparing for my upcoming finals and every college student knows that finals week can be very stressful. I studied really hard for my Ethics final because I was struggling to maintain a C average in that class. The very same week that finals were held my gynecologist placed me on Lupron to control my Endometriosis and considered another surgery to treat it. The day before I took my Ethics final, I started getting some abdominal symptoms. I didn't think anything of it because I had those types of symptoms in the past with my female issues, emotional stress from school and dealing with Asperger Syndrome. I signed up for an online literature class and about a day or so after finals week the professor of my online summer literature class wanted to meet with students that signed up for that class in her office to go over our class syllabus and what we would need for the class.

When finals week ended, I truly did not feel good at all. I felt fatigued and slightly nauseous. I went home, rested and tried not to focus so much on my symptoms. Lacey wanted me to go to Florida with her to visit with Dustin because he was working there at the time, but I was debating on whether that would be a good idea or not. I had paid for a trip to an amusement park later that week. When the pain first hit me on the Friday after finals ended, I had no intentions of going to the Emergency room and had plans on visiting my gynecologist on Monday if the pain did not subside.

When Mom got home from work on Friday evening, she was concerned about me. I told her that I was in pain but that I thought that it was not anything serious. Mom asked me to describe my pain. I told her it was around my belly button, and it moves around to my lower right groin area. I told her that I thought that medicine I was on for my endometriosis was causing it, because I had had this type of pain before.

I stayed in my room most of the weekend and tried to work on my assignments for my online literature class. Lacey and Mom were both concerned about me. Lacey asked me how I felt about going with her to visit Dustin. Just to be on the safe side I told her that I decided to stay home and planned on making an appointment with my gynecologist for Monday morning and that I was going to try to make it to the event that I paid for.

The rest of the evening wore on and it was still an around the clock pain medication routine for me and every time that I would get up to go get something I would be walking hunched over.

"Lauren, you are walking like someone with appendicitis," said Mom. She checked my abdomen and said I was tender exactly where the appendix is also. She told me I needed to go to the ER.

Monday morning, I got up after a night of no sleep and decided I should ride to work with Mom and get checked out at the Emergency room just in case I could not get in with my gynecologist. As I walked to the bathroom to take my shower, I noticed Dad in the hallway. Confused and concerned he asked me about my pain. I told him that I felt like I needed to be checked out anyway. I walked into the kitchen to fix some breakfast and take my medication; Mom was sitting at the table having her morning coffee before she left for work.

"Mom, I said as I got out the Milk to pour on my cereal, I feel like I need to ride to work with you and get checked out. This pain is not getting any better and I feel worried that it could be something serious. Mom told me not to eat in case I did have appendicitis, and she thought it was a good idea. You need to finish getting ready so we can get on the road.

I finishing getting dressed, brushed and flossed my teeth. I packed a suitcase full of essentials with all of my electronics that I use, my stuff for my literature class, and stuff that I would take whenever I travel except for my medications. I felt a little nervous about what was wrong, but I needed to know what was wrong. Whenever I got to work with Mom, she checked me in and immediately the other nurses took my vitals, gave me a shot for nausea and pain, and drew my blood. My blood count was elevated, meaning that there was some type of infection going on somewhere in my body. Due to my history of endometriosis the ER doctor ordered an ultrasound of my female parts. The doctors changed shifts so I had a second doctor. When the ultrasound was completed that the first doctor had ordered it showed large ovarian cysts which I thought was my problem. The second doctor told my Mom that even though I was not reacting like the typical patient with appendicitis (not much pain) the doctor told mom that she was not comfortable discharging me without getting a CT scan of my abdomen because she could not visualize my appendix on the ultrasound.

I had the CT scan of my abdomen and the doctor told me it was fine if I wanted to wait for the results in my Mom's office where I could be more comfortable. Mom was the nurse manager of the Emergency Room and I sat with her while she did her work. Mom called Dad to tell him that the ultrasound revealed that I had big cysts on both of my ovaries. I gathered up my things thinking that we would be heading home soon. Just as Mom hung up the phone with Dad, the ER doctor came running back to Mom's office with the report of my CT scan and said, "Sorry, Lauren, you aren't going anywhere, you have appendicitis." She called the surgeon on-call and they started getting me ready for surgery. Mom immediately called Dad back and told me the changed diagnosis, and that I would be going to surgery.

Immediately Dad finished up what he needed to get done on the farm and got to the hospital as quickly as possible just to see me before I went into surgery. Dad just walked into the main entrance of the hospital as the operating room nurses wheeled me on the stretcher from the Emergency Room toward the surgery department.

I stayed in the hospital for three nights after my appendectomy until my white blood count back returned to normal. My appendix had abscessed, so I also had a drain. While I was in the hospital, I received intravenous antibiotics and antibiotics in pill form. My surgery was done laparoscopically, meaning it was completed with four poke hole incisions in my belly, one of them contained a drain attached to the site of the appendix, which I had to keep until I went back for my followup with my surgeon that performed my appendectomy. My surgeon said that since I didn't get checked out quick enough that my appendix had abscessed and that's why I had to wear the drain and stay longer in the hospital. The side effects of my Lupron that my gynecologist started me on kicked in immediately after I woke up from the appendicitis surgery and they were terrible.

The whole time that I was in the hospital recovering from appendicitis and after I came home from the hospital the side effects of Lupron caused me to feel nervous, hallucinate, gave me hot flashes, and mood swings that were worse than any of my previous meltdowns and even dangerous. I tried diligently to read the book for my literature class, but I was too mentally disturbed from the medication. The day that I came home from the hospital I wanted to jump out of the car while we were waiting in the drive through line at McDonalds and I would normally never have those feelings. When we got home from the hospital Mom immediately called my gynecologist and told her she was taking me off the Lupron because it was making me crazy and to consider some other treatment for my endometriosis.

I healed from my appendicitis surgery and was able to work on my online literature class. That was a very hard literature class and I worked very hard on it nonstop. This class kept me very busy from the remainder of May until July. For the third year in a row in June of that year Lacey and I went with our cousin Amber, her daughter, and one of her daughter's friends on our cousin's beach vacation. It was a nice break to get away from working on my literature class to go to the beach and have fun. These cousin vacations are still some of my favorite memories.

July ended my literature class and students had to take an in-person test on everything that was covered in the class. I experienced a rocky start to the beginning of the class with the appendicitis and lupron side effects but was able to succeed in the class and earned a B average.

A week before school started back for the fall 2010 season Lacey took me and one of our family friends to an amusement park. I was thrilled to be able to go there and felt really excited to be able to ride their tallest and fastest roller coaster. Upon returning home from the park, it was time to get ready for my final year as a college student. For the fall semester I signed up for a one credit Microsoft word computer class, a senior level bible class that was required for all students in order to graduate, a gospel history class, a Theology class, and a Physical Science course. I had already completed most of the credits required for the University Studies degree.

During the first chapel service of the school year all graduating students for the Spring semester walked through the chapel wearing a cap and gown to show that they would be graduating in the Spring. It felt good to know that I would be graduating in the Spring yet at the same time I felt a bit sad. The school semester went on and I continued with the usual struggles that I had every semester in school. I was also beginning to suffer from school burnout from going nearly four years of school all year long without taking breaks.

I continued to have meltdowns and struggled to retain my composure at all times while in class. I had a facebook account at the time and one day before I left for class, I logged onto my facebook account on Mom's computer and noticed that someone that bullied me when I was younger because they misunderstood me was going through treatments for infertility and that there were several posts saying that they were praying for this person. That made me feel jealous and frustrated about how that person was able to succeed in life as compared to me when I felt like I done my best at all times while feeling tempted to give up on my goals. I expressed my feelings about the situation unkindly. Through the times that I have experienced flares of my Autism where Mom and Dad nearly had to take me to the hospital I received no prayers, get well messages or cards from anyone. This is the real reason that I feel jealous of others like this person when they are experiencing physical health issues. There is so much stigma associated with autism spectrum disorders and mental illness. This is not anything that should be taken lightly, and we need to be there for those with Autism and mental illnesses just as we are for someone with a physiological illness such as a heart problem. Lacey saw the post on her phone and contacted Mom about it. Mom was very concerned about me and told Lacey to suspend my facebook account. Mom felt like I needed to stay away from social media and just focus on school and living my life.

The end of the fall 2010 semester, I was finally able to take a full month off from off-season classes that were offered at the college for the first time since I was a student there. This was because I had previously taken all of the off-season classes that were offered, and I had less than twelve credits to graduate. It was Lacey's first full year as a married woman and her third year as a full-time nurse. For Christmas of that year Mom bought her a computer because Lacey had verbalized her interest in working on her graduate studies.

Soon it was time for my final semester ever as an undergraduate student. When it was time to return to school for the Spring semester I had already pre-registered for all of my classes. I signed up for a one credit website design computer class, a science class, child psychology class, and a repeat of ethics class because I wanted to improve my grade and another Bible class. The associate dean of the Counseling Psychology program moved away, and the college had to get a fill in as an associate dean of the program until they could find a full-time associate dean of the program. The subtitle of the science class that I signed up for was called Cancer and Emerging Diseases. I thought that would mean Emerging Chronic Diseases and was hoping to learn something about Autism by taking that class. It was actually about emerging infectious diseases caused by viruses and autoimmune disorders such as lupus, but

I got a good grade in the class anyway. My child psychology professor was amazing, and I earned an A in that class. For our research project I chose a rare disorder that causes OCD and Tic symptoms in children which is called Pediatric Autoimmune Neuropsychiatric Disorder Associated with Streptococcus (PANDAS) and earned an A on the project. The disorder is caused by the Streptococcus bacteria.

Near the end of February of the 2011 Spring season in addition to struggling with my classes I received some of the worst news of my life at that point. I was sitting in the student lounge in the Bible department waiting for my 11am ethics repeat class. I was scrolling through facebook on my phone out of boredom instead of studying for ethics class. I received a message from Chris' older sister saying that he passed away unexpectedly at midnight the previous night. I immediately called Mom at work and told her what happened.

"Mom, I said as I called her in a near panic trying not to scare anyone else.

"What's wrong Lauren," said Mom as she answered my call.

"I just got a message on facebook from Chris' older sister saying that he passed away unexpectedly last night," I said trying to remain calm.

"Are you sure Lauren," said Mom.

"Yes, Mom I am sure," I said, pacing the floor.

"Lauren said Mom. Whatever you do please try to remain calm and make it through all of your classes and I will be home as soon as possible.

"Ok, Mom. I love you; I said ending the call and walking in late to my Ethics class.

Later that night and into the following day I vented on facebook about losing Chris and several people commented on my post saying that they were sorry that this happened and that they were praying for his family as well as me. The next few days, I felt angry and had meltdowns that caused me to break out one of my front teeth that had a crown placed on it. This cost me and my family a lot of money in dental visits as well as frequent visits to the dentist for the next two months.

Spring break of that year Mom, Dad, Lacey, and I went to Florida to visit with Dustin. It was the first time that I ever travelled on vacation for Spring break. While we were there, we went to a Theme Park and a fair in the area and I got some amazing roller coasters added to my goal list. Mom and I were unfortunate and caught really bad colds. I felt very frustrated about having a cold on vacation and it caused me to have a meltdown and stemming.

When we got home from Spring break, Lacey and Dustins' dog, Smokey, disappeared one day while he and Dad were together in the garage. Smokey was really a family dog. We all loved him and he loved us. Everyone looked for him, everywhere. I was determined to help them find their dog. This is where the talents of my Asperger Syndrome came into play, and I feel very thankful that I was able to use my talents for helping Lacey and Dustin find their dog. I created a flyer with a picture of the dog, describing everything about the dog in complete detail from the breed, height and weight, other physical characteristics, the dog's personality, medical history, where and when it was last seen and our phone numbers. Plus, I posted the flyer on facebook and set the post to public. The ad that I created I used an online system that works like an amber alert system for lost pets and posted the flyer in an ad on facebook that was set to public. It was very expensive, but it was well worth the effort. Two weeks later someone found the dog and called our house while I was in class; he was in the the next county over. Dad and Lacey went to the person's house and found that it was Lacey and Dustin's dog. If I had not posted that descriptive ad on Facebook and the online lost pets system Lacey and Dustin would have never gotten their dog back. Dad later learned that one of our neighbors had stolen the dog and taken him to her mother's house near where he was found.

The remainder of the semester moved quickly, and I had to order my cap and gown for the graduation ceremony and other stuff. During finals week everyone that was going to graduate from the college had to practice marching in and out of the chapel for the portion of the graduation ceremony that would be held in the chapel. Graduation is a two-day event there. The first day of the graduation is held in the chapel and family members are allowed to come to that event. The second day of graduation is held in the college gymnasium. On the first day of graduation events there was a meal for all graduating students in the cafeteria where all students got a gift bag with a T-shirt and other items. Mom took off from work to come to both of my graduation events with Dad, Lacey, and Dustin. I went home for a little while after the graduation practice that was held in the chapel that morning and had to return later that afternoon for the ceremony inside the chapel building. Mom, Dad, and Lacey both attended the graduation ceremony that was held in the chapel that afternoon. After the ceremony we happened to run into Dr. Metcalf.

"You must be Lauren's parents," said Dr. Metcalf.

"Mom and Dad, I said," This is the president of the school, Dr. Metcalf."

"Nice to meet you sir," said Mom and Dad as they both shook Dr. Metcalf's hand.

"I just want you to know that I am very proud of Lauren, " said Dr. Metcalf to Mom and Dad. She is a wonderful student that works really hard."

The next morning, I had to be at the college gymnasium early enough to get seated while Mom, Dad, Lacey and Dustin came later. The ceremony started and Dr. Metcalf along with some other faculty gave the graduation message and prayer. Soon it was time for students to march on stage to receive their diplomas. When it was time for me to march on stage and receive my diploma, I felt a surge of excitement run through my body.

"Go Lauren, Lacey's voice echoed from the audience as I walked on the stage to receive my diploma.

After everyone received their diplomas, the ceremony was over, and graduates took pictures with their friends and family. Mom, Dad, Dustin, and Lacey wanted to take pictures with me just as the other graduates took pictures with their families. Nan was unable to make it because Mom felt it would be too challenging for Nan to get around a large, crowded gymnasium.

That afternoon Mom and Dad held me a graduation dinner at home with all of the family, and it was a true blessing. After that I just wanted to relax around the house for the next few days. It was at that moment that I felt like a true adult for the first time and needed to let that reality sink in.

CHAPTER TWENTY-ONE

Favoring one person over another is not good. But a person will do wrong for a piece of bread. (Proverbs 28:21 NIrV)

At age 30 years old I still had trouble controlling my emotions and suffered from Anxiety related to Asperger Syndrome; I suffered from constant pain from female problems and other problems in my lower body that were very painful. Life after graduation from college continued and I did not apply for a job like I had planned to do. As the summer went on, I still went swimming at the pool at Uncle Melvin and Aunt Yevette's house.

I still lived with my parents because of the drug problem in our area and of the fact that I felt like I could not afford to live on my own without facing financial debt. Mom and Dad were not crazy about me living on my own. I still experienced hormonal fluctuations that caused me to experience severe stemming and uncontrollable meltdowns at certain times in my menstrual cycle. There was a restaurant that opened a few miles from my house in 2011 that was open on Thursdays through Saturdays that served Thanksgiving style meals and hot hotdogs and hamburger type meals with fries. I enjoyed eating at that restaurant because it allowed me to visit with others and meet other people. I considered helping out at that restaurant just to give me something to do. Nan needed people to stay with her at night and it was usually Mom and Dad that would stay with her. If I were going to go to the restaurant near our house, I would take Nan meals if Mom and Dad were busy.

I still had uncontrollable meltdowns despite all efforts to control myself should I feel upset about anything. October 10th of 2011 was our annual church homecoming and there was a dinner after the service. I cannot handle sitting still in a traditional church service. I was feeling excited to eat a delicious meal after the service, so I just ate a snack with some milk before leaving for church because I wanted to save some room in my tummy for the large meal after church. During the main part of the service, I got bored because the service lasted longer I and turned on my phone to play angry birds and didn't realize that the sound was on. Mom felt embarrassed about me turning on my phone and tried her best to control the situation. Before the meal started, I started feeling panicked and worried about other stuff in addition to Mom's reaction about the issue with my phone and tried to control my meltdown but could not do it and just went in the bathroom and cried hoping to stop in time for the meal with no luck. After spending a while in the bathroom trying to stop crying, I just went on home and Mom and Dad later brought me my meal. Mom continued to feel embarrassed about how I reacted that day and she later told me that there was a woman there that had a urinary tract infection and could not get to the bathroom because of me. The next time this happens I plan to just turn my phone on silent mode with apps and notifications and drink a protein shake and some water to hold me over, so I won't feel hunger related mood swings. That day I was experiencing mood swings related to low blood sugar from not eating fulfilling food to keep me satiable until the church dinner. I would advise people to stay hydrated by keeping a bottle of water nearby even though it may seem inappropriate and either drink a protein shake or eat something light with protein packed in it before an event such as this. When I was younger my mom always felt like regular and nutritious meals helped with my meltdowns.

My gynecologist wanted me to take something to help get my endometriosis in control, but I knew that there was nothing that I could take that would not give me serious side effects. At the end of November of 2011, I had my second surgery for my endometriosis, and they were able to destroy a lot of the Endometriosis growths and release the contents from a baseball sized cyst that was growing on my left ovary.

"Well Mom, what did they find in surgery this time," I asked Mom after waking up from my second surgery for Endometriosis as the nurse wheeled me back into the room where Mom and Dad were at.

"They said that your Endometriosis was severe and that the next time you come in for surgery that you would need to have a hysterectomy," said Mom.

I went back to my doctor about two weeks later for my first followup appointment and she gave me a prescription for a type of hormone that was a lower dose than what was in the Lupron shots. The low dose hormone that I was prescribed stopped my periods, but I still had the mood swings and chronic pain that was caused by endometriosis. One of the side effects of that hormone pill that I was taking caused me to get constant colds.

We continued to celebrate the holidays with the usual guests. Melvin and Yevette's youngest son Jonathan and his girlfriend had just had a new daughter and they brought her to celebrate Christmas with us. For Christmas of that year, I got my first iPad, and it took me a while to learn how to use it. Initially, I was frustrated but then I got addicted to it and now I use my iPad constantly. Mom also bought me a gift card from a new spa that Aunt Yevette opened up for a one-year membership.

Soon it was time for the New Year and the winter season. My gynecologist wanted me to try acupuncture for my mood swings, pain, and endometriosis in addition to the hormone medication that I was taking. I tried acupuncture for several months and it did not work as well as I would have liked for it to work. It was very expensive and was not covered by insurance. Dr. Singh retired (but my family still remains friends with him and his family). We have periodic lunch visits. As for 2012 I tried to stay busy despite being on disability. I didn't the idea of having to be on disability because I knew that I was gifted in ways that no one had seen yet. In February of 2012 it marked the one-year anniversary of the passing of Chris, and I still think about him every day.

The spa included a gym with exercise equipment, several rooms in the back for spa treatments, a room for exercise classes as well as a retail section in the front of the spa which consisted of nutritious snack foods, and personal care items. Yevette happened to meet one of the other customers that came to her spa on a daily basis. Like me, this girl was diagnosed with Asperger Syndrome. I met her in February 2012 and liked getting to know her. I exchanged phone numbers with her and told her to call or text me anytime. She was an only child who was raised by her father, and she did not drive. I usually stopped by the Spa to work out after my acupuncture appointments.

One day when this girl came to the spa, she had a serious meltdown and hit stuff, including me. I felt deep concern for her as I witnessed her meltdown. The girl's father helped her to calm down. Her asked me if I was ok, and I told him that I was.

She recovered from the meltdown, and we had a good conversation. I knew that she could not control that meltdown. I liked getting to meet other people with Asperger Syndrome.

A few weeks later during the early part of the Spring of that year a major tornado came into a county near our area and destroyed many homes and businesses and I felt so blessed that it did not cause any damage to our area. I was worried that we would be affected by the tornado, but we were not.

Uncle Melvin had a knee replacement surgery the week of Easter of 2012 and he stayed with us while he recovered from his surgery. Mom was still working as a nurse at the time, and she would help take care of him whenever she got home from work in the evenings. I helped him some with his physical therapy exercise which was not a big deal for me because I really liked exercise and fitness, and yoga type exercises.

I was out of college for exactly one year at that time. I still felt determined to make something out of myself even though I was technically disabled. I had considered going back to school to earn a master's degree and hopefully doing something to work with kids on the autism spectrum. I continued researching treatments and felt determined to take the healthiest approach to treating every condition that I was diagnosed with. I continued to sell enough Avon to buy my personal products, such as bright colored lipstick and to earn enough money to buy lunch and gas for when I went to my many medical appointments.

I started planning my amusement park trips for the year. Lacey volunteered to go with me to an Ohio park in the middle of May of that year and even though we had a great day at the park I had a meltdown on the way home. When we were almost home irrational and uncontrollable thoughts of jealousy toward Lacey as she called Dustin to discuss stuff on the way home ran though my head even though I have always loved her very much. I still did not find my match yet and it was hard for me not to feel jealous that Lacey had found her match.

"Lauren why are you crying," Lacey asked.

I did not respond to her because I felt worried that she would not understand the reason I felt upset. When I got home Dad was disappointed and concerned with me for getting upset. That only made things worse, and I cried and wrung my hands the entire evening without telling anyone why I was upset.

A month later I wanted to go to a roller coaster club convention about five hours south of us because we frequently vacation in that area. Mom and Dad went with me to that one instead of Lacey because she was attending a music festival in our area that she already paid for. The trip was nice, and I got to meet other coaster enthusiasts and add a new coaster to my growing bucket list. Whenever we went back home from that trip life continued as normal. Mom went back to work and continued to stay with Nan on a nightly basis. I went to the local public pool as well as Uncle Melvin and Aunt Yevette's pool. Their house that they lived in at the time had a pool and I went there every day to swim. I continued to eat at the restaurant near our house every day that it was open. By the time summer approached in 2012 I stopped attending my acupuncture sessions because I felt it was not helping me and all I was doing was wasting my money and time.

During the fall of that year, I was recommended Restoril by my gynecologist to help me sleep and I refused to take that stuff without consulting with a psychiatrist due to my history of side effects from medications. The Psychiatrist at the local mental health clinic knew about my health history of Autism/Asperger's Syndrome and felt that seeing a counselor if I wanted to would work just as well as seeing a psychiatrist and that I should just visit my Primary care provider. They felt that I would do ok on Restoril if I wanted to take it even though I decided against it and just wanted to take Atarax instead when needed because it has always helped me in the past. I told Mom and Dad what the doctor said, and they also agreed.

During the 2012 presidential election President Obama got reelected as the president of the United States and around that same time Adam Lanza broke into Sandy Hook Elementary School in Newtown, Connecticut and caused a massive school shooting and later shot and killed himself. Adam Lanza was supposedly diagnosed with Asperger Syndrome and at that time many people began to think that people with Asperger Syndrome were at a higher risk of murdering other people. That bothered me a lot and a few times I felt like I had to let people know that I would never murder anyone. I later learned that it was thought that Adam Lanza suffered from another psychiatric condition in addition to Asperger Syndrome.

The 2012 holiday season was uneventful for my family. We celebrated Christmas with the usual guests, but little did I know that it would be the last Christmas that we would spend with Aaron and Jonathan. Soon it was time to ring in 2013. Prior to 2013 Nan had to have someone check on her and give her medications and food daily but by that time she had several mini strokes and her memory and health declined.

I still continued to have meltdowns that were uncontrollable at times, and I was still taking hormone pills to control my endometriosis and Zoloft to control my anxiety. I still had pain and hormonal symptoms without bleeding. When Dr. Singh retired, I used my gynecologist as my primary care doctor until I could find a new family care provider.

In March of 2013 Mom, Lacey, and I went to a concert about three hours away from where we live. When we got to the concert venue we stopped by the bathroom before heading into the main concert venue. Lacey felt like we should use the family restroom instead of the women's restroom because the line for the women's restroom was too long.

I am very private when I have to use the bathroom and do not like for anyone to have to come in on me for any reason, even if it is my mom and my sister. I am very slow when I have to use the restroom and was also diagnosed with a a condition known as Pelvic Floor Dysfunction. PFD causes bowel and urinary symptoms that are very frustrating and embarrassing to deal with. Lacey and Mom went first to use the bathroom and I decided to wait until they were done. While I was in the bathroom a woman continued to knock on the door and it really annoyed me.

"I will be done in a few minutes" I said," rushing up trying to use the bathroom and washing my hands to the point where I walked out of the bathroom with wet hands from rushing up.

"I am so sorry," I said to the woman who knocked on the door while I was in the bathroom.

"Lauren don't worry about it," said Mom as she ushered me into the main concert venue.

"Mom, that woman was very rude," Lacey said to Mom as we headed to our seats in the main venue.

On the way home from the concert Lacey continued to tell Mom about how frustrated that she felt toward that woman's unkind reactions to me over taking too long in the bathroom.

"Mom, people like that woman that pounded on the door when Lauren was in the bathroom really frustrate me. I really try to look out for Lauren's well-being and safety. I just wish I would have been of better support to Lauren when we were younger, " said Lacey, still continuing to feel frustrated about how that woman reacted to having to wait on me to get done in the bathroom. I just did not know how to handle her or what to do for her."

"Lacey, " said Mom, "I understand how you feel. I feel as if I have made my fair share of mistakes in trying to help Lauren."

About a week or so later I found out that New Kids on the Block were going on tour again for the summer of 2013 and I wanted to see them in concert again because they are still my favorite group. I wanted Lacey to go with me to that concert. Because the concert was the day after my birthday, I thought that would be a great way to celebrate my birthday. Tickets for the concert went on sale the week after Easter and I asked Lacey to check her schedule and to see if she could get off from work on the date of the concert.

I had a meltdown with irrational thoughts about going to the concert and that I didn't deserve to go. Lacey tried to reason with me, and I was eventually able to calm down.

Whenever the tickets for that concert went on sale I immediately logged onto Ticketmaster and bought the tickets. This was another case where I got so fixated on something that I wanted to achieve and felt unrealistic worries about whether I would achieve it or not.

Something else that happened that Spring that I find interesting. The DSM V was released, and Asperger Syndrome was no longer considered as a diagnosis by itself. All of the autism spectrum disorders were lumped into one category of disorders called autism spectrum disorder and labeled based on severity with Level one being the least severe and Level three being the most severe. Many people that worked with people with autism spectrum disorders did not agree with this change of diagnosis codes as addressed in the DSM V but the way that I have always looked at diagnosing a medical condition is that getting effective treatment for symptoms is more important than labeling the disorder.

By the end of May of 2013 Mom cut down to part time work at her nursing job and in the first week of June of 2013 all of the staff in the emergency department threw her a surprise retirement party. The surprise party was held in the hospital cafeteria and Dad, Lacey, Nan, Aunt Sylvia and her family, Amber and her fiancé, and me met Mom in the hospital cafeteria.

A week later we received terrible news that Melvin and Yevette's youngest son Jonathan had passed away. Three weeks later my Nan's younger brother, my great Uncle passed away and later in the month of July my cousin, Aaron, Melvin and Yevette's other son passed away (40 days apart). Ever since we were little I always got along with Aaron, and he was always able to help me feel better if I was having a bad day no matter what happened. Aaron thought it was amazing that I was a roller coaster fanatic and he always liked asking me questions about roller coasters. Neither Aaron nor Jonathan cared that I had Asperger Syndrome and both of them loved me for who I was, and I loved them, they were great cousins, loving and supportive.

Two back-to-back funerals were very challenging for my family, especially Uncle Melvin and Aunt Yevette. This time when the family came for a visit it was not as calming even though I enjoyed their presence to keep me calm during the week of both funerals. I handled the grief of losing both Aaron and Jonathan well, but it did flare my anxiety, my mood swings, my pain from endometriosis and my joint pain. It was a terrible time for all of us.

Two weeks after the passing of Aaron it was time for the New Kids on the Block concert that I bought tickets for in April and my 32nd birthday. That concert was near where my dad's older brothers lived and Dad rode with us so he could visit with his older brothers while we were at the concert. We stayed with my aunt and uncle while we were there, and it was for sure a nice break from the two back-to-back losses that we had suffered from that summer. Lacey and I went to a zoo with a waterpark because there happened to be a small roller coaster there that I wanted to add to my list in addition to attending the concert while Dad visited with his brothers.

Exactly one week later I attended a Temple Grandin speaking event three hours away from where we lived with Mom and her best friend Melanie who was one of my home economics teachers in high school. It was a fun event to attend even though we only attended part of the event. Before the event started, I met Temple in a separate room, took a selfie with her, and she signed a copy of one of her books for me. Temple spoke for the first hour and ten minutes or so of the morning event and Eustasia, Temple's mother, spoke for the second half of the morning event. I really enjoyed listening to what both of them had to say about autism spectrum disorders. The second half of the event that was held that day was to help professionals in the social work and education fields to obtain continuing education credits required for their jobs. While at the convention Mom bought a package of really interesting books about Temple and Autism Spectrum Disorders that I could not wait to read when we got back home that evening. Whenever we got back home that evening, I started reading one of the books that came in the package that Mom purchased at the convention.

Nan's health continued to decline and by October of 2013 she needed someone to stay with her 24 hours a day. Mom stayed with Nan whenever she was not working. If Mom did not stay with her Aunt Sylvia stayed with her. Aunt Sylvia and Uncle Dewey moved back to Kentucky the year that I graduated from high school.

The holiday season of that year came, and we celebrated Christmas with Nan at her house because Nan no longer left home easily. All of our local family came to Nan's house for us to celebrate Christmas. It was her last Christmas with us. On January 26th of 2014 Nan turned 96 years old and she passed away a week after Easter 2014. I was sad whenever Nan died but at the same time, I knew that she had lived a very long life, her life had become so difficult for her, and she was in a much better place.

One day during the first part of June, I went to our local public pool by myself. It was a nice day, and everything was fine until I was on my way home. On my way home I noticed that a policeman pulled up behind me. With me being on the Autism Spectrum I was so scared that I was literally shaking when the policeman pulled me over that I reacted unkindly to him. I really thought that he was going to take me to jail for something that I did not do.

"What did I do," I asked as the policeman came up to my driver side window and asked for my license, my anxiety clearly visible with my shaking hands and feeling out of breath. My heart raced so fast that it felt uncomfortable against my chest.

"Someone called and reported you because you were driving on yellow line and driving slow and I just wanted to make sure that you were not drunk," said the policeman.

"I am not drunk, and I would never drink and drive. I have Asperger Syndrome. It's otherwise known as High Functioning Autism, and I have worked my butt off to be able to overcome a lot of obstacles. I graduated from a Christian college, and they do not allow students to do anything that is against Christian living," I said as I showed the policeman my license and my college transcript.

"I should have written you up because of the way you reacted but since you are driving with your seatbelt on and were not drinking, I will let you go this time and I am sorry that I upset you," said the policeman.

"Thank you, lord, I prayed as I drove home.

Most policemen do not understand how to approach anyone on the Autism Spectrum. Should this ever happen to me again I have purchased an autism awareness sticker and placed it on the lower left side of my driver's side window. The autism awareness sticker explains what Autism is and what can happen if someone in the car is approached suddenly by a policeman as in this case. It does not cause any visual distractions but it's noticeable enough to be seen by anyone who approaches my driver's side window.

About a week later in the second week of June 2014 Mom and I went to eastern Pennsylvania with Dad to a car show so I could go to a nearby amusement park. I was excited to ride all of their roller coasters. Dad went to the car show in the area that he wanted to go to and enjoyed it. While we were there, I kept Mom and Dad up at night going to the bathroom while we were in the hotel room at night and that woke them up. When Dad got annoyed with me for getting up and down all night to go to the bathroom and for complaining of constant pain in my lower body it caused me to have meltdowns and stemming. Dad was concerned about me getting upset and wringing my hands and not being quiet enough in the hotel room and he expressed concerns about going on further trips. For the remainder of the trip, I continued to worry unrealistically about whether or not he would take more on any more trips if I asked him to and tried my best to stay calm under all circumstances.

About a week after we got back Lacey and Dustin announced that Lacey was pregnant after five years of marriage. I was nervous about the idea of Lacey having a little one to raise because I knew that it would mean a change in our family routine. Change in routine of any type brings serious anxiety in anyone with any form of Autism. I felt jealous of all of the attention that Lacey would receive once the baby came and reacted unkindly with meltdowns and stemming.

Lacey turned 31 years old that year and for her birthday Dustin took her to a place where you find out the gender of the baby earlier than normal. When they got to their appointment Lacey and Dustin called our house with excitement to tell us that their baby was a boy.

"Hooray," I heard Mom, yelling with excitement from the living room.

"Is it a boy or a girl," I asked out of curiosity.

"It's a boy," said Mom.

Even though I continued to feel jealous of Lacey and reacted horrible I did my best and got her stuff for the baby whenever it was time for her to have him. I was not jealous of the baby because I knew that he was a separate person.

The holiday season came, and it was the first holiday without Nan and the second holiday without Aaron and Jonathan. Everyone came for the holidays at our house once again, but how changed it was for our missing loved ones. For Lacey's Christmas present I bought her stuff for the soon to be born baby boy. Mom had officially retired from her nursing job around that time also.

CHAPTER TWENTY-TWO

So put your hands to work. Strengthen your legs for the journey.
(Hebrews 12:12 NIrV)

As January of 2015 arrived in Lacey went for her weekly doctor appointments with her Obstetrician and had already requested Maternity leave from her nursing job. On February 8th, 2015, Lacey and Dustin welcomed their newborn son Oakley into the world. Even though I was very jealous of Lacey most of my life because she did not have Autism and was able to get married and hold down a job, I felt like Oakley was the first major blessing in my life. I loved him so much and he was so precious. I loved rocking him and soothing him whenever he would cry. Oakley had severe colic and I did not like to see him in discomfort.

One day I walked in Lacey and Dustins' house because I really wanted to hold Oakley and rock him even if I did wake him up.

"AAAHHHHHH" Oakley screamed as I picked him up long enough to wake him up and get him back to sleep.

Oakley's first few months of life passed and soon it was Springtime and time for his first Easter. That year we had some really bad weather, and our church was damaged from floods, so we were not able to have church at our church on Easter Sunday of 2015. We went to Church with Dustin's parents at their church and went to an Easter Dinner at a restaurant after the Easter service at their church. That Easter was so different, not being in our own church and not having a big dinner after church with our extended family. But it was good to be with people we loved, and we felt very close to Dustin's parents.

The weekend following Easter of 2015 we were scheduled to have the first ever Autism walk in our area. I was excited to participate in the walk, but it had to be canceled due to bad weather and was rescheduled to the first week of June 2015.

A few weeks later I was at the pharmacy getting my monthly medications and while I was waiting in line to pick them up my and pay for them, I happened to run across Shanna, a girl that I graduated from High School with. Shanna and I struck up a conversation. Shanna was the person who organized the County Autism walk and organization.

"Since you have Autism would you be willing to give a speech on your experience with Autism and give some advice on dealing with the disorder at our Autism walk," asked Shanna.

"I would love to," I said happily. I prayed for years about being a light for others with Autism and at that moment I felt as if my prayers were answered.

Shanna was always nice to me in High School even though many of the other kids that she hung out with bullied me because I was different and because they did not understand my situation. Shanna was a cheerleader and a senior salute in high school. She became a respiratory therapist and landed a job at one of our local hospitals. She is married and has two sons. Like me, her oldest son was diagnosed with Pervasive Developmental Disorder/Asperger Syndrome, which is now classified as High Functioning Autism.

"Mom, I said as I walked in the door with my medication. I saw my friend Shanna at the pharmacy, and she asked me if I would be willing to give a speech on my Autism experience at the Autism walk and I told her yes."

Mom was encouraging and thought it was great. I immediately began work on my speech for the Autism walk. I wrote out my speech and read it over several times. Then I typed it out and printed it out. Mom proofread it, thought it was good, but suggested a little tweaking.

A week and a half before the Autism walk and my speech, Lacey and our cousin Tara went with me to a New Kids on the Block concert that I purchased tickets for back in January. Mom babysat Oakley while we went to the concert. I purchased the tickets with money that I saved up and prepaid my credit card bill for the tickets via an app on my tablet. Whenever I get to do something like this it always makes me feel good because I don't have much of a social life.

June 7th, 2015, we had the first ever County Autism walk in the area. It was the first time that I ever spoke publicly about my experience with High Functioning Autism. It was an overcast day and I drove there early while Mom, Lacey, and Oakley met me there shortly afterward. After all of the people that signed up for the event and attended claimed their T-shirts it was time for me to give my speech.

"May I have your attention please, said Shanna as the time for the walk neared. I would like to thank everyone for coming to the first county Autism walk and before we start the walk, I have asked Lauren to talk to everyone about Autism a little bit before we get started. I have known Lauren for a long time, and She has Autism. Are there any questions before I hand Lauren the microphone?"

Shanna handed me the microphone and I began my first ever speech on my experience with High Functioning Autism wearing bright red lipstick that matched our Autism walk T-shirts. I described my experience with High Functioning Autism, when I was diagnosed with the condition, the symptoms of the condition and the symptoms that I have experienced, and what worked best for best for me. Talking about my experiences helped me in dealing with Autism symptoms and helped me to learn more about everyday social stuff. It also felt like a key was unlocked that day because I started to realize more stuff that I was never told before. For example, it was still taking time for me to realize that normal people say things that they do not mean when they feel tired, frustrated or upset about something. I was always brutally honest about something whenever I felt upset in addition to stemming. This had nothing to do with the event, but it was something that was unlocked in me when I gave that speech and it happened for no reason. It was as if God wanted to reveal more lessons about social stuff to me.

"Lauren, you did amazing, " said one woman in the crowd. She asked me about what she could do about her son's special interests. I enjoyed talking with her and since his special interest was dinosaurs, I suggested letting him enjoy his special interest unless it endangers his health. I also suggested she use his interest in an educational way.

Lacey and my family thought I did a great job and told me so. Lacey suggested we go out to eat to celebrate. We all went out to eat and enjoyed delicious Mexican food and fried ice cream for dessert. *"A well-deserved dessert for Lauren,"* Lacey posted on facebook with a picture of me at the Mexican restaurant with her cell phone after the autism walk with a video of my speech. Several people complimented on the video that Lacey posted of my speech.

I still went to the local public pool or at Uncle Melvin and Aunt Yevette's house. Sometimes I would have to help Mom babysit Oakley at times while Lacey and Dustin worked. I would use Nan's old house on days that I wanted to work on crafts.

In the fall of that year, we did go to the beach and spent a week there. No one else in my family went out to the beach with me because everyone had to stay inside and babysit Oakley because he was still a baby. I got frustrated over that and it caused me to get meltdowns and stemming behaviors. The amusement park nearby got a new coaster and that added me a coaster credit.

I developed another intense special interest with another major singer in addition to my interest in New Kids on the Block and roller coasters. I saw videos of this particular singer on facebook and you tube and thought to myself, *"Wow he is very talented and cute."*

Christmas of 2015 arrived, and it was Oakley's first Christmas. His main Christmas present from me was money that I deposited into his savings account. He also got lots of clothes and toys from all of us. It was fun having a baby at Christmas!

Following Christmas I saw that there was going to be a concert near us in April of 2016 and I really wanted to go to the concert. I bought tickets for the concert in January of 2016 and Lacey went with me. It was the week after Easter of that year. Not long after the April concert the same singer announced another concert fairly close to us in the middle of August 2016 and I had to purchase tickets to that concert. Lacey agreed to go with me to that concert too because she knew that I was obsessed with this singer, and she wanted me to be happy. Summer of 2016 I went to the pool every day that the weather was nice and to the gym daily. Going to the pool was the best therapy for my chronic pain and Autism.

June of 2016 we had our second annual autism walk in our area and I was glad to talk about my experiences with the disorder for a second year in a row. Shanna was still the host of the event. I had people video me with my Ipad and phone speaking. It was a hot morning in June of 2016 and my iPad and phone kicked off due to heat for those that were videoing me, which frustrated me. Because of all of this I had a meltdown after the walk ended and stemmed. When I returned home later I uploaded the video from both my iPad and my phone to facebook while both devices were charging. About an hour later when both devices were charged, I checked facebook to see what people had said about my speech.

"*Oh No,* I thought to myself as I started crying and stemming. *I busted my butt off to put that speech together and not very many people have commented on my speech. Why are people on facebook so much more interested in other stuff and not someone like me?*"

"Lauren honey why are you crying and wringing your hands," asked Dad as he walked in my room to check on me.

"Only a few people have commented on my video of my speech that I uploaded to facebook, " I said, continuing to cry and stem.

"Who told you that your speech was not good today?" asked Dad, trying to reason with me.

"No one said it to my face or said any negative comments about it on facebook but there have not been any comments about it on facebook," I said.

"I thought you did really well," said Dad, trying to help calm me down.

A few hours later I was wrong about my 2016 Autism speech. I checked facebook and noticed that several people had shared my post on my speech and that there were several good compliments on it under my original post and what other people shared about it.

"Lauren, you described my son's symptoms completely," said one woman in one of the comments on my video when someone else shared it on facebook.

About a week after the Autism walk of 2016 Mom and Dad went grocery shopping and out to eat at a nearby restaurant. While they were at the restaurant eating, they happened to run into Linda, one of Mom's childhood friends who was also a retired nurse. Linda told Mom and Dad that she had seen the video of my speech on facebook and felt really inspired by it. She told Mom that her daughter always had some type of problem and based on what she heard me say, she wondered if her daughter may have some form of Autism like me.

Mom told me about seeing Linda and what she said, I felt so happy. I have prayed that God would use me to be a light for others with Autism and to help me with my autism and at that moment I felt as if another prayer was answered. It means so much to me to think I have impacted someone in a positive way. I hope that I can inspire other people through my speeches, whether they are neurotypical or autistic.

When Mom finished telling me about Linda and what she said I added Linda as a friend on facebook. She always comments on my posts. Her posts are so positive and inspiring. I really appreciate her so much.

Near the end of the summer of 2016 Mom, Dad, Lacey, Oakley and myself went on a camping trip with my aunt (Dad's sister) and uncle, their family and a couple that were good camping friends of Mom and Dad. We went to sand dunes near Lake Michigan. Our family rode over the dunes and it was a lot like a coaster. There was an amusement park nearby, that I wanted to go to and I already pre purchased tickets for it. The amusement park was only about 30 minutes away from where we were staying, and it had six roller coasters that I was able to add to my list.

The day of the second concert, I happened to have a meltdown earlier in the day over some stuff that I was worried about which almost kept me from being able to go to the concert if I hadn't calmed down. I was tired from the meltdowns but I still enjoyed the concert. Concerts are my favorite thing to do besides coasters.

The summer faded away into fall and soon it was time for Halloween. I decided to dress up as Donald Trump and carried a sign that said "make our (community name) great" since he was running for president and that was his slogan to make America Great. Lacey and Oakley dressed up as Dr. and Mrs. Frankenstein. I went trick or treating with them and everyone thought it was hilarious that I was dressed up as Donald Trump.

Soon it was time for Christmas of 2016. Concert tickets for New Kids on the Block and another concert went on sale, and I purchased tickets for both of them. Because of my ticket purchases, I did not have a lot of money left over to purchase holiday gifts for my family. I just deposited some money into Oakley's savings account as his Christmas gift. I was semi-dating a guy at that time, and he went with me to the one concert because he told me that he liked the singer too. Lacey was not able to go because she had an appointment to get her taxes done. I felt thankful that this guy was able to go with me to the concert, but the relationship never developed into anything more than going to the concert together.

The winter season passed, and it was soon time for Spring. Our family came in from Pennsylvania and they stayed at Nan's old house which remained fully furnished through Easter weekend. They got to meet Oakley and we all got to visit. It was a really nice weekend.

The week after the New Kids on the Block Concert I had my fourth and final female surgery which included a hysterectomy, leaving only my right ovary. I do however still experience hormonal fluctuations that can worsen mood swings even though they don't seem to be quite as bad. Due to my stage four Endometriosis, I sought out expertise from a surgeon in a major medical center in the state that specialized in complex cases of Endometriosis and other female problems to perform my surgery. The surgery was performed laparoscopically, and the surgeon was able to repair damage to my bowel from Endometriosis and excise it from my bladder. This was the first time that I ever had relief from the pain I suffered from for so long even though I still suffer from the joint pain and mood issues.

Two weeks after my last surgery, it was time for the annual autism walk in the area and I was excited to speak at the event again. This was my third time speaking at the event and as they say the third time's a charm at doing something. I believe the third speech was the best one that I had done up until that point even though I was still somewhat recovering from my surgery.

At the end of September, we went on a family vacation to Walt Disney World for our first time ever and I loved it. Oakley loved it too, but he was too little to enjoy anything other than meeting the characters and I took several pictures of him meeting the characters and selfies with myself and the characters. Dad saw me applying lipstick and eye makeup one day and wondered why I was putting on makeup to go to an amusement park and ride roller coasters. I told him I wanted to look cute for character meet and greets and on ride photos. I felt blessed enough to add another bunch of roller coasters to my growing list.

Prior to going on this Disney trip, I did some research and found out that I was able to get a Disability Pass for rides and character meet and greets due to my Autism and at Disney world its free. For everyone that gets a disability pass the other members in the group can use the pass too. The Disability Pass works the same way as the traditional fast pass system does. Anyone that has a chronic medical condition, including any form of Autism is eligible for the Disability Pass system as long as they have a note from a medical provider that states that they cannot tolerate standing in line for long periods of time. Based on my experiences this is beneficial and I would highly encourage anyone with any medical condition to take advantage of Disability services at any major amusement park or tourist attractions.

The Christmas season came quickly, and we did the typical stuff for the holiday season. After we finished opening gifts on Christmas morning Lacey and Dustin gave the big announcement that Lacey was pregnant with a baby girl and that she was due in May. She had known since before we left on our Disney trip. Once again I felt jealous of Lacey's ability to have a family. I also felt like I would never love another baby like I did Oakley. I experienced meltdowns of course and I know my Mom and Dad were concerned.

The time flew by and soon it was time for my precious niece to make her entrance into the world. The week before Lacey went to the hospital to deliver my niece was the fourth annual autism walk in the area. Shanna was also pregnant at the time with her second son, and I presented her with a baby gift whenever I finished my speech. On May 25th, 2018, Lacey gave birth to my niece, Owynn Mae. I was able to see her in the hospital before she and Lacey were released to come home. Whenever I saw her for the first time in the hospital, I was not only able to hold her, but I was lucky enough to get a video of Oakley wanting to hold her.

Like new babies do, she was wiggling and kind of grunting, he said "what her want me to do?" He was hugging and loving her the whole time. When he said that Lacey cried tears of joy and I squealed with excitement while videoing them with my phone.

I still liked swimming at the local pool on days that it was hot, and I wanted to go to another concert. I was hesitant about asking Lacey to go with me because she had just given birth two weeks or so prior to the concert so I asked my friend Courtney to go, and she went with me. The rest of the summer was fun, and we got to visit with family and an amusement park too.

As the fall of 2018 continued, I signed up for and paid for a yoga teacher trainer course that lasted for about six months at a yoga studio nearby. I loved yoga so much that I wanted to teach it and I do consider yoga one of my special interests, just as much as I love roller coasters and music stars like New Kids on the Block. Oakley was three years old, and he became aware of the fact that I was different and that I had a special interest in roller coasters. One day whenever we were babysitting Oakley and Owynn, Mom was cleaning off the counter tops in the kitchen and Oakley happened to see a coupon with a picture of a roller coaster on it. He grabbed it and immediately came running into the living room where I was sitting while reading a book.

"Naurna, Naurna, " said Oakley as he showed me the coupon with the picture of a roller coaster on it. Are you going to ride this?" Oakley had not yet learned how to say my name properly, so he called me Naurna. He also learned to go and get Mom or Dad if he ever witnessed me having a meltdown.

"Yes, if we ever get to go there," I said looking at the coupon.

Fall passed quickly and soon it was time for the holidays. Owynn was about 8 months old and just as I started doing for Oakley, I made it my goal to deposit money into her savings account every Christmas, Valentines Day, Easter, and Birthday. I did not spend much money on gifts that year because I spent all of my money on the yoga teacher training course and a trip to Disney World with Aunt Yevette and Uncle Melvin and their granddaughter the week before Christmas 2018. One of the Disney parks got a new coaster that I wanted to ride and add to my list. We flew to Disney World for the trip and as we passed through security at the airport on the day, we were coming back home I lost my driver's license while walking through the security line. It was overly crowded that day because it was Christmas Eve and people were wall to wall against each other trying to get through the airport. I was rushing to get through and was not aware that my license was missing until it was almost time to board the plane. Prior to boarding the plane, I double checked my carry-on bag to make sure that I had all of my electronic stuff and other important stuff such as money and credit cards. When I noticed that my license was missing, I panicked and had a total meltdown in the airport. Even though I was told that I was able to go to the courthouse on the next business day and get another copy of my license I still felt upset and stemmed by wringing my hands. It was a miracle that I was still able to fly home based on me being so upset and when Mom and Dad found out how I reacted they were very embarrassed. In order to avoid stuff like this in the future I hope to be able to plan ahead when traveling and have an app on my phone to scan an ID while entering security without having to get it out.

The yoga teacher training program started in November, and we skipped December due to the holidays and resumed in January of 2019. The program lasted until May of 2019 and the classes were held on Friday evenings and all day on Saturdays and Sundays from 8am until 8pm. The classes were held on the first weekend of every month. I did not have any meltdowns at any of our class sessions nor did I feel as if I was being discriminated against for my disability. Our homework assignments consisted of reading several yoga books, sitting in and observing some of the yoga classes at the studio and participating in yoga classes at the studio.

The weekend of our January class, I woke up, got dressed, ate and brushed my teeth. Then I gathered my stuff and went downstairs to the garage to put my stuff in my car. As I was putting my stuff in my car, I noticed a strange and eerie looking dog outside. That set off my sensory fears that I did not have for years. I screamed a blood-curdling scream, and I ran back up the steps. Mom and Dad were so startled. I told them of the scary looking stray dog outside that I was terrified of. They were aware of the stray dog but reassured me that it seemed friendly, and that I had probably scared it worse that it scared me.

Despite the incident with me getting spooked by the dog I was able to make it to my yoga teacher trainer class on time without any problems that morning. This incident with the dog reminded me of what it felt like when I felt terrified of the owl picture in our house and the picture of the wildcat hanging in the school gymnasium when I was in elementary school and the other unexplained fears.

Spring of 2019 arrived, and it was soon time for the yoga teacher trainer program to end. 2019 was the fifth-year anniversary of the autism walk in our area and Shanna continued to allow me to talk about my Autism experience. Owynn turned one year old on May 25th of that year, and we had her birthday party at our church fellowship hall. I deposited money into her savings account as her birthday present from me. Since Lacey was busy because she was starting a graduate school program, I asked one of our close family friends to go with me to one of my concerts and an amusement park and my friend Courtney to go with me to the New Kids on the Block concert. I continued to go to the local public pool every day that it was hot outside. Dad went to a car show in July in Missouri and Mom, and I went with him because there was a six flags park nearby that I wanted to go to. I went to Six flags while I was in Missouri with Dad and rode all of their roller coasters minus one coaster. There is one thing that I have learned to do in order to avoid meltdowns when I am staying in a hotel. I have decided to make sure that I have headphones to watch movies, read books, and listen to podcasts and music. I always make sure that I have plenty of that downloaded to my tablet ahead of time and make sure that both my phone and tablet stay charged at all times.

I was sick with a severe respiratory tract infection on my birthday that lasted for over a month. I purchased concert tickets for Lacey for a singer that she likes for her birthday that came two weeks later and she really liked it. The summer passed and it was soon time for the fall season. I went to another car show with Dad and while we were there, I purchased Holiday gifts for Oakley and Owynn at the nearby outlet mall. I also purchased concert tickets for myself, and Lacey and Dustin as Christmas presents for 2019 and upgraded my coaster fan club membership to a family membership to include Lacey in the club as another part of her Christmas present from me. I had many plans for 2020 like I normally do, and I had no clue that a serious pandemic like COVID 19 would affect the lives of everyone around the world.

Me holding Oakley as a newborn

Me holding Oakley in the spring of 2018

Me kissing Oakley in winter 2016

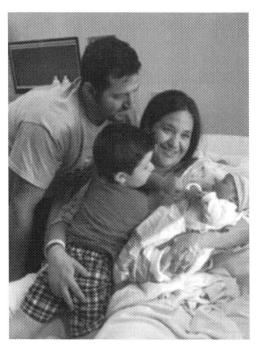

My sis and her family holding a freshly hatched Owynn

Me with some friends and family at the 2019 autism walk for our area

CHAPTER TWENTY-THREE

What is your life? It is a mist that appears for a little while. Then it disappears. (James 4:14 NIrV)

An unwelcome guest arrived in the lives of everyone worldwide in the spring of 2020, called COVID 19. The COVID 19 pandemic caused devastating effects on almost every part of the globe and affected the economy in the United States and worldwide. COVID 19 first began in China in December of 2019. COVID 19 virus (Coronavirus Disease) is in the same category of viruses that caused the global SARS (severe acute respiratory syndrome) outbreak in 2003 and MERS (Middle East Respiratory Syndrome) in 2012. COVID 19 is the nineteenth virus in the coronavirus group of viruses and was also named after the year it was discovered. Coronaviruses have been circulating for more than forty years and are a cause of the seasonal cold that most people get.

COVID 19 first first gained headlines on the news in January 2020, and I did not think it would become a major issue. Lacey and I went to a concert one night in the middle of January 2020 and the concert was lots of fun as usual. I felt very blessed to attend that concert because little did, I know that it would be the only one that I would be able to attend that year.

Oakley turned five years old on February 8th, 2020. He had a Nerf Gun themed birthday party. Around that very same week I read the news section on the roller coaster fan club website, and it stated that China was shut down because of the COVID 19 virus that had been spreading since December. The roller coaster fan club had an international event planned in China that was already canceled due to the COVID 19 lockdown in the country. Two weeks after Oakley's 5th birthday party Mom and Dad went on a 10-day trip to Florida to see my dad's sister who lives in Florida in the wintertime. While Mom and Dad were gone, I kept Owynn and Oakley for about two hours one night while Lacey and Dustin had business to conduct. On the night that I babysat Oakley and Owynn I started planning roller coaster trips for the summer, where I would like to travel to, and how much it would cost to do it.

Mom and Dad came back home near the first week of March 2020 and at that point businesses were gradually shutting down due to COVID 19 entering the United States. I had to go to physical therapy for a problem with my hip and one day when I went to therapy the receptionist had to get my temperature upon check in to the appointment to make sure that I was not sick in any way. The lobby was closed off and patients had to wait in their car before coming into their appointment and had to wear a mask and sanitize their hands while in the treatment room.

Around the second week of March all of the concerts that were scheduled for the summer 2020 season were cancelled or rescheduled until 2021 because COVID 19 had now entered the United States. The concert that I purchased Lacey tickets for was completely cancelled and another concert that I bought tickets for was rescheduled for 2021. I was able to get my money back on the concert that I purchased Lacey tickets for and as for the rescheduled concert I did not get my money back.

From the middle of March until the end of May the United States and Canada were placed under lockdown and all non-essential businesses had to close down. Even Dentist offices and physical therapy centers had to close down, which I did not agree with because I do consider these to be essential businesses. I had to miss my six-month Dental cleaning because my Dentist office had to be closed down due to lockdown restrictions.

"I don't like that I have to miss my six-month Dental visit," I said, complaining and twisting my hands when I found out that my Dentist had to close his office for COVID 19 restrictions.

"Your teeth are in good shape because you take such good care of them, and it will be ok if you have to miss your cleaning," said Mom, trying to reason with me.

I thought this lockdown was only going to last about two weeks. It ended up lasting for about two and a half months. Schools across the nation were closed down and students had to access class via zoom meetings and parents had to drive to school to turn in packets of assignments that were due each week. Students got lunches at the beginning of every week. Important milestone events such as weddings, birthday parties, prom, and graduations were not allowed to be celebrated in the traditional ways. Easter fell in the middle of the nationwide COVID 19 lockdown, and I had already purchased stuff for Oakley and Owynn's Easter baskets one month before the pandemic lockdown.

I was hoping that I would get to go to several amusement parks over the summer because I saved up my money for that. I was taught that growing up in a Christian environment that it was wrong to complain about anything, but I didn't like being dishonest about my feelings and hiding my feelings, so I constantly complained about the negative effects of the COVID 19 pandemic lockdown.

Owynn turned two years old on May 25th, 2020, and due to COVID 19 restrictions we were not allowed to have her a birthday party. She just had birthday cake at home with the family only. Since that was the case Lacey got her a new kitten for her birthday because she loves cats. I deposited money into her savings account just as I have done for both kids every major holiday since they were born.

I was hoping that the public pools would be open for the summer in our area, but they were not able to open due to government restrictions on COVID 19. Uncle Melvin and Aunt Yevette moved into a different house and their new house did not have a pool, so I was not able to go swimming anywhere. Not being able to go swimming when the weather is super-hot outside is miserable.

The first week of June of 2020 gyms were able to open back up. As soon as our local gym opened back up, I started back going on a regular basis. A few stores at our local mall opened back up and most of them were bare and due to COVID 19 restrictions dressing rooms were not open. I refused to purchase clothes if I went shopping because most dressing rooms in clothing stores were not open. Beauty salons opened back up but as mandated by most state board laws, all cosmetologists were required to wear masks when working on clients and clients were strongly recommended to wear masks.

As the summer went on, I was able to go to the beach with Lacey, Dustin, and the kids on the week of my birthday. That was nice but we had to wear masks everywhere that we went outside of our condominium or the beach. Wearing a mask in hot weather is uncomfortable and it makes it feel difficult to breathe at times.

Anytime that anyone traveled during the summer of 2020 they had to take the punishment of taking two weeks off of work without any pay to quarantine from possible exposure to the COVID 19 virus.

Since I was not able to spend the money that I had saved up for amusement parks I felt very disappointed about that. When we got back from the beach, I spent the money I saved on an expensive beauty treatment that I wanted to get done and it worked.

School started back in August of that year in a non-traditional way. All students in our area went to school via zoom meetings once a week and had to complete a set of assignments to be turned in every Friday. Oakley entered Kindergarten and he had to miss the majority of the first semester of school due to COVID 19 restrictions and lockdown. When there were in person school days school would only be in session for a few days per week. He didn't like not being able to see his friends. Lacey had to work so most of the time so it was Mom helping Oakley with his homework assignments.

Oakley did not like doing cyber school. Mom had to get after him to get his work done. Kindergarten is a hard age to do online studies. He just wanted to play. The two times that I helped him with his homework he reacted the same way even though he did a good job at working on the assignments He is a very smart little boy and does good in school. He cried about having to do schoolwork at home. He is a very happy and healthy kid but seeing him complain about doing homework reminded me of how I used to have a lot of problems in school. Oakley truly functioned much better with in person learning than he did with remote learning.

In mid-September of 2020, I went to the zoo with Lacey, Dustin, both kids, and another couple and their children. It was a very hot and crowded day. Masks were required to get inside the zoo and the social distancing policies were enforced. I disliked having to wear a mask in very hot weather but I was willing to so I could enjoy spending time at the zoo with my family while taking precautions for protecting myself against COVID 19. I would sneak my mask off every so often just to feel the breeze. Wearing a mask made it difficult to wear any form of makeup besides eye makeup because it caused me to smear makeup all over my face and the mask, which I thought looked kind of gross. I have slacked on wearing makeup since the pandemic came, but I still wear red lipstick when I can.

For Halloween that year our community had a drive through trunk or treat at one of the churches instead of the traditional trunk or treat. Lacey had to work that night and I went trick or treating with Dustin and the kids. I was dressed up as a Covid medical worker in all of the protective gear.

Everyone got ready for the holiday season COVID 19 style and social distancing. We were not able to have Thanksgiving or Christmas with other relatives due to COVID 19 restrictions. Oakley was still in and out of regular school for the semester continuously due to COVID restrictions. I wanted to travel to the Smoky Mountains but my family were not not keen on going because they knew several people who contracted Covid there. I was so disappointed.

I was so sick and tired of quarantine and social distancing. I cried and stemmed for days.

Since we were not able to travel to the Smoky Mountains area like I wanted to, I decided to spend more money than I normally do for the kids on Christmas. I deposited money into their savings accounts as usual. I also bought them a basketball goal (which they still love), and they each got a special basketball. I purchased Oakley Pokémon cards, a game and a case for his Nintendo switch, and some clothes. I purchased Owynn, a box that doubles as a Barbie doll house, some Barbie dolls, and some clothes. I had been wanting a new iPad for quite some time and I saved up enough money to purchase one and a keyboard to go with it.

Mom got me the newest historical doll from the American Girl line of dolls. I absolutely loved the doll. It was my first ever American Girl doll and I loved it! It only made me want more of them. She sleeps with me every night just as my stuffed animals from when I was younger do, including my beloved Papa Smurf.

Soon it was time to ring in 2021 and I was more than ready to put the pandemic behind me and move on. It was then that I really decided to work on my book. I wanted to write a book based on my experiences with High Functioning Autism for as long as I could remember, and I felt determined to do it. I purchased a printer for my new tablet in hopes of being able to get my book completed by the summer, but I did not get it completed like I wanted to.

I purchased tickets for a local concert that I wanted to go to in the Spring. It got pushed back until July because of COVID restrictions that were still in place. I heard at that time that the COVID 19 shots were available for some people, and I really really wanted one. I felt so much determination to get back to normal that I called, emailed, prayed, and asked to be placed on waiting lists to get COVID shots.

One morning in the first week of February 2021 I woke up around 10am. I had been feeling hopeless about ever getting the COVID 19 shot series before I possibly got exposed to the virus. Mom came into my room with a pleased look on her face. She told told me she got appointments to get our the vaccine the next day! I was so excited and happy. I just wanted everyone to get their vaccine and get rid of the darn plague.

The next morning Dad drove Mom and I to the place where the COVID 19 shots were being given because they both had things to do that day after our appointments. Dad already gotten his COVID 19 vaccine because of his age. Mom and I got our vaccine, and I felt so thrilled to get mine that I took a selfie of myself getting my first dose of the COVID 19 shot and posted it on Facebook and Instagram. That day the weather service for our area issued a major snowstorm warning for our area.

About two days later we celebrated Oakley's sixth birthday at Lacey and Dustin's house. Lacey and Dustin got Oakley a cake as well as some Nerf guns. Mom and Dad got him clothes and I just got him a card with a receipt of money that I deposited into his savings account for his birthday as well as his and Owynn's valentine cards.

A full week later it continued to snow and there was ice and snow all over our area. On the night of February 14th, Valentines Day 2021 our power went out around 9 pm. I was miserable and in a panic. Uncle Milt invited us to come to his house to sleep because he had a wall mount gas heater that provided heat and Mom took our oil lamps. I was awake the entire night. I tossed and turned the whole night, I stemmed all night, Mom couldn't sleep for me. She came and lay on the couch, talked to me and tried to sooth me to no avail. When morning came, I went back across the road to our house. It was very cold and dark, but I just wanted to be home. Even in the daylight hours, the house seemed dark.

We were without electricity for several days. The ice storms were so severe, we could stand on our porch and hear the trees falling, fortunately we had no damage done to our house, but the trees were damaged in our yard and later, Dad had to hire someone to come in and trim the trees, and one had to be cut down behind our house to keep it from falling on our house. There was such damage done from the falling trees that power company workers were out day and night, but it was so extensive, it took a while even with many crews working around the clock.

One day during the power outage Mom and Dad wanted me to babysit for Owynn and Oakley for a few hours while Mom fixed dinner in the little kitchen, she added in the basement which had a gas range and was purchased a year prior. The basement also had a gas heater, but it was total darkness because there are no windows. It took longer for her to fix dinner because she didn't have all ingredients for the meals down there and she had to use the old antique oil lamps and battery-operated lanterns. Dustin was working and Lacey had to go out for something that day.

Lacey and Dustin had heat in their house from the gas fireplace and had a generator for electricity in certain rooms in their house. I was so bored and had a meltdown with stems while babysitting the kids. I did everything possible to keep myself from stemming and having a meltdown while Oakley and Owynn colored in their coloring books and played with their toys. I fed the dog and took it outside to use the bathroom, put away the dishes, and folded the laundry, and none of that helped as much as I would have liked it too.

Oakley and Owynn wanted me to color with them in their coloring books. As I opened a page in one of their coloring books I started gnawing on a marker. Both of the kids noticed that I was biting on the marker.

"Naurno, what are you doing," asked Owynn. When she was a toddler, she always called me Naurno.

"Nothing," I said, continuing to gnaw on the marker.

"It's okay Lauren, said Oakley as he put his arms around me."

"Lauren please stop wringing your hands," said Dad when he came in and witnessed me wringing my hands from having a meltdown over frustration about the electricity being out.

"Dad, I don't like this, and I wish the electricity would come back on, " I said, frustrated because I could not see to read, having to take a shower with a flashlight in cold water, and freezing out of my mind. I am so terrified of the dark."

"None of us like it either, " Dad said, trying to reason with me. It is just something that we have to deal with.

My cousin Clint's electricity had gone out a couple of days before ours. He borrowed Dad's generator and bought one (they were very difficult to find), but his wife had learned how to use Dad's and he had to go to work, so Clint brought his new one to us to use. There was a lot of trading supplies and cords to manage three different households. Uncle Milt had his gas heat. Fuel for the generators was difficult to find because the pumps didn't work without electricity. When Dad, Dustin or Lacey went to purchase the fuel for the generators, they would be gone for hours sometimes trying to locate accessible fuel. The noise from the generator was so loud. It was hard to sleep with the noise and Mom and Dad were constantly having to add fuel to the generator. Finally, after five days of dealing with my longtime fear of the dark, not being able to read as much as I would like, poor sleep, and having to take cold showers, our electricity came back on.

"Are you happy, now?" Dad asked the night that our electricity came back on.

"Yes," I said.

"Lord, thank you so much for turning our electricity back on," I prayed whenever our electricity came back on.

The big thaw from the snow and ice storm began to melt it made sounds as it melted off of our house and from the trees. Something that was really bizarre was that ice was causing trees to nearly fall on people's houses. One tree in our backyard was about to fall over and a tree in our front yard had branches breaking from it that fell onto our driveway. Dustin and Oakley cleaned up the tree branches in our driveway and Mom and Dad had to hire someone to cut down the tree in our backyard that almost fell over.

The major snow and ice storm melted and then we had some major flooding in our area that caused just as much damage. Many people in our area were still without electricity and the floods only worsened further power outages. That left many people in our area without electricity for almost a month. Our neighbors didn't have electricity for twenty plus days. One of our friends would come to our house ever couple of days and get a hot shower in our basement. Our phones were out for almost a month, but I was very thankful that our electricity came back on when it did.

Near the end of the month Aunt Yevette invited Mom, Lacey and the kids, and me to go with her, her granddaughter, and some of their friends on a trip to the Smoky Mountains. I wanted to go for quite some time. We went and it was a great relief. I went shopping at the nearby outlet mall and purchased myself some new clothes and some gifts for Owynn and Oakley for their Easter baskets. Things were still not quite back to normal and many COVID 19 restrictions were still in place in the area.

When we returned back home from our trip to the Smoky Mountains, I went to my appointment to get the second dose of the COVID 19 shot in the series. I went to my appointment and was thrilled to finish up with my COVID 19 shot series because I thought that would be the key to being able to return back to normal. I filled out my paperwork and handed the people my driver's license and when it was my turn to be called back to get the shot, I asked one nurse to take a picture of me receiving the shot. She said she would be happy to, and as the other nurse gave me the shot the nurse that checked me in and read my information snapped a picture of me receiving the shot.

"Got my second dose of COVID 19 shot. I can't wait to get back to normal. I want to go to lots of theme parks this year and ride roller coasters," I said in a facebook post with the picture of me receiving the second dose of the COVID 19 vaccine.

Soon it was time to start thinking about going to theme parks for the year. Mom and Dad were planning to go to Virginia on a camping trip in the summer with some other couples that they are friends with and frequently camp with. I chose to go with them because they would be camping in Williamsburg, Virginia. I wanted to go so I could go to Busch Gardens theme park and get their roller coasters added to my bucket list.

I asked Mom and Dad to let me go to Virginia with them so I could go to Busch gardens. Dad felt hesitant about letting me go because he was still traumatized by the trip in 2004 where he drove me to Pennsylvania and thought that I had a bad meltdown at the amusement park when actually I had the worst meltdown the day before. They allowed me to go with them so I could go to Busch Gardens, and I am thankful for that.

Lacey and the kids were supposed to go with us so she could go with me to Busch Gardens. She had to work, and I just told her that I would have Mom go with me to Busch Gardens. Mom and I took an Uber to the park from the campground. Mom does not ride roller coasters, but she was glad to be with me. I rode all of the roller coasters that were open at Busch Gardens, including the one that I wanted to ride when I went there in 1995 on my eighth-grade class trip but was unable to ride at the time. While we were in Virginia, I enjoyed doing all of the other things that Mom and Dad did with their friends even though we did not think that I would like it.

When we got back home from our trip to Virginia the COVID 19 pandemic worsened again, and the Delta Variant was the dominant strain of the virus in our area. It was highly contagious and very deadly for those that did not take precautions. I felt very frustrated because I was hoping that things would return to pre-pandemic life. I had two concerts in July 2021 that I really wanted to go to that were rescheduled from 2020 and from April 2021 due to COVID 19 restrictions. Lacey and Dustin went with me to the concert that was the first week of July and Lacey drove me to the one that was later in July, but she brought Dustin's niece to go with me inside the concert venue while she stayed outside in the car and worked on schoolwork.

"I don't think you should go to that concert because of the COVID 19 delta variant," said Mom the day before I went to my second concert in the month of July 2021 out of sheer concern. I did not listen to her because I wanted to go to that concert because I knew that I could not get my money back for the concert and since it was a singer that I really liked I was determined to go.

I went to the concert but wore my mask the entire duration of the concert and washed my hands religiously. I wanted to wear my bright red lipstick, but I couldn't wear it because it was hot and any makeup other than eye makeup would smear all over my mask. I did not come into contact with the delta variant of COVID 19 that night.

The next day as I attended my surprise birthday party, I was able to reflect on my accomplishments as I still continue to overcome the challenges of living with High Functioning Autism. I felt so overwhelmed by the amount of love and kindness from my family for throwing me a surprise birthday party that all of my problems seemed insignificant. Ever since I was old enough to understand the power of prayer and realized that I had a disorder I prayed that God would help me to live a normal life, such as being able to have a job that I like, hopefully fall in love and get married to a guy that shares my values and interests. God has answered my prayers but not in the way that I asked for and that is okay. God has answered my prayers in allowing me to author this book based on my experiences with High Functioning Autism and talk about my Autism experience at our local Autism walks. I will always have problems to some degree with High Functioning Autism and I hope that my journey through living with the disorder will inspire others to live their best and healthiest life possible. We should do something meaningful with our lives on earth despite a diagnosis of High Functioning Autism because each day that we have is a gift.

Symptoms of (HFA/AS) plus benefits and tips

Here are examples of symptoms associated with High Functioning Autism/Asperger's Syndrome.

1. Poor eye contact.
2. Odd walking gait.
3. Clumsiness, poor coordination and poor fine motor skills.
4. Poor posture.
5. Does not handle disappointment.
6. Hyper or hypo sensitivity to lights, sounds, texture, smells, etc.
7. Talking too loud or too low when speaking.
8. Intense interest in a particular subject area to the point where they will talk about it nonstop and fixate on the topic.
9. Inability to give and take in a friendship or relationship.
10. Inability to relate to others and poor social skills.
11. Poor emotional control, usually referred to as meltdowns.
12. Anxiety over changes in routine.
13. Anxiety and depression symptoms.
14. Inability to understand sarcasm. This means that they believe everything that they see, hear, or read about from others.
15. Difficulty with processing information when given instructions, working on an academic task, etc despite normal to above average intelligence.

16. Low self-esteem and self-confidence.
17. Hypo or Hypersensitivity to pain.
18. Feeling emotional over things that most people would recover from.
19. Fatigue that sometimes gets misunderstood as laziness. This can overlap with shutdowns.
20. Sleeping issues.
21. Staring at other people if they find something interesting. This is considered to be rude.
22. Shutdowns if they are tired, stressed, etc if there is no meltdown. This means tuning out everything in their surroundings for a certain period of time.
23. Repetitive motions.

What are some examples of the good traits of people with Asperger Syndrome/HFA?

1. Honesty.
2. They stand up for what they are passionate about.
3. They are non-judgmental.
4. They are honest about everything and will never pretend about anything even when upset.
5. Social status is not always important.
6. They have good attention to detail, good at memorizing details and facts. Normal people do not have this ability. I used to be told that I have a photographic Memory. I am also really good at memorizing facts.
7. If they are given the chance they can succeed. They already have the determination that the average person has to work to attain but find it difficult to complete anything that they do not like.
8. I learned from Health Class in high school and from several other resources that kids with mental illness and low self-esteem are at higher risk than other kids for making poor decisions, drug abuse, unwanted pregnancies, etc. I am a firm believer that this is not entirely true.
9. They are very naive.

10. If they are angry or upset, they will never try to bully, gossip, or lie to try to get back at someone. Despite uncontrollable emotions with self-injurious stemming and uncontrollable rage with crying they usually don't lash out rude remarks at others. They always tell the truth even when they are upset.
11. They are just as happy to be alone as they are with people.
12. They are very loyal and trustworthy.
13. They are highly intelligent despite having academic learning disorders and trouble keeping jobs.
14. Though it's a lifelong disorder and symptoms may intensify at times; it will not worsen overtime like many other chronic conditions. Many people learn to adjust and deal with symptoms with maturity.

Me and my sister at the autism walk 2022 and me

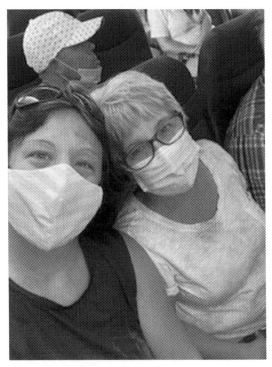

Mom traveling to the beach for a family vacation
in the midst of the pandemic in 2021

HFA/AS FACT: AUTISM SPECTRUM DISORDERS ARE NOT CAUSED BY POOR PARENTING.

Here are my personal tips and tricks for ASD people and parents/spouses. These may not work for you but most of these have worked for me.

1. Accept yourself or your Autistic child or spouse.
2. Be realistic and encouraging when trying to achieve goals.
3. Pray for those afflicted by Autism. Growing up in a Christian environment I learned the importance of prayer.
4. Lead by example. Even though Autistic people may not always understand the way others act they do pick up on small details.
5. Always stick to your promises and have a plan B handy. For example, if you promised your child that you would do something fun with her and for some reason you cannot do it on the day it was planned don't hesitate to ask someone else to do it. This excludes emergencies and inclement weather.
6. As for fixations that can lead to worry and Anxiety such as the potential for changes in routine and disappointment when things don't go as planned, be supportive.
7. Before judging someone on the autism spectrum for acting out examine how you are acting. (Matthew 7:1-5)
8. Always remember the golden rule to do unto others as you would have them do to you. (Matthew 7:12)
9. Never say anything out of anger near an Autistic person because they tend to take everything literally. (Proverbs 14:17) Be careful on how you approach humorous teasing around Autistic people. They also interpret this literally too.
10. Redirection works better than punishment for meltdowns. Punishment always made my meltdowns worse. When your loved one is having a meltdown Don't use comments such as "You are too big to behave this way," or "You are being very rude," etc. Use comments such as "Is there anything I can do to help you feel better," etc and always do your best to stay calm

and patient. Also allow them to talk when they feel like it and listen to them without judging them.

11. Keep some form of information in a handy location such as in your car's glove compartment that lets people know that you or a loved one is on the Autism spectrum if you experience an emergency. Some smartphone apps allow users to pull up their medical charts without a passcode in an emergency.

12. Never criticize the parents or spouse of an Autistic person. Say something like "I'm sorry you have to deal with this and is there anything I can do to help you." And always pray for the person and his or her family.

13. Be an Autism advocate.

14. Warn the person ahead of time for potential planned changes in routine but do not warn a long time in advance or the day of the events. Some examples of routine changes can include an assembly at school, having guests in the house, etc.

15. Teach the person ahead of time how to handle common emergencies that will occur from time to time in ways that they can understand such as jump starting a car battery or changing a tire.

16. When teaching them skills or helping them with homework assignments they can appear lazy or as if they are not listening. They don't understand things the way a normal person does even if they are trying. This is related to sensory processing issues in their brain. If this is the case, be patient and try to understand and figure out ways for them to learn best even if it does not work well for other people.

17. Encourage them to overcome any sensory issues or fears but take baby steps if needed.

18. School systems should be willing to understand each special needs child's needs and be willing to get them individual tutoring services at certain times during the school day to help with homework assignments from all classes. If the child is enrolled in all special education courses the teachers should

help to get them reintegrated into a regular education classroom setting if they are high functioning.

19. Advocate for an aide for your child if needed. If your child has an aide, make sure that the aide understands autism spectrum disorders.

20. Consider getting accommodations when applying for jobs and career training programs and make sure that your boss/professors and coworkers are understanding of yours or your child/spouse's disability.

21. Allow your child to help in making decisions that are best for his or her educational and treatment goals.

22. Bullying of any form toward anyone with High Functioning Autism is wrong and it is not the victim's fault. If you or your child/spouse is being bullied, speak up and report the issue to the appropriate authorities.

23. If you cannot afford traditional health insurance but do not qualify for Medicaid benefits look into programs that can help you pay for your medical care needs. Everyone on the Autism spectrum needs to have access to affordable health care programs in order to treat Autism and comorbid physiological and psychological disorders.

24. I have experienced worsening Autism meltdowns and heavy periods every month since I first started my period at age 11. Always keep track of your daughter's periods and seek help if you notice severe mood swings and worsening meltdowns and monitor her for any unusual pain. There are many options for controlling period symptoms. PMS does worsen Autism symptoms in females.

25. Medications should be used with caution in Autistic people.

26. Autism training courses should be required for teachers, mental health professionals, medical professionals, and emergency responders.

27. Pastors should consider talking about certain topics differently if they have Autistic people in the congregation and consider making the church as sensory friendly as possible.

28. Always ask people on the Autism spectrum if they would like to join with you for a social situation and be okay with their social quirks. Don't force them into the situation or ignore them.

29. If an Autistic person complains of chronic symptoms, please listen to them even though they appear as if they are attention seekers or hypochondriacs. Sensory and cognitive issues can cause them to overreact.

30. Embrace your loved one's special interest as long as it does not affect their well-being or that of their families. If it's an expensive special interest, teach them how to budget on everyday things in order to save for their special interest.

31. If you travel, research and take advantage of any disability services.

32. Learn ways of putting your special interest to good use.

33. Invest in modern day technology and keep your software and apps updated regularly on computers, tablets, and smartphones yet set limits on social media.

34. Outside of school/work, and homework assignments invest in a good pair of bluetooth headphones to use if your child/spouse hates doing household chores or for when you travel. This helps me when I have to do household chores and for having trouble sleeping in a hotel room when we are traveling and for these reasons, I am thankful for the use of modern technology. Bluetooth headphones allow you to listen to music, audiobooks, podcasts etc if they are connected to a smartphone or a tablet nearby in addition to reducing noise.

35. Keep a diary of your worst symptoms. I've done it and it's hard to keep doing it continuously but if you stick with it, it's amazing to discover what causes the worst of your symptoms. But I do still have meltdowns regularly.

36. Pursue whatever helps yourself or your loved one to deal with your Autism symptoms. This could be the key to unlocking effective new treatments for others with autism spectrum disorders.

37. Life is short, and you should embrace your ASD child or loved one's unique abilities and fascinations.
38. Don't sweat the meltdowns and social awkwardness.
39. Encourage them to take care of their health with exercise, good eating habits, no smoking, alcoholic drinking, or drugs.
40. Try yoga as a form of exercise. There are many different levels and types of yoga.
41. Genuine happiness and a good attitude are the best treatment for High Functioning Autism.
42. Practice mindfulness.
43. Don't give up hope. There is a light at the end of the tunnel.

I have come up with a term that I have described as behavior shaming. *Behavior shaming* refers to judging a person whose actions and feelings are out of the norm for a particular society or situation. We live in a society that often shames people for how they act or how they look. The term for judging someone who is too fat or too skinny is called *body shaming.* It is considered rude if we tell someone that they look too fat or too thin. Most people do not get into trouble for judging a child or an adult with autism for having a meltdown and I feel like this is discrimination. Behavior shaming based on my personal experience does not work for disciplining a person with any form of Autism. It always made me feel worse about myself and feeling bad about myself worsened or caused meltdowns.

I have observed that people on the Autism Spectrum tend to be judged unmercifully as compared to those with other conditions. Ableism is common amongst people with any form of Autism, and I have experienced it at many points in my life. Autistic children from wealthy families are often viewed as spoiled rotten when they have a meltdown and kids from lower social economic backgrounds are viewed as abused or neglected by their parents.

Blessed is the person who keeps on going when times are hard. After they have gone through hard times, this person will receive a crown. The crown is life itself. The Lord has promised it to those who love him. (James 1:12 NIrV)

Although High Functioning Autism has a list of symptoms and certain criteria have to be met to get a diagnosis, the disorder affects each person differently. Some people may have all of the symptoms, and some may have only a few of the symptoms. Some people may be affected by certain symptoms worse than others. Autism also shares some of the same traits as attention deficit hyperactivity disorder (ADHD), obsessive compulsive disorder (OCD), and Tourette Syndrome. These disorders are also comorbid disorders of Autism. Some of the most successful people on the planet were diagnosed with autism spectrum disorder or suspected to have it. Some examples include Bill Gates (the founder of Microsoft), Elon Musk (the creator of Tesla), Steve Jobs (the co-founder of Apple. We know Apple in this case does not mean fruit. It means iPhones).

This is a phrase from Temple Grandin that I would like to use, and she is right. "If we didn't have Autism we would still be living in caves." (Temple Grandin)

Here is a phrase that I made up myself about Autistic people.

"If we didn't have Autism, we would not have iPhones." (My quote)

Lacey told me one day after one of my many speeches at our local annual autism walk that I was the pioneer of High Functioning Autism for our area. Lacey has told me in the past that she thought that I had High Functioning Autism for a reason and that she genuinely HATED it for me that I had to suffer from this disorder.

If you feel that you or a loved one has an autism spectrum disorder, please seek advice from a qualified medical or psychological provider and work with them to find the best treatment plan for you or your child/spouse. The goal of any treatment plan for autism spectrum disorders should be to help the person to be more functional, not to make them more socially acceptable. The goal of this book was to teach others about what I learned based on my experiences with autism spectrum disorder and how to supplement other therapies in addition to traditional medical or psychological treatment.

GLOSSARY

Web Resources:
American Psychiatric Association: www.psychiatry.org
Autism Speaks: www.autismspeaks.org
Autism Treatment Center: www.autismtreatmentcenter.org
Autism Society: www.autismsociety.org
Cleveland Clinic: www.clevelandclinic.org
Centers for Disease Control and Prevention: www.cdc.gov
Mayo Clinic: www.mayoclinic.org
Temple Grandin: www.templegrandin.com

Books:
Diagnostic and Statistical Manual IV
Diagnostic and Statistical Manual V
John Donovan and Caren Zucker: In a Different Key: The Story of Autism
Melanie Boudreau: Toppling the Idol of Ideal
New International Reader's Version of the Bible
Steve Silberman: Neurotribes
Stephen Shore: Beyond the Wall; Personal Experiences with Autism and Asperger Syndrome
Temple Grandin and Tony Atwood: Asperger Syndrome and Girls
Temple Grandin: The Unwritten Rules of Social Relationships
Temple Grandin: Thinking in Pictures

Tony Atwood: Asperger Syndrome, A Guide For Parents and Professionals
Mitzi Waltz: Pervasive Developmental Disorders; Finding a Diagnosis and Getting help.
Raun Kaufman: Autism Breakthrough
Barry Neil Kaufman: Son Rise; The Miracle Continues

Printed in the United States
by Baker & Taylor Publisher Services